Due Date	Return Date	De Date	Return Date

Scholars of the Heart

by the same author

*

MEN DRESSED AS SEAMEN

(*Christophers*)

VIEW FROM ATLANTIS

(*Constable*)

COUSINS AND STRANGERS

(*Harvard U. P.*)

COASTLINE

(*Hugh Evelyn*)

SCHOLARS OF THE HEART

Essays in Criticism

S. GORLEY PUTT

FABER AND FABER
24 Russell Square
London

First published in mcmlxii
by Faber and Faber Limited
24 Russell Square London W.C.1
Printed in Great Britain
by Ebenezer Baylis and Son Limited
The Trinity Press, Worcester, and London

To

MPA, EKW, LVH

Sabbatical greetings

CONTENTS

III. Professor Emeritus

ACKNOWLEDGMENTS

A first version of these essays appeared in the *Orion* miscellanies and in the pages of *The Times Literary Supplement*, *Essays in Criticism*, *Cornhill*, *The Wind and the Rain*. In places I have also adapted material first contributed to *Time and Tide*, *Tribune*, *The Oxford Magazine*, *Folio*. I am grateful to the editors for their encouragement then and for their permission to reprint now.

S.G.P.

PREFACE

When assailed by the frivolous tolerance of middle age, one's first beneficiary is usually oneself. What has happened to the narrow-minded austerity of youth? I blush now to recall that, reviewing Lytton Strachey's *Characters and Commentaries* for *The Granta* at the savage age of twenty-one, I once advised critical scriveners to save energy for a deathbed destruction of odd papers, lest the piety of more squeamish survivors should later assemble them into a book. Alas for the critical rigour of twenty-one! It fades as slowly and as surely as physical prowess. There comes a time when, with the easier optimism of lowered sights, we no longer ask: 'What good will it do?' Instead, we ask the more indulgent question: 'Where could be the harm in it?' And instead of waiting for the incautious literary executor, we hurry unaided into reprint.

If pressed for a more positive exculpation, I could only confess a private relief in putting one's name to some pieces (numbers 1, 2, 3, 4, 5, 6, 10 and parts of 11) which have appeared in the stately anonymity of *The Times Literary Supplement*. I do not quarrel with the editorial tradition of that paper. Yet the irritation of an author who is tempted to cry 'Coward!' must sometimes be matched by the embarrassment of a critic who is obliged, for the moment at least, to stay in hiding.

For the selection of essays here brought together I can claim no special doctrine. If I have repeated one idea more than another, it is the not very exciting conviction that an unpretentious moral flair has served the English spirit as an acceptable substitute for the knack, so enviable in other nations, of being 'artistic'. When, visiting Florence, I am asked what we English can set up to rival that infallible Italian grace discernible as easily among modern errand-boys and typists as in Michelangelo's David or your favourite Madonna, I am inclined to remember Italian social history and reply, perfectly seriously: 'The bus queue'. Putting it another way, one may say of certain West-country villages and market-towns (so attuned to the mild pastoral country in which they are set) that there is not one distinguished building or tolerable picture in the place, and yet in time become near-besotted by their decorous unplanned and convenient beauty.

I can accept, in the spirit of Arnold's 'touchstones' or even Housman's scalp-tinglings, the blazing magic of something very like 'pure' poetry. I can see well enough that when the young Henry Howard, Earl of Surrey, raided Vergil to create the English lines

And lo! moist night now from the welkin falls
And stars declining counsel us to rest

he achieved something that was not falsified by Tudor social brutalities and is as potent now as when he wrote. I can see, too, that an over-scrupulous interest in even so harmless a concept as 'decency' can, when translated into aesthetic terms, have its unattractive side—sanctimonious, censorious, priggish; just as the sensation-mongers in turn can at weak moments lapse into the precious, the vulgar and the slapdash. But I should be false to my instincts and my training if I did not confess that as a novel-reader at least I cannot rid myself of that English moral-aesthetic muddle (if you like to call it so). That lively old rascal Norman Douglas had a ferocious sanity which illuminated even his most cantankerous prose; but if you try to sell me the social gospel of those merry contemporary entertainers for whom the comic spirit is nourished on a general loathing and a particular set of club regulations, then I start yelling for Bunyan to amuse me and wondering if the angry young existentialists may not have been right after all. I can imagine Albert Camus more comfortable in the company of Pilgrim Christian than at Brideshead.

A word about my three groupings. The first four papers in 'Old Tutors Revisited' contain backward glances at writers who were prominent, either personally or as names in the weather-reports of the climate of opinion, during my pre-war undergraduate days. I have tried to peer at them through the eyes of new readers of the 1950's and 1960's, and if they look a trace out of focus the fault must be attributed not to them but to the effects of my self-imposed squint. The last essay in this section seeks to present a sample of the post-war generation who, spurning his environment, shows himself a truer disciple of the English Liberal school than he may yet realize.

'Scholars and Sometime Scholars' brings together some pretty disparate novelists; and for me 'Professor Emeritus' could only be Henry James. My gropings after system in *The Illusion of Involvement* may serve as an example of the occupational itch of novel reviewers to perform the less distracting task of appreciating in terms of amplitude the collected works of one author. I had reached this stage by the war years, and read some rum things in my mess-deck hammock. James himself I had rediscovered during those gaunt naval days following upon night watches, when unimagined strains brought about an altogether surprising flowering of the virtues of patience and application. (That I was not alone in this was evident from the flight of James items from the second-hand bookshops, which must have caused mingled pleasure and annoyance to the faithful when they discovered that a war-time 'come-back' had anticipated the muted centenary celebrations of 1943.) By the time I had finished pondering why this master-analyst of the human predicament had ever fallen out of favour, he was already back in the swim. I then turned to sample other novelists who had entertained large numbers of readers without attracting much recent critical attention. I discovered that some of the moral flair nowadays acknowledged, almost to satiety, in Henry James had also informed the writing of such still outmoded figures as Maria Edgeworth and Anthony Hope. I found it interesting to speculate on the kinds of enjoyment offered by the popular but unliterary Upton Sinclair and the literary but non-popular William Gerhardi. (Because the works of writers in this section are not always easily familiar to the sort of readers who could be trusted to know E. M. Forster or Cecil Day Lewis by heart, so to say, I have here indulged a rather closer documentation of my interpretations.)

Although I have acknowledged elsewhere* my long debt to Dr. F. R. Leavis, I certainly cannot claim to have applied with anything like professional rigour the admirable standards he taught his pupils. The tough integrity of his approach still makes most of the rest of us look like a bunch of knee-ducking Osrics. For my own part, I have been so long away from the authoritative atmosphere of academic commentary that I have lapsed into the more comfortable stance of an unorganized enjoyer of books and cannot even feel entirely guiltless when asked why anyone who can put pen to paper should spend time writing about other men's works. With the warnings sounded in Sir Charles Snow's Rede Lecture still ringing in our ears, we amateurs may even join the professionals in wondering how much the practice of our secondary art may not have been driving sharp little contributory wedges between 'The Two Cultures'. To scriveners thus chastened, Dr. Helen Gardner's book *The Business of Criticism* (1959) seemed at first to bring messages of forgiveness and hope. 'The torch rather than the sceptre would be my symbol for the critic,' she writes. 'Elucidation, or illumination, is the critic's primary task as I conceive it. Having made the initial act of choice, or judgement of value, I want to remove any obstacles which prevent the work having its fullest possible effect.'

But it does a little depend on where one comes in, so to say. 'Having made the initial . . . judgement of value.' First catch your hare! May it really be assumed that we are competent to make, unaided, such acts of choice? Even if we falter, we are warned not to turn to the sceptre-bearers who go in for 'the erection and application of standards by which writers and their works are to be given their ratings', because 'the attempt to train young people in this kind of discrimination seems to me to be a folly, if not a crime.' Again, it depends on where one comes in. If Dr. Gardner should now be asking why a generation of critics had ever arisen to hand out, like diplomas, their miniature sceptres into hands not always as steady as their own, it is only fair to recall just what state the dimmer sort of torch-bearers had landed us in, in those far-off pre-*Scrutiny* days. The

* In *Five-Finger Exercises: A Sample of English Poetry*. *Moderna Språk*, Stockholm, 1957, and *Technique and Culture: Three Cambridge Portraits*, in Essays and Studies (New Series, Vol. XIV), English Association, 1961.

excesses of the less intelligent wielders of *Scrutiny* sceptres may well have raised some academic eyebrows—but what of the third-rate pupils who lit their smoky tapers from the torch-bearers? Witness the time, not so very long ago, when the English literary scene was overrun by whimsical will-o'-the-wisps all busily telling us that whereas the blank verse of 'A' was a gently undulating plateau, the blank verse of 'B', on the other hand (it was usually 'on the other hand') scudded like a little yacht before the breeze. As Dr. Gardner herself points out, 'methods of literary criticism develop through dissatisfaction with older methods,' and even her strictures on the sceptre-bearers show her to have partaken, consciously or not, of the fruits of their own revolutionary advance from maudlin chit-chat.

Reviewers and critics, like anthropologists or theologians, go on squabbling happily enough among themselves. It is only by a piece of occupational bad luck that their tantrums come more regularly before the public eye. They do, in general, agree on what they are *trying* to do. What that is, I leave to the magisterial pronouncement of my 'Professor Emeritus' (from Henry James's 1914 essay on 'The New Novel'):

'The effect, if not the prime office, of criticism is to make our absorption and our enjoyment of the things that feed the mind as aware of itself as possible, since that awareness quickens the mental demand, which thus in turn wanders further and further for pasture.'

1

Old Tutors Revisited

1

FROM IRON TO FEATHERS

Cecil Day Lewis in his Generation

'If anyone had told me, during those agreeable bouts of poetic appreciation, that I should one day succeed Sir Maurice Bowra in the Chair of Poetry, I would have taken it, not only for the most unprophetic raving, but as a joke in very doubtful taste.' Thus Mr. Day Lewis, reaching Oxford in 1923 ('looking rather beautiful in a depraved way') and three-fifths of the way through his autobiography. At this point, one can almost hear, nowadays, the respectful disbelieving titter of a polite audience. In tone, as in substance, the remark is indeed a far cry from the words of the young schoolmaster-poet who joined the Communist Party in 1935 (in Cheltenham, of all places), who nerved himself to say, in *Transitional Poem*, 'It is becoming now to declare my allegiance,' and who could throw off, in *The Magnetic Mountain*, such lines as:

> *Scavenger barons and your jackal vassals,*
> *Your pimping press-gang, your unclean vessels,*
> *We'll make you swallow your words at a gulp . . .*
> *We can be much ruder and we're learning to shoot.*

'Not of the princes and prelates with periwigged charioteers'—this second disclaimer was not Mr. Day Lewis's, but that of the present Laureate, who must now have sonnets ready and waiting, like chocolates in a slot-machine, for royal comings and goings. And Mr. Day Lewis himself has already published a nativity poem for a prince. Beyond Masefield stands the yet more warning figure of Wordsworth: 'Bliss was it in that dawn to be alive.' Well advanced, now, towards the ruminative state, Mr. Day Lewis can write, the day after his fifty-fifth birthday:

'Placid and orderly though my life has become'. 'Oh, black frost of my youth, recalcitrant time,' he had once written.

Pondering these instances of change in the tone and tempo of a poet's life, an impatient reader of *The Buried Day* (1960) may at first find himself asking where, now, is the authentic ring of that old 'Auden-Spender-Day Lewis' period? How sick they must have become of that label, all three of them! The first-named has removed himself from the field by becoming an American citizen, but either of the remaining two, a saddened *laudator temporis acti* might now guess, could well inherit the Laureateship. 'Placid and orderly' the whole life, now revealed, may seem to have been, to any such hasty reader who turns fretfully from Mr. Day Lewis's earlier verse to the smooth-flowing pastoral prose of his autobiography. Have they all, these militants of the 1920s and 1930s, resolved to view their between-war days through a diminishing glass?

Any such baffled reader, smartly on the watch for acknowledged and unacknowledged inconsistencies of tone, of faith, of politics, would in sober fact be convicting himself of a woeful insensitivity to the courage and skill with which a man of unusual verbal integrity has told his story. For *The Buried Day* is not only a fascinating document, a record full of names, memories, attitudes spanning the past forty years of troubled life in British social and political history; it is also a quiet reticent work of art in its own right. Mild, tolerant, sensitive, the author has chosen to slur over (without quite erasing) certain strong emotions, while basking in the earned and recommended tranquillity in which they are recollected. (And if the recommendation came from the Laureate-to-be, Wordsworth, it did at least come from a major poet.) Mr. Day Lewis has had the literary tact to remember, throughout his autobiography, that what is proper matter for passionate lyric verse may be sad stuff indeed when squeezed out, under no transfiguring pressure of feeling, in the literal historic truth of narrative prose. Rightly to judge the nature of his present achievement, a fair-minded reader would do well to reflect on the nature of this new medium to which the author has turned.

In the first place, it may be admitted at once that within its deliberate limits this autobiography *has* the ring of authentic honesty, even—or perhaps particularly—in those passages in which the lowered sights and moderate demands of middle age are most ruefully acknowledged. Admissions of childhood fears, of moral cowardice, of inglorious anxieties: these are all here, it is true, but they could be matched by similar revelations by writers who have not shared Mr. Day Lewis's sensibility. Such admissions, from the stance of middle age, are as easy to make as those testimonies to past illiteracy so smugly claimed by prosperous aldermen when they give away the prizes at the local school. It is not at *this* level of remembered feeling, certainly, that life has gouged in the author's face those deep criss-crossing lines which scar his smiling face in the frontispiece portrait. To learn of *these* matters, we should—quite properly—turn to his poems. Sometimes the prose narrator will take us to the brink, as when he stands with his stepmother at his father's deathbed and discovers '—not for the first time or the last—what a poor substitute pity is for love, how agonizingly and ineffectually it strains to become what it cannot be'. But he does not, in prose, push us over the edge.

Mr. Day Lewis must have remembered, when he sat down to his autobiographical task, that we are all normally prepared to admit greater degrees of intimacy in what we hear or read, in direct proportion to the degree to which the context of narration recedes from immediate factual 'actuality'. We can bear to sit down and read other men's opinions, directly expressed, when we would be bored stiff if the authors were in the same room talking to us—or 'at us', as we would undoubtedly complain. Yet even the printed word can make us feel uncomfortable when a living man or woman ventures to describe events or states of mind which a squeamish reader deems to be too deeply personal. Such matters, nevertheless, he is perfectly capable of swallowing if they are removed from the context of private life and granted the 'universality' of fiction or poetry. The thinly disguised hero of an autobiographical novel, or the unidentified speaker of some passionate lyric, may be allowed to blurt out emotional truths which in a straight autobiography sound 'cheap' and which when conveyed in live conversation are enough to mark the man down as an exhibitionist, a regular cad. And if seekers after the pleasures of vicarious laceration should be disappointed by Mr. Day Lewis's unwillingness to reveal the deepest scars of his public and personal life, they must blame their frustration not on the author's lack of candour but on his good sense, as a professional writer, of when to do one thing and when to do another.

Mr. Day Lewis, then, has wisely taken pains to ration both the trivial incident (acceptable in the smoking-room, but not in an autobiography) and the heart's deep secrets (acceptable in novel or poem, but not in an autobiography). The slumbrous droning of childhood summers, the antics of family eccentrics, the 'intense yet unsentimental' friendships of school and college life—all these things will awaken nostalgic echoes in the hearts of many readers, but they are hardly likely to conclude that the young poet Day Lewis was in essence very different from themselves—merely a trifle thinner-skinned, perhaps. Many undergraduates feel pleasantly goofy when punting in the summer; they will recognize that when the young Day Lewis, also punting, felt 'porous' to nature, he is telling them in better words what they felt, rather than claiming to have felt something only a poet can feel.

The author was born of Anglo-Irish stock; his father was a curate of the Church of Ireland, his mother died when he was four. Throughout 'the long acrimony of adolescence' young Day Lewis sought for a personal identity, finally selecting that of the Poet. Forced by the accident of death into baring towards his father the feminine streak in his own nature, he veered from early hero-worship to a later resentment against emotional demands and 'hurt' looks: that normal stock-in-trade, in fact, of maternal—rather than paternal—blackmail. No wonder that he admits to lapses into namby-pambyness as he pored, in that sad widower's household in Notting Hill, over clerical tailors' catalogues with their 'pictures of morbidly spiritual-looking clergymen wearing . . . exotic vestments, such as alb, amice, chasuble'. No wonder that he was to feel, at Oxford and again when he in turn came to be a professional mentor, 'an almost passionate distaste for the adolescent'. No wonder, in spite of this resentment, that he found at the university a shaping pressure from mature society, while he himself was 'concealing with fantastic aplomb his anxiety, his sense of inferiority, his almost total cluelessness'.

The Oxford story is tenderly and wittily told: the menace of college secretaries and Learner-Bores, the emergence of real friends in the figures of Charles Fenby and Rex Warner, the first—now detested—volume of verse (*Beechen Vigil*, 1926), the meeting with Auden. 'Sardonic, restless, intolerant, but basically romantic and naïve still', young Day Lewis found Auden dogmatic and intellectually bossy. But he was roused to emulation and later felt 'the glint of mutual rivalry'. Perhaps it was the Auden who said 'the poet must look like the stockbroker' who most effectively sluiced young Cecil's mind of notions concocted from fidgety afternoons among the brochures of clerical tailors. At any rate, Auden was but one of many in whose company the author was making 'fruitful experiments in the chemistry of personality'. And the 'Auden-Spender-Day Lewis' label may now indeed be decently laid aside when we learn that, after all the pre-war commotion wrought by that triple incantation, the three poets met together under the same roof for the first time as late as 1947. It was the critics, and not they themselves, who had declared them to be a Movement.

After Day Lewis's 'doomed-to-failure spirit' had been duly rewarded by a fourth in Greats, he was rescued from dejection by a series of school posts—Summer Fields, Larchfield, Cheltenham. Those eight years yield one splendid shopping-list catalogue, deserving quotation:

'a world of bells and tattered books and football boots and crazes and blackboards and piercing screams; of ink smells, chalk-duster smells, smells of mud and mown grass, and the mousey smell of little boys; of draughts, radiators, chilblains, stringy meat, steamed puddings; of dismal walks in the rain; of boring jokes and catchwords endlessly repeated . . . a world of rewards and punishments, reach-me-down justice and covert partiality, of sadly unoriginal sin: a world where, under controlled conditions, the workings of the herd instinct may be observed in all their pristine innocence and mindless brutality, but where also, as in an accelerated film of plant growth, one can delightedly watch rapid unfoldings of intelligence, courage, inventiveness, sensibility.'

By now Mr. Day Lewis was married and soon had a young family to think about, as well as his schoolmastering chores. His political conscience and the poetic impulse were alike uncomfortable in the strait-jacket of a life which was becoming, on an outside view, almost a caricature of the bourgeois. At Cheltenham, when a colleague happened upon *Transitional Poem* and objected to the subject matter, the poor young author was obliged to blurt out: 'But they're love poems, addressed to my wife.' Almost as respectable, given the time and place, was his slow gravitation towards extreme left-wing views. 'In a tricky, darkening decade we were a generation which had not vision equal to desire . . . we lived too much in the future, and in abstractions'. The word 'generation' recalls the title of Mr. Alastair Cooke's book on Alger Hiss: *A Generation on Trial.* Any reader who recalls those years of anti-Fascism, of the Popular Front, of the intellectuals' sick-hearted impotence in the face of Britain's inglorious role in that tricky decade, will hardly need to question the pages which explain this poet's flirtation with Communism. It was to Auden that he wrote the lines:

> *A mole first, out of riddling passages*
> *You came up for a breather into my field,*
> *Then back to your engineering . . .*

—but they might with equal force have been addressed to whatever dedicated agents of direct action may have sought to enlist the verbal support of a sensibility nourished on the Anglican Church, Sherborne, Wadham and Cheltenham.

On this whole phase of his public and private life, Mr. Day Lewis writes with a sympathy thrown into perspective, but not falsified, by hindsight. A romantic Marxism, documented more by Russian films than by Leninist strategic directives, was filling 'the hollow in the breast where a God should be'. Those were the days when dons and poets, clerics and town councillors, could all espouse with divided minds the progressive interest, coaxing from their uncertainties a faith 'naïve, poorly focused, yet passionately conceived'. What if they looked like those characters from a *New Yorker* cartoon who sat hunched up in a smoke-filled room saying: 'All that now remains to be done is to seize power'? They were making their protest in the only manner for which their liberal gentlemanly training had fitted them. It would be foolish, from the fake security (on the domestic side of politics, at least) of these present cause-less days, to under-estimate the effect they all had on the conscience of their country. Whether to join the International Brigade in Spain or to edit *The Mind in Chains* may well have been, for this particular sensibility, an acute personal choice. Any contemporary young poet who feels tempted to shrug an existentialist shoulder at all this pother would do well to read how Mr. Day Lewis 'prevaricated and procrastinated', seeking 'an interplay and consonance between the inner and the outward life, between public meaning and private meaning'. He found the consonance only because in the murkiness of those times both alike were in hopeless muddle.

These are paragraphs of candour at a level where candour is unusual. 'On veut bien être méchant,' wrote Molière, 'on ne veut point être ridicule.' The 1930s were, for many unhardened spirits, a time when impotence and ridiculousness had not yet been subjected to the crucible from which they have emerged, to universal acclaim, as Albert Camus's *absurde*. Without intending any such thing, *The Buried Day* demonstrates that there was heroism, of a sort, in those squalid pre-Munich days. The author's own release came from his decision to give up amateurish politics in favour of a more professional devotion to poetry; and the choice was made possible in 1935 by the discovery—*ridicule* enough—that as 'Nicholas Blake' he could earn a liberating salary as a writer of detective stories.

In a cottage near Axminster began the next phase: free from schoolmastering, free from the awkwardness of attitudes based on politics only half-believed. But the date is 1938. Outside, the war; inside, 'a new, dominantly sensual love', lightly touched on here. It was to be a thorny road, after all, for the pastoral muse. At this point the author retires—apart from a postscript over-autumnal in tone, to be sure, for a writer who in this very book has shown himself to be in midsummer working order. 'Certainly I take things less hard,' he admits. But in this new guiltless repose there is surely material, still, for guilt to work upon? Enough, be it hoped, to stir Mr. Day Lewis to a complementary volume. 'We take but three steps from feathers to iron,' he once quoted from Keats. In his new 'Transitional Poem' from iron back again to feathers there is a quality of stoicism, less hard than iron, less musty than feathers, which gives ground for the expectation that in verse and prose alike there is still, for this subtle writer, 'A Hope for Poetry'.

2

THE LIMITATIONS OF INTELLIGENT TALK

Aldous Huxley's Essays

The name of Huxley has long glowed with a scientific lustre. Yet if the word had been dropped into a cultivated conversation during the 1920s and 1930s it would probably have been taken for granted that the speaker was referring to Mr. Aldous Huxley in a literary context suggesting the higher Bloomsbury. Today a similar exercise in name-dropping would doubtless call up the benign figure of Sir Julian Huxley in a scientific context suggesting biological contributions to a television Brains Trust. If one may posit so basic a change of assumptions in knowledgeable circles, then the brothers Huxley may well serve to illustrate the remarkable shift of balance between 'The Two Cultures', to use the phrase made common currency by C. P. Snow.

It is true that Mr. Aldous Huxley's pre-war novels boldly introduced many scientific words and concepts; but they were in the main introduced via a set of literary conventions which are at least as old as the works of Thomas Love Peacock. It is a fair supposition that if Mr. Huxley were starting his literary career in the 1960s, and possessed the same ease of familiarity with scientific thought, he would no longer feel the need to gild his gingerbread. Scientific essayists are no longer required to stick in bits of 'literature' if they wish their works to reach a reasonably wide audience. Is it not rather the custom, nowadays, for our poets and novelists to stick in a bit of 'science'?

The whirligig of time has indeed brought in his revenges. We are all so much more attuned to the voice of the specialist, these days, that even the most advanced reader of the weeklies is prepared to listen not only to a biologist but also to a theologian. The smart scepticism of pre-war intellectuals no longer shocks us. On the contrary, it sounds painfully old-fashioned to our sober ears. The most spectacular manifestations of physical science, so far from making the words of pre-enlightenment moralists look deliciously ridiculous, have sent a doom-ridden generation searching desperately, and in the most unlikely places, for guidance. If the Age of Steam developed under the aegis of the Goddess of Reason, the Atomic Age is sending some of its baffled beneficiaries scuttling after Zen Buddhism. A worried frown has replaced the lifted eyebrow as the proper expression for pundits.

So that when we re-read essays from *The Olive Tree* and note that in 1936 Mr. Huxley's favourite eyebrow-raising adjective was still 'strange', it all seems centuries away. 'In the desert, I should infallibly have invented the Greek mythology. The Jews and Arabs discovered Jahweh and Allah. I find it strange.' We sad heirs of disillusion do not find it strange at all. And when, in a serious study of D. H. Lawrence reprinted from the same volume, Mr. Huxley refers to Lawrence's 'restatement of the strange Christian doctrine of the resurrection of the body', that betraying adjective 'strange' places him, to a solemn 'anything-is-possible' 1960 appraisal, not up among the *enfants terribles* but way back on the rickety rationalist Olympus of Edward Gibbon. Rickety, that is to say, when *we* are invited to view the 'crimes and follies' of mankind from Gibbon's standpoint: for of what crimes and follies unthinkable in Gibbon's day has not the race shown itself to be capable during our own lifetime? When a mountain is shaken by an earthquake it may be demonstrated that the cause of the disturbance lies deep beneath the very plains themselves; yet the mountain-dwellers may still come to the conclusion that even on the mountain they are not as safe as they once thought.

Mr. Aldous Huxley's *Collected Essays* (1960) may well introduce him to a new generation of young readers who will need the publisher's reminder that he has produced, over forty-odd years, some ten novels, two plays, two biographies, five volumes of short stories, two of poetry and no fewer than nineteen classified as 'essays and belles lettres'. Ignorant, perhaps, of *Point Counter Point*, unmindful of the status (to use a fashionable word) occupied in pre-war years by the author of

Brave New World, what sort of picture will new readers be able to build up of the mind and the man behind these half-hundred slices from prose written over a period of a third of a century? If they trouble to look up the dates of these essays, what common attitudes will they find in the author of *On the Margin* (1923) and *Adonis and the Alphabet* (1956)?

First, an unruffled confidence. Confidence that the author has something valuable—and usually provocative—to say about almost any subject under the sun; confidence, too, betrayed at times in references *de haut en bas* to other writers in other ages. The man who could in 1923 refer to Donne as 'that strange old Dean of St. Paul's' can write with equal aplomb in his 1959 preface of work in which,

'following Montaigne, I have tried to make the best of all the essay's three worlds, have tried to say everything at once in as near an approach to contrapuntal simultaneity as the nature of literary art will allow of.'

The words are more portentous, but the know-all tone is that of the author's earlier and lighter vein, as, when discussing in 1923 two conceptions of love, he said: 'without presuming to pass judgement, I will content myself with pointing out the defects of each.'

Secondly, facility. Everything has been grist to Mr. Huxley's mill: books, paintings, music, politics, philosophy, anthropology, sex, drugs, or cats. The stones grind away indifferently—much as the plumbing regulator in certain Continental trains may be moved, by English-speaking travellers, 'indifferently to the left or to the right'. Ideas seem to go in at one ear and out at the other. It is so, magnanimously, with the author; and after a time it becomes so, distressingly, with the reader, too.

Thirdly (and surprisingly, perhaps, for so omnivorous, so very egg-headed a pundit), frivolity. When Mr. Huxley quotes other writers, whether D. H. Lawrence or even John Humphrey Noyes of the Oneida Community, they sound insistent (ill bred? vital?) in the midst of the embedding prose, which is sometimes elegant, sometimes slapdash, but always light-handed.

Confidence, facility, frivolity: these are the attributes of much good talk in educated circles in England; especially, perhaps, after-dinner talk. Mr. Huxley's essays are pre-eminently a kind of chatting at what might be called a high level of expected response. 'I sing the sofa,' wrote that very serious-minded poet

William Cowper. 'I sing anything at all about anything at all,' says Mr. Huxley among the nuts and wine, 'and I promise you that however many out-of-the-way sources I may quote and however wickedly provocative I may be, I shall never be so ill bred as to degenerate into a lecturer or a preacher.' If in the end all this should become a trace tedious, it will be as an amiable, garrulous don might become tedious, by being over-allusive and under-engaged.

At times the passing thoughts are perceptive as well as entertaining. Glancing with Mr. Huxley at early Victorian fashions in dress and coiffure, we feel good sense in the reminder that the nude young ladies of Etty's paintings look unusually indecent because 'we imagined that that egg-faced type came into the world complete with flowing draperies'. At other times over-allusiveness and a careless piling up of paradoxes have led Mr. Huxley into positions of downright wrong-headedness. Thus in the otherwise entertaining essay 'Sermons in Cats' (1931) he suggests that 'primitive people' lack the conventions and traditions of 'civilized people'. Now the convention-ridden nature of primitive society must have been well known to so widely read and widely travelled an author. But what of it? The analogy serves its passing purpose. We shall soon move on to some other light-fingered allusion. Lightness is all: yet the total effect of some of these semi-facetious lay-sermons is to make one value more the humourless gruff seriousness of a Lawrence or the consistent, if curmudgeonly, prejudices of a Norman Douglas.

The climate of opinion in the years after the Great War favoured a wonderful sprouting of much fancy and some imagination: irreverent, basically materialist, in general optimistic. The glum aftermath of World War II has fostered no such crop of brilliance. Yet if the changes of intellectual fashion have been unkind to Mr. Huxley's gay juggling dexterity (unkinder, in these selected essays, than one would ever have supposed from grateful memories of the individual volumes here represented), there are some compensating advantages. We may now be disposed to reject the trimmings; but our appetite for the serious conclusions of Mr. Huxley's roving intelligence has become, if anything, sharper. We are less liable to scoff with him, but we are readier to learn from him.

Shorn of their 'wicked' asides, his travel essays still make good reading. Not all our neo-Puritanism can destroy the pleasant freshness of the author's observation as when he notes (in 1936) the 'pale mauve or shell-pink sock-suspenders' on the brown calves of Arab dignitaries; or detract from the felicity of such a phrase as 'importunate fidelity', applied to the child beggars of Tunisia. We may be less amused than we once were to find a tour of Mexico being used as a starting-point for meanderings through the encyclopedia; but we are probably more patiently prepared now than we were in 1934 to listen to straight descriptions of Central American villagers—to whom, in our chastened mood, we no longer feel so very superior.

Moreover, Mr. Huxley has himself taken advantage of the tougher appetites of a new generation of readers. The biologist who muses in the Mojave Desert in 1956 may be less entertaining than the coruscating author of *Wordsworth in the Tropics* (1929), but as readers we are for our part more vulnerable than those feckless ghosts of thirty years ago to the chilling sentences:

'Nature is blessedly non-human; and insofar as we belong to the natural order, we too are blessedly non-human. . . . The non-humanity of wild flowers, as of the deepest levels of our own minds, exists within a system which includes and transcends the human. . . . In the home-made realm of symbols we are separate and mutually hostile partisans. Thanks to words, we have been able to rise above the brutes; and thanks to words, we have often sunk to the level of demons.'

The last two of these quoted sentences from a 1956 essay might be matched anywhere in the anthology; but the first two sentences hint at a possible philosophy which the entranced reader of, say, *Point Counter Point* would have sworn the author could never possibly embrace. In several of the post-war essays, indeed, the knowingness may remain as an inescapable flavour, but the giggle has gone. In his latest work Mr. Huxley sometimes even forgets to shrug his shoulders, sometimes forgets his cherished amateur status and begins to read us the first few pages of a serious lecture from the signs of the times.

What has happened? Whatever it is, it has happened not only to Mr. Huxley but to us all. To that extent, at least, he is still writing as a more than usually articulate representative of the ordinary cultivated contemporary. It is hardly surprising that since we seem not to know, nowadays, which branch we *are* sitting on, the essayist and the reader alike have become a little less agile with the saw.

Quoting D. H. Lawrence to the effect that as novelist he considered himself superior to the saint, the scientist, the philosopher and the poet, since 'only in the novel are *all* things given full play', Mr. Huxley adds, in his preface: 'What is true of the novel is only a little less true of the essay'. Let our memories of the inventiveness of *Antic Hay* or the underlying passion of *Brave New World* serve to give the lie to so mistaken a notion! For although it might be rash to claim for Mr. Huxley's own novels an illustration of anything like the full range of Coleridgean Imagination, it is certainly true that even at their best his essays can juggle with no more than the fixities and definites of Coleridgean Fancy.

When Mr. Huxley seeks to persuade us, so to say, that 'l'essai, c'est l'homme', he is in fact making the best of a case for little more than a practised ease of articulation, a journalistic agility deft enough to pin down the flittering musings of an almost over-volatile mind. Surely not even Mr. Huxley could allow himself, within the charged atmosphere of a novel, to get away with the flat uncharacterized pronouncement of such a sentence as: 'If I could paint and had the necessary time, I should devote myself for a few years to making pictures only of olive trees.' Put it in a novel, and the speaker of such a sentence becomes at once a figure of fun; put it in an essay, and the reader can hardly avoid embarrassment. For this primness is Addison in his most maddening mood. The development of the novel since the days of *The Spectator* has saved us from too much of this sort of thing, except in the heaviest of quotation marks.

Alas, the lightness with which Mr. Huxley could in 1959 transfer Lawrence's serious statement quite out of context and relevance is yet another example of that frivolous garrulity which has tricked out so much of his writing with the false transitions of a conjurer. What is now so surprising, taken in extended sample, is the uncritical looseness of so much of his writing. One had remembered Mr. Huxley as an elegant stylist. Yet here, flung together, his chosen pieces reveal an astonishing abundance of clichés, a litter of 'that is to say' and 'whichever the case may be' and 'mention in passing' and 'propagandists would have us believe' and 'I will cite only one more'.

He is, and has been, a master of the paradoxical phrase. Yet taken from their slim volumes and shuffled together, his paradoxes reveal themselves far too often as wearisomely distended by verbose afterthoughts. Can this really be so? Were these hackneyed bits of padding really present at the time of the first appearance of *Music at Night* and *Ends and Means*? It seems so. Among the nuts and port, or even at a Rotarians' hasty luncheon, many of Mr. Huxley's paragraphs might still raise a tolerant laugh. In cold print, they prompt instead the priggish questions: 'Is it really true that any one thing is no more or less important than any other thing? What *does* this man stand for?'

There would be little point in grumbling now about the elaborate facetiousness of some of Mr. Huxley's early pieces if the tone had not survived into his more recent and more serious essays. 'Me personally the unflagging pleasures of contemporary cities leave most lugubriously unamused'—this is from an essay in a 1929 volume. A recent piece from *Esquire* magazine opens with the words: 'The reading of yet another book about modern psychological theories is always, I find, a rather exasperating experience.' If the word 'rather' denotes a weakening of fanciful *élan* the words 'I find' betray that same old weary superiority, quite as complacent as Addison's. This would be less bothersome if the succeeding sentences in the *Esquire* essay did not constitute so admirably launched an attack on pretentiousness in the works of some second-rate and second-hand psychologists.

It would be a thousand pities if the old Huxley tone should prevent a modern reader from enjoying the new Huxley content. For the running commentary of Mr. Huxley's intelligent talk does most wonderfully capture the sort of things cultivated Englishmen have been thinking during his lifetime, but never expressed with such effortless flow. When H. G. Wells came to write his autobiography, he flattered his readers by adding the sub-title: 'Discoveries and Conclusions of a Very Ordinary Brain'. It is both humbling and a fillip to one's pride, in re-reading Mr. Huxley's essays, to note how faithfully he has in fact marched along beside the kind of fashionable views he once seemed to be forming.

3

THE STRENGTH OF TIMID HEARTS

E. M. Forster

Mr. Forster's last novel, *A Passage to India*, was published in 1924, the year of the Wembley Exhibition. Meanwhile, we have cherished such little scraps in the way of reviews and memories of travel and reprinted talks as he throws us from time to time, and read essays and monographs about him. To these latter we turn in the hope of finding a sensible structure of criticism to tell us reasons why we enjoy his books as much as we do. Is he, on the basis of only five novels, as important a novelist as we think him to be? It is so difficult, in the face of competition from more prolific, more graspable novelists, to maintain him at the level where we should like to keep him. Rose Macaulay's little guide-book* made us feel that she, for all her devotion, was in the main expressing better than we ourselves could express the agreeable opinions we have always had; Professor Trilling's companion piece† goes in for statement of themes and tracking down of attitudes, yet fails to construct for us the platform our admiration has been demanding. We fall back into the pleasing bewilderment of paying Mr. Forster the highest honours for representing we know not precisely what, for writing beautifully we cannot see how, for being major in a manner so beguilingly characteristic of minor.

The first novel, *Where Angels Fear to Tread*, was published in 1905, when the author was twenty-six. Mr. Trilling comments that this is not a remarkable age at which to have written a first novel, 'unless the novel be, as Forster's was, a whole and mature work dominated by a fresh and commanding intelligence'.

* Rose Macaulay: *The Writings of E. M. Forster*, 1938.

† Lionel Trilling: *E. M. Forster*. Third Edition, 1951.

Maturity, subtlety, intelligence, discrimination—these are the counters shuffled hopefully to and fro by the critics and appreciators, and they are all applicable enough. Yet after spanning the twenty odd years of his career as a novelist, we are left with the original notion that, sly and modulated and witty as Mr. Forster's manner may be, what really wins our assent is not the beautiful intelligence but the beautiful simplicity of heart. This is where he wins us, and this is where he makes it so difficult for his admirers to pin down and display his credentials for greatness.

There is a scene in *A Room With a View* (1908) where the English tourists, returning from some prudent Italian excursion, are overtaken by a storm; their carriage just misses being struck by a falling tramline-standard, and in the sudden relief at their narrow escape, 'the floods of love and sincerity, which might fructify every hour of life, burst forth in tumult.' Which *might* fructify every hour of life—the phrase is central for an understanding of Mr. Forster. We are decent enough folk, he is always saying, and we really do have in us a great fund of loving-kindness and tender mercy, but heigh-ho, what *does* become of it? When Mr. Forster asks these questions, his readers feel as if they are standing in the crowd when Hans Andersen's child announces that the Emperor *has* no clothes: we recognize at once that the child is right and that everybody else is wrong, and yet when we turn to make up a list of prominent citizens it is difficult to see the child figuring as an equal among the aldermen. So right do we feel Mr. Forster to be, so admirable when he speaks out and so disarming when he hesitates, that we want to pop him up with Tolstoy and Henry James; but when we have set him there he looks so uncomfortable, and begs to be let down in a tone so aggrieved, that we wonder what on earth possessed us to put him there in the first place. Down he comes, and at once we fall in love with the grace of his relaxed omniscient humility, and strive to push him, like a protesting Pope, towards his throne.

Mr. Forster is a dictatorial Liberal who insists on seeing both sides of every question; it is for this quality that many will wish to enshrine him and we may suspect that it is this quality that makes him look so quizzically unsuitable when enshrined. 'Niceness,' as Mrs. Leavis has said of him, 'has its drawbacks.' Like his own Rickie, 'he suffered from the Primal Curse, which is not—as the Authorized Version suggests—the knowledge of good and evil, but the knowledge of good-and-evil.' We might suppose, then, that uncertainty of purpose keeps our author mascot-size when we should like him to be a totem-pole? But, no; Rose Macaulay could condense from his writings a credo in which many of his readers would join: 'He believes in personal relationships, in individuality, in beauty, in affection, in liberty and in democracy; he disbelieves in nationalism, empire, militarism, catch-words, Christianity, oligarchy, dictatorship, big business, schoolmasters and a number of other things.' In the early short stories, indeed, she found:

'abstract and brief chronicles of the earlier novels. In them Reality, Life, Truth, Passion, Gaiety, Nature, Youth, call the thing what you will, fights for its life, in various garbs and with various weapons, against Unreality, Death, Sham, Conventionalism, Dullness, Pompousness, Age.'

All this is definite enough for any categorist—indeed, only the author's technical skill has prevented his characters from being mere mouthpieces. If there still remains a feeling of weakness, it is not to be explained simply as a matter of uncertainty or omission. It is a weakness inherent in the very nature of Mr. Forster's attitude to the qualities he asks us to inspect. There is a fineness of perception that enables him to be a devastating social critic. He can catch his victims at the very moment when, imagining their mentor to be aesthetic, they vulgarly poke fun at an ugly house, or when, imagining him at another moment to be a jolly sun-worshipper, they discover with what genuine devotion he reverences Pallas Athene no less than Eros. This same correcting process of discrimination, this liberal tendency to allow the exception not only proof of but also equality with the rule, can sometimes weaken to the point of danger the effect of Mr. Forster's arguments and the attraction of his chosen qualities. If bad things are generously allowed the benefit of the doubt, good things are sometimes deliberately scratched in a mood of anti-generosity, as if to demonstrate that there is no trickery. There are times, in short, when we his readers, convinced by the Forster arguments and in tune with the Forster mood, nevertheless feel ourselves to be better advocates than the author or his characters—and this makes for uneasiness all round.

In an essay published in 1938,* Dr. F. R. Leavis complained that 'intelligence and sensitiveness such as *Howards End* at its finest represents need not be so frustrated by innocence and inexperience as the unrealities of the book suggest'. Exactly: if we have been, in the main, persuaded of the validity of Schlegel culture, we cannot see why the younger sister at any rate has to break away from it into the so very unlikely arms of Leonard Bast. Professor Trilling, noting the symbolism of the blood that falls on Lucy's Italian pictures (in *A Room With a View*), claims for the true lover of art a sincerity greater than that allowed by Mr. Forster himself, the arch-advocate: 'the art of the timid is not life: to the courageous the pictures have had blood on them from the first.' Again, if Stephen Wonham is Nature's child, it is surely needlessly hurtful to be taught that he can survive only at the expense of poor Rickie, the seeker after truth. And the cruellest disappointment of all, the worst moral 'let-down', is in *A Passage to India*, when Fielding and Aziz, having failed to make any impression by words or deeds against the barriers separating East and West, cannot even make a personal contact, cannot release even for a moment their 'floods of love and sincerity'. Anyone who shares Mr. Forster's faith in personal relationships, and especially any reader who has been converted by Mr. Forster himself to that faith, must protest that the defeatist ending is not inescapably inherent in the situation, but indicates a failure of creative vitality:

' "Why can't we be friends now?" said the other, holding him affectionately. "It's what I want. It's what you want."

'But the horses didn't want it—they swerved apart; the earth didn't want it, sending up rocks through which riders must pass single file; the temples, the tank, the jail, the palace, the birds, the carrion, the Guest House . . . they didn't want it, they said in their hundred voices: "No, not yet," and the sky said: "No, not there." '

In an essay of 1939 on the subject of Mrs. Miniver, Mr. Forster causes that lady from the 'top drawer but one' to cry ' "*touchée!*" with her little ringing laugh, and pass on untouched'. Alas, he can cause his own heroes and heroines to cry '*touché!*' when pierced by the arrows of passion or intelligence, and nevertheless pass on as if untouched, or much less touched than

* Reprinted in *The Common Pursuit*, 1952.

we, their rallied and convinced advocates, would have them be. What seems to have happened is that the sympathetic liberal mind, distressed by dogma and shrinking not so much from convictions as from a continuing courage in them, can sometimes with wisdom decline to see much difference between off-white and dark grey—a paralysis of the finer discrimination with results as disastrous in personal relationships as in morals or politics.

The vague dissatisfaction arising from the disparity between the Forster ideals and the Forster achievements, as reflected in the five novels, may count for weakness; but these waverings and hesitations of attitude are redeemed by a gift refreshingly simple, a gift having nothing to do with moral niceties but all to do with a novelist's art. For Mr. Forster is a modest but secure master of dialogue. He can, from his first pages to his last, make his characters talk intelligently and naturally at the same time: a feat difficult enough in life, and all but unattainable in novels. We know the very tone of their voices—Miss Bartlett of *A Room With a View*, Tibby of *Howards End*, Ansell of *The Longest Journey* and the rest. Of the characters of *Where Angels Fear to Tread* Dr. Leavis justly commented that they 'are all very simplified figures, seen from the outside; it is only in a very qualified way that they engage us (though they engage us enough for a measure of poignancy)'. But even in this earliest novel (and how much more so in *A Passage to India*) they are all so *speakingly* alive that when they take up the challenge in some mild encounter, the outcome of which is nevertheless of great significance, we do for the moment share in the match, cheering or fretful as the fortunes of the game change. How will Miss Abbott deal with her love for Gino? Will Rickie acknowledge his half-brother? Will Cecil Vyse, in *A Room With a View*, be sent packing? What exactly, in *Howards End*, is the strange power of Mrs. Wilcox? When will Adela Quested speak out?

Caught up in these and similar interests as we listen to the talk, enjoying wit and scenting out the humbug, we are so beguiled, so involved in the conversation, that it does not occur to us until the novels have been laid aside that all these young people and uncles and cousins and servants and husbands have been deftly arranged in ranks, sometimes changing sides and sometimes trying in vain to remain neutral, but always in the event for or against one or other of the good or bad causes collected in Rose Macaulay's list. Then and only then do we recall that these people, so wonderfully alive when they are talking, seem rarely to engage in activities, even of the less boisterous kinds, not somehow connected with the issues at hand. And (in the earlier novels at any rate) when outside events do impinge, when Gerald is 'broken up' in the football match or the train goes over Rickie's knees, they can be as pat and unconvincing as the horrid crimes hinted at in Henry James's drawing-rooms, and serve, by their fantasy, to muffle for a moment the continuing talk round the tea-table.

If we can accept the view that Mr. Forster's recurring theme is the desirability of releasing 'the floods of love and sincerity', and if it can be agreed that his quick ear and urbane style combine to furnish an equipment more than equal to the tasks of dialogue and argument, then the disparity between what the author deems desirable and what he can permit his characters to achieve in the world in which they live can be taken as the measure of his 'criticism of life'. Dr. Leavis has made this acute observation:

'Pre-eminently a novelist of civilized personal relations, he has at the same time a radical dissatisfaction with civilization—with the finest civilization of personal intercourse that he knows; a radical dissatisfaction that prompts references to D. H. Lawrence rather than to Jane Austen.'

The reference to Lawrence has to be qualified by allowances of different aims and methods, and Dr. Leavis did so qualify his comparison. But it serves to bring to a recognizable head that vague feeling of 'something lacking' at which other critics have hinted. It is not so much that Mr. Forster himself remains a spectator of life—for it would be silly and impudent to hazard how far he or Lawrence or any other novelist sought to live the life he valued most. But his men and women, lined up on the field, too often remain non-playing players. They see, one after another, that the best thing in life is to play, and play without counting the cost. But those who do play look slightly ridiculous from the sidelines where the author and the rest of the characters and we ourselves are all standing.

'Not possible' is perhaps the sad message of *A Passage to India*, expressed in Fielding's withdrawal and, more symbolically, in the petering out of the triumphal Indian procession after the trial scene. 'It was a victory, but such a queer one.' The problem of the next step is stated but not answered: 'Where was the procession going?' An earlier attempt at a direct statement of passion was a failure: the embrace of Agnes and Gerald in *The Longest Journey* may cause Rickie to limp away rapt in wonderful visions of Love (coloured valleys, pure flame, virgin snow, springs of creation, torrent of song, and so on), but the brief embarrassed description of that embrace is woefully inadequate. Here, as in so many other instances in this author's work, it is the attitude towards a feeling, rather than the feeling itself, that matters. 'The man's grip was the stronger. He had drawn the woman on to his knee. . . .' One almost visualizes a crane. 'Her face had no expression. It stared at the intruder and never saw him. Then her lover kissed it. . . .' *It!* We are not far from Henry James's *The Velvet Glove* with the immortal Berridge's 'application of all his recovered wholeness of feeling, under his moustache, might express'. (It is surely a tribute to Mr. Forster's freshness of outlook and universality of theme that we recall so rarely that four of the five novels were Edwardian in time.)

Mr. Forster's heroes are the sort of men Forrest Reid's boys might have grown into, if Forrest Reid had allowed his boys to grow up. This is perhaps another way of saying that the Forster novels are the sort of novels the Forster short stories did in fact grow into. About the Forster stories and the Forrest Reid novels and autobiographies there plays the same Grecian light, made manifest in the same strong simple colours. Pan is the most natural of strollers through woods and fields so freshly viewed, and we wonder why we had hitherto enjoyed living in a mist. Yet when the pagan boys have grown into liberal men, they strain to peer through the moral mist with eyes already less clear than those of Pan or the pagan boys, because they brim a little with nostalgia and the vision is slightly 'off the beam'. Thus Rickie in *The Longest Journey* persuades us, and himself, that he is nostalgic for Cambridge; but when we see him with his half-brother Stephen Wonham, it is clear that he is fascinated by an earlier state of bliss of which Cambridge was but a reflection.

After Cambridge, Italy serves as the symbol of release from suburban (and donnish) limitations. 'The traveller who has gone to Italy to study the tactile values of Giotto, or the corruption of the Papacy, may return remembering nothing but the blue sky and the men and women who live under it.' But it is with the *effect* of Italy and Italians on the British visitors that Mr. Forster is mainly concerned. In *A Room With a View* no one Italian scene or person stays for long in the memory; in *Where Angels Fear to Tread*, Gino wreaks havoc with the Herriton sense of proportion and the Herriton wickerwork of morality, but he himself, when he comes most to life before us, comes to life as an animated symbol—of earth-earthy love when he dandles his offspring, of earth-earthy cruelty when he twists a broken arm. In each instance it is the effect on other people that matters, and the author seems not to speak from inside Gino himself.

Coolly the Forster characters lead us to the conclusion that heat is good; the author's brain tells him and us that passion is worth more than intelligence; with delicacy he counsels us to beware of those who, like Miss Bartlett, ask 'Are not beauty and delicacy the same?' Surely there can be no harm in accepting the gifts of our senses? Surely our 'need for a sympathetic gesture is so great that we care not what exactly it signifies or how much we have to pay for it afterwards', and we yield at times, like Lucy Honeychurch, even to the pressure of Miss Bartlett's hand? Alas, we are taught, but not shown. Pan keeps his heart to himself and becomes a liberal humanitarian, proposing to tread in carpet slippers the antic hay. And when the time came for Mr. Forster to draw the portrait of a hero, he chose not a passionate world-forsaking lover but a quiet thoughtful don who saw how important love should be, who wrote 'I have seldom been out of love', who was 'the best man who ever lived', but who felt most and lived best within the confines of King's College, Cambridge.

The uneasiness, after all, is the uneasiness of truth itself. Romantic novelists by the dozen have imagined a world in which we would willingly, but do not, believe. Others, gifted less than Mr. Forster with the destructive accomplishment of wit, have turned to rend, as illusions, the true notions of their youth. It is the measure of Mr. Forster's art as philosopher and novelist that he can show us in the lives of decent baffled cultured folk, as imperfect as ourselves, the residual possibilities of courage and of love.

4

PAN IN ULSTER

Forrest Reid

Nothing can be more exasperating, to certain soberly constituted minds, than the sight—or even the prospect—of a solitary human being quietly enjoying himself. Let him be noisy, or in company, and his pleasure in the world can be made acceptable to, albeit unshared by, the most censorious disposition. The self-sufficiency is the irritant. At once we become possessed of a sense of moral outrage, be the pleasure in question never so innocent. '*Look* at that awful man, smoking his pipe among the snowdrops! Why does he not busy himself with something useful?' It is a vexation as intemperate and disproportionate as when we happen upon someone asleep in a deckchair while we, wide awake, contemplate the plight of the western world. Before long we are in danger of espousing the cause of the Marthas of this world, claiming that we, too, could all appreciate the beauties of life if we were not already, in a spirit of resentful self-sacrifice, fully occupied with kitchen tasks while Mary, her hands disencumbered, pulls pious faces in the drawing-room. If a writer should harangue us on Mary's behalf, we may disagree with his conclusions and yet find it in ourselves to applaud his crusading zeal—for is he not in this very activity showing himself, so to say, to be gainfully employed? But let him *be* such a person, let him be seen picking up pretty pebbles without bothering to assume the role either of a licensed poet or an instructive professor of geology, and he is in danger of arousing in his readers an indefensible but powerful antagonism.

Forrest Reid's self-sufficiency, as man and writer, won for him a small, loyal body of like-minded friends and readers. This same quality, rather than any self-imposed restriction of theme, has limited his following and allowed him to be esteemed as a specialist novelist writing for a very small, esoteric minority. It will be a singularly undeserved misfortune if his novels are to be set aside for the self-conscious satisfaction of those who may wish to see in him the excuse for a cult. For his prime subject and only enduring interest was that one universal experience common to every mature reader of every possible shade of opinion—youth. Moralists or artists, dull or diverting, purposeful or negligent, we have all been young; we can all remember childish fears and schoolboy raptures. To enjoy Forrest Reid it is only necessary to overcome that stubborn resistance to the notion of a grown man still enjoying, with unbroken continuity, pleasures we ourselves had forgotten and must now strive consciously to recapture. The resistance is unmistakably there, but it is peculiarly difficult to spot; it is as though our sentimental pleasure in the sight of children playing rounders on the beach were to be marred by shock and envy at the discovery that one of the 'children' was a fully grown man.

Forrest Reid died in 1947. Five years later a memorial plaque was unveiled outside his unpretentious Belfast home, a semi-detached house of the type so often singled out by witty novelists who, themselves resentful products of the *petite bourgeoisie*, see beauty in slums and palaces and shrink from all intervening habitations as from some unrelieved waste land. Here he lived and worked, read and wrote, cooked and dreamed. From this house he set out daily on his walks. Like many people who live alone, he enjoyed company—for to an independent bachelor, company is normally of his own choosing and therefore especially welcome. It is true that his abiding interest in the world of boyhood led him to seek out the company of sturdy lads whose words and gestures, mingling with his own recollections, would reappear again and again in his books. But it would be quite inaccurate to imagine, or seek to establish, an exclusive interest on Reid's part in such companionship. Kenneth Hamilton, hero of one of Reid's most attractive essays, was only one member of the Hamilton family to whom he figured as 'Uncle Forrest'. To the rest of the family he was not a faun-like creature from the Isles of Greece but the neighbour who lived alone in Ormiston Crescent instead of *en famille* on the Malone Road, who came in regularly for bridge on Tuesday, Thursday and Saturday evenings, concentrating with a wholly professional zeal on winning the rubber, and who only partially kept at bay with tobacco smoke the odours of his evil-smelling dog, Nix.

Forrest Reid lived a simple, indeed a humdrum life. Oddly enough, that is the only biographical fact about him that need have significance for literary critics. Unlike so many writers who have turned their backs on the values of the contemporary world, living flamboyantly unconventional lives and enshrining in flamboyantly unconventional prose very ordinary notions, Forrest Reid spoke and wrote with grave simplicity about a system of values which, if adopted, would turn the world's ideas gently but firmly topsy-turvy. How little interested he was in changing men's outward behaviour (apart from his scrupulous attention to good manners) may be judged from his own quiet acceptance of provincial life, his disinclination to mingle in literary or political circles, his devotion to such unrevolutionary pastimes as bonfires, croquet and jig-saw puzzles. He hated fuss and every form of pretentiousness. Just as some people quietly accept and try to carry out the tenets of Christianity without wishing to become priests or missionaries, so Reid believed in and sought, in Belfast, to live in accordance with the spirit of Greek Mediterranean culture. He prayed to Hermes—and he was as surprised as most of us are when, on one occasion at least, his prayers were answered.

Living in the private world he so beautifully unveiled in *Apostate* (1926), Forrest Reid would invite selected spirits to share his little kingdom but he was never roused to proselytize. In this respect he differed in temper from Norman Douglas, that other *inglese italianizzato*, who huffed and snuffed—to our great benefit—at the Anglo-Saxon mood. For Reid, mild practice was enough; any preaching in his books is sufficiently embodied in the attraction of the alternative way of life he sets before us. Nor was he immune from crotchets and contradictions: Mediterranean in outlook, he was none the less an Ulsterman by birth, and he could be as testy as the best of them. To those who showed no native aptitude for the classical virtues or who were impervious to the charms of the golden age of youth and adolescence, Forrest Reid could turn a face the very reverse of inviting. 'Socrates was the greatest man who ever lived!' he once informed a damsel who had wandered into his tiny bedroom and saw the ikon of his saint hanging above the bed. Then the young lady was rash enough to ask: 'Why?' 'Because he was!' he snapped, and that was that.

In one way or another, sometimes directly presented and sometimes obliquely approached in lyrical, melodramatic or frankly day-dreaming guise, Forrest Reid's theme is that of a boy's open enjoyment of the natural world—its sights and sounds and colours, the warmth of the sun and the independence of animals, the sparkle of the sea and the smoothness of human bodies—persists into and beyond middle age, beneath thickening layers of pretence and apparent indifference. He hated to acknowledge the passing of youth. It was bad enough to lose agility, to grow from feckless colt into stolid old dray-horse. But it added insult to injury when the loss was not honestly bewailed, when the world pretended that it was happy to put away childish things. 'I don't believe it,' he said in effect; and his young heroes are surrounded by various types from the adult world, ranging from parents who seemed to have succeeded in growing a second skin, to others—uncles and tutors and country friends—who felt some measure of kinship, sometimes even to the point of dreaming themselves back into their boyhood bodies.

There is a scene in *The Bracknels* (published in 1911, and in a revised version, *Denis Bracknel*, in 1947) where the strange child Denis is surprised at night by his tutor in the act of pouring a libation to the Moon in a thicket near his home:

'Half an hour ago Rusk had asked himself how far it was all real, how far a mere exploit of boyish romance: but somehow as he watched it now, alone, at this hour and in this place, with the dimness of night and the stillness of motionless trees all around him, stretching away into what might have been the very womb of the past, he found it difficult to see it in the light of anything childish or trivial. . . . What, then, was the relation of this naked pagan boy, with body bared to the whiteness of the moon, to the young Presbyterian who sat Sunday by Sunday in his father's pew?'

The adult is sympathetic, but honestly perplexed. A not dissimilar scene occurs in *Young Tom* (1944), where Tom, watching a friend stripping for a river bathe, takes it in his stride and is quite unmoved by speculation or wonderment. True, the boy's thoughts have to be put in faintly hortatory language by his adult creator, but the keyword of the passage is 'natural':

'He had simply emerged from his soiled and much-patched clothing like a butterfly from a chrysalis, and the contrast between his fair hair and the golden brown of his body and limbs appeared to the smaller boy as attractive as anything could be. In fact James-Arthur, merely by divesting himself of his clothes, had instantly become part of the natural scene, like the grass and the trees and the river and the sky, and the dragonfly asleep upon his water-lily.'

It may be objected that, in the main, Forrest Reid's novels about boyhood (excluding some early titles, and those already quoted, they are: *Following Darkness*, 1912, rewritten as *Peter Waring*, 1937; *Uncle Stephen*, 1931; *Brian Westby*, 1934; *The Retreat*, 1936) have only one theme, and betray a sorry limitation of interest in a creative writer. The force of this perfectly valid criticism may be diminished by two considerations. First, Reid was most successful as a novelist when he wrote simply and fearlessly as an Ulster-born Pan, and least effective when, as in *Uncle Stephen*, he muddied his canvas by the admixture of mystical fantasy of a more Teutonic shade, offensive alike to the squeamish and to the more jovially 'pagan' reader. Secondly, in lines aptly quoted by Mr. Burlingham,* Reid made it very clear that what to some readers must remain an attractive byway of literature he himself considered to be the great arterial road not only of writing but also of living: his reiterated 'theme' was, in fact, his own 'poetic criticism of life':

'If I had never written a line, and were never again to write one, that would not alter my conviction that the years of childhood, boyhood, and adolescence are the most significant. What follows is chiefly a logical development—the child being father of the man.'

It is well to admit that a writer who made himself the acknowledged exponent of the mind and imagination of boyhood was naturally full of special affection for those bright qualities of feeling and intelligence we can all, following Wordsworth, detect in the 'natural piety' of youth before 'Shades of the prison-

* Russell Burlingham: *Forrest Reid*. A Portrait and a Study. 1953.

house begin to close/Upon the growing Boy'. Once this none too formidable nettle has been grasped, there is a chance that an author who has so far chiefly appealed to lovers of a clear prose lit now by gleams of a stoical irony and now by the smile of one who glories in the world about him, may also find favour with a widening public.

For may the great god Pan forbid that Forrest Reid should ever fall into the hands of cult-mongers! In life he detested the over-literary approach. His little house was crammed with books but he could snort, in his cherished 'Philistine' moods, at literary coteries. When asked why he did not move away from Belfast, he replied: 'I live here simply because I was born here. Most of my friends are here and it is a good place to live.' Then he would add: 'You never meet *anyone* here!' He hated to be visited as 'Forrest Reid the novelist'—he wanted his friends to come back, to keep up the talk over tea or whisky, to listen to his gramophone records. He was inclined to like drudgery, had a vein of Ulster severity, and was apt to change ostentatiously into his walking shoes when a caller embarked on insincere aesthetic theories. He could use the vocabulary of his young playmates when occasion demanded: 'Oh, what an awful whopper!' he would say, when artificial views were aired. But behind all the irascibility and addiction to pranks there was a steady discriminating affection for all those, living or dead, who could see goodness and love innocence. His best readers will be those who can share, if only for an hour, his tough, pedantic simplicity of heart.

5

WHY CAN'T THE ENGLISH?

Looking back in friendly jeering

Mr. Martin Green's portrait does not adorn the jacket of his book. This is (for once) a pity. *A Mirror for Anglo-Saxons* (1961) is bound to stir up a deal of controversy, and it would be pleasant to know what the thirty-four-year-old author looks like. Does he, by any chance, resemble the type-figure he presents, in the manner of Overbury or Earle, of the essential Englishman?

'He is small, neat, quick-moving, with a fresh-colored, neat-featured, unemphatic face, without physical stateliness, wheeling a bicycle, carelessly dressed, open-necked, plain-mannered, shrewd, skeptical, friendly-jeering in tone, hostile to all elaborateness or eccentricity, unwilling to talk his emotions, but quick in his sympathies, soon intimately related to you, jealous of his masculinity, a family man, essentially private, needing and creating around him the atmosphere of decency, kindliness, cleanliness; the sort of man who asks skeptical questions after the meeting.'

It is within some such package that Mr. Green is prepared to bundle up the few remaining manifestations of British 'decency', a quality he has found surviving significantly in only four men: D. H. Lawrence, George Orwell, F. R. Leavis, and Kingsley Amis. It should be added that although the kind of 'decency' Mr. Green yearns after is confined to the Northern counties, there seems little hope for any of us, whether we live above or below the Severn-Wash line, since two of his heroes are dead and the other two are Cambridge dons.

It would be very easy indeed, and very foolish too, to dismiss

Mr. Green's book by launching upon it the sort of onslaught he has delivered against most things in contemporary British culture. His picture (for polemical reasons, if for no other) is necessarily partial, and an equally partial reply would serve to counter many of his thrusts. But it is to be hoped that British readers of *A Mirror for Anglo-Saxons* will not be nettled into a merely defensive posture.

The kind of stance Mr. Green adopts towards his reader is precisely that which his type-figure might adopt (though why he should see himself as wheeling his bicycle instead of riding it is a puzzle, and may even offer a clue to the whole book); and a 'friendly-jeering' response is called for. This is a serious and important book, not less so for the frankness and—curiously—modesty of its tone. This young man is hurt, and weeps; he is frustrated, and kicks against the pricks; he reaches out for comfort, and when he finds it in another civilization he is generous enough to acknowledge it.

The fact that his personal salvation should have been found in America, of all places, is likely to arm many otherwise sympathetic readers. Had Mr. Green waxed lyrical beneath the ilex and olives of the Mediterranean much would have been forgiven him: he would be repeating the approved Grand Tour discontents and would win the approval of those of his countrymen who cry ' "Let's pretend it's Capri" in Hyde Park' and do not recognize how degraded a figure they cut, seeking to inject a fake vitamin extract into a body the real ills of which they have not begun to understand. By selecting modern America as his pep-pill this penetrating critic of our own malaise is likely to find the statement of his diagnosis shouted down by rearguard cries of the inane 'Let's play Greece to their Rome' variety. Or perhaps such readers will not get so far: the fact that the book, presumably by some economy of publishing technique, preserves its original American spelling, will be enough to make them throw up—and in—their hands.

There is no avoiding it; this nettle must be grasped before the intention and merits of the book can be discussed at all. The author is an Englishman who loves his country with a frenzy engaging heart and mind alike. He dislikes the 'official' version of England, dislikes its voice, its niminy-piminy backward-looking loss of courage, its new 'unwillingness to take great things greatly', its bogus gentility, its thinning of the blood. His objections crystallized when he discovered America; not because he swallowed America whole (for he can be pretty tart about America, too) but because once the weight of much moribund tradition had been lifted from his neck he could look back from the less muzzy air of Michigan and see more clearly just what he loved in the England of his own genuine traditions, and just what sort of tawdry fancy-dress nostalgia was sapping its lifeblood, muffling its confidence, disappointing its friends. When one has made this first effort of adjustment to Mr. Green's standpoint—and it is by no means easy—the honesty of his intentions becomes clear, the strangely self-effacing quality of his effrontery can win indulgence and even admiration. And a reader of the old school who is patient and open-minded enough to read through to the end may even find himself saying, with unexpected pride: 'Only an Englishman could have written like this.'

A Mirror for Anglo-Saxons is made up of seven essays, linked together by brief autobiographical passages explaining where the author was at the time and why he wrote as he did. It sounds arch, conceited; it is, in fact, a straightfaced laying of the cards on the table. It is helpful to have these casual, almost naïve comments, and they contain some of the best writing in the book. Mr. Green does not thrust his personality on the reader, but something of it seeps through.

'I was born into a lower-class family, none of whose members, on either side, had been even to secondary school, but at eleven I took an examination . . . and was sent free to the county grammar school. . . . By eighteen I was a gentleman, beyond hope of reprieve. I had been radically separated from my home and relations; not by any crude snobbery, but by a genuine and inevitable introduction into a new mental world. . . .'

After Cambridge and military service the author found a teaching job in France, and then a teaching fellowship at the University of Michigan. Finding himself 'in a nation where everyone expected things to get better', he stayed for three years, escaping 'that dull, dim, echoing, frightening weightlessness' and breathing in 'the sense of eagerness and effort and choice and achievement'. Returning home in 1955 he wrote an essay for the Anglo-American magazine *Quixote*, full of amusing yet serious sketches of his fellow-passengers on board a Cunarder, 'unluridly dead, in the English manner, just inoffensively unalive'; of the 'deeply offensive' B.B.C. quiz-programmes with their 'port-wine voices, shrill or gruff, soaked in a sweet, rich arrogance of caste, identifying lines from *Alice in Wonderland* . . .'—and so on. Another job, this time in Turkey, produced 'Home Thoughts about Two Homes from Abroad', and in this piece the attack on false standards at home is developed in vividly telling phrases. ' "Sell all your goods and give to the poor", delivered in an Oxford accent, becomes a perfectly conservative idea.' Or again: 'Whatever is contemporary is merely correct; though one knows that as soon as it becomes history one will be told that it was all magnificently muddled, maliciously colorful . . . in the inimitable British manner.'

After Turkey Mr. Green returned to America, having forgiven Michigan for their contumaciousness over his Ph.D. (one aspect of American culture, one surmises, that he does not long to see at home?) and having decided, very sensibly, that however much other nations may try to explain away the causes of America's expanding economy the great joy of living there is to concentrate not on its causes but on its effects. Back at Ann Arbor, he wrote his third essay on the theme of the British Establishment. Fair-minded enough to acknowledge that 'in no country in the world is the career [of a gentleman] so open to the talents as in England', he gives us a somewhat jaundiced account of the process by which, profiting by the sort of social reforms he himself would presumably have fought for, he 'slid over from Gracie Fields to Anthony Eden'. By twenty-one he was B.A. Cantab., a 'gilded youth'. This seems to have worried him a lot, and partly for the warm-hearted reason that Mr. Green does not seem to think of himself as in any way marked out by inherent intelligence, as opposed to acquired 'status'.

It is at such a point that one longs to draw the author aside and assure him that other victims of the English Tripos have felt themselves a bit out of things when they go home for the vacations, without necessarily wanting to blow up the society which enabled them to profit (presumably) by three years of Cambridge, even if they 'saw through Lord Peter Wimsey at sixteen'. Cannot Mr. Green get it into his head that his problem is more personal (and therefore more difficult) than sociological? Can he not be brought to admit that most people, Etonians or county scholars, are just not as bright, or as sensitive, as he is? It is certainly vexing to discover that one cannot make political purses, so to say, out of intellectual sows' ears; but pretending that all sows' ears *ought* to be silk purses does not get one very far. Indeed, the writer makes one feel 'friendly-jeering' enough (wheeled bicycle or no) to say, straight out: 'By your own standards, most people are fools anywhere, chum.'

The fourth essay, on cultural images in England and America, pays tribute to Mr. J. D. Salinger and slogs away again at the 'voluntary self-dramatization and self-diminishment' at home; but to a friendly-jeering reader the most significant paragraph may well be that in the introductory pages which confesses to Mr. Green's new respect for 'urbanity'. He attributes it to his move from Michigan to an Eastern college (his new urbanity restrains him from mentioning the name) and to the personal influence of such people as John Crowe Ransom. Others may recognize the mellowing influence of age and success. It is true that campus life in America, given the luck of the right place and the right people at the right time, can be as comfortable and exhilarating (at the same time!) as any community in the world. It is also true that this is precisely what some young Fulbright refugees from Ohio State, say, may be finding this minute at Cambridge, Eng. The grass is always greener. . . . And Mr. Green would have been less than human if he had not found his nerves and sensibilities soothed, at thirty-one, by some of the very things which ruffled his cock-o'-the-north feathers at twenty-one. Complacency, after all, is an acquired taste.

So far, all has been (so far as England is concerned) destructive. In the concluding chapters, Mr. Green tells us what he admires in his native land, to which he returned in 1958 having 'completely ceased to be English, completely severed my connexion with all that I had been, all I most naturally was'. By this time, naturally enough, he was taking himself a little more seriously than before. He is no longer merely a sensitive recording instrument, but remembers to tell us how many brandies he drank in the Tewkesbury hotel he so much disliked. It was lucky indeed that at this stage of his disillusion he should have made or renewed contact with Dr. F. R. Leavis. We are given a moving and at times beautifully perceptive tribute to this untired veteran of the sort of moral civil war in which Mr. Green himself has been, so far, no more than a skirmisher. It is unlikely that we shall be given an account by Dr. Leavis himself of the same conversation, if only because of the scrupulous private code to which Mr. Green pays due homage. Those of us who are less scrupulous would be curious to know what the most sensitive eyes in Cambridge recorded when they rested, ten years later, on Mr. Green.

Quoting Mr. Richard Chase to the effect that in America a 'provincial, anti-intellectual, protestant moralism . . . finds its comic self-awareness in writers like Kingsley Amis, its literary-critical champion in F. R. Leavis, and its prophetic voice in D. H. Lawrence', Mr. Green accepts this trio (throwing in George Orwell for good measure) as types of the 'decent man', as opposed to the outmoded gentleman. Alas, it is sad indeed to note that so unhackneyed a revolutionary as Mr. Green should already, in stating his own positives, have fallen into the same errors of exclusiveness which marred the society he loathes. As we read on we see the liberal revolt hardening into ludicrously old-fashioned Jacobin jargon. 'Decency means cleanliness, in the most literal sense'. (Those twittering ladies on board the Cunarder were hardly, one supposes, *dirty*?) Decent people enjoy 'the propriety, the communality, the conjugality, of marriage'. (What is indecent about Mr. William Gerhardi or Mr. E. M. Forster?) They are lower-middle-class, travel third class (surely we had become 'second' by 1958?), are privates, not officers. When Mr. Green 'carries on' like this, he is simply silly. He would be better advised to go on teaching other gilded youths (if that is what a Cambridge degree must necessarily involve) how to 'want to be shown someone we can admire and love dealing with life in a way we can admire and love' (without toppling over backwards, one might add, into Norman Vincent Peale).

Mr. Green's own strongest card tends to get lost in the final shuffle. It is, surely, to act as a sensitive interpreter of those qualities in American life of which we in this country stand most in need. He is clearly growing tired (as one should, at thirty-four) of making rude gestures. He has it in him to make positive ones. Taking a last fling at our pusillanimity, he writes: 'It is because they think of themselves as "gentlemen" who aren't quite gentlemen that they resent Americans' spontaneity and self-confidence; if they could find something else they really are, and really want to be, that resentment too would disappear.' This is good constructive stuff, and Mr. Green is well equipped to build where he has demolished.

Much of this book is eloquent, and it will doubtless provoke much eloquent rebuttal. The temptation to quote more sentences is strong; the temptation to argue about them is even stronger. To take first a couple of minor samples: Mr. Green complains about the gossip and snobbery in the British press, but does not mention the social news in his American papers, pages and pages and pages of it, often inflated accounts of local 'teas' given by some sociable matron to 'honor' a pair of visiting cousins. Why is this good? Is it simply that the size of our island brings it about that we are all (North-countrymen included) treated to last night's London sprees, when we should, by analogy with those 'honoring' matrons of Omaha and Kalamazoo, be tuning our ears to the click of teacups at Piddletrenthide or Salford?

And there are times when one longs to agree with Mr. Green that much so-called 'gentlemanly' behaviour is nowadays a sham, without wishing to empty out baby with bathwater and condemn the real traditions of service which these frauds are wrecking. Granted that there is very little *noblesse oblige* about the flashy expense-account cheats who are making it difficult for 'decent' people (and not *all* of them are destitute, Mr. Green!) not to flinch when seated in certain makes of shiny motor cars; yet this is something we ought to be fighting by applying more stringent standards (even the *old* ones) on the home front, without feeling the need to call for aid upon the moral resources of Texas or Los Angeles.

Two rather more substantial lines of argument (or, rather, complement) may be indicated. First, how does it come about that, if the British way of life is as rotten as Mr. Green in the main depicts it, a growing number of American Fulbright scholars are returning to this country either for good or for second and third long visits? *These* people are not millionaires or travel snobs entranced by olde worlde villages. They have sailed their little personal Mayflowers in the opposite direction precisely because, like Mr. Green, they love their own country but enjoy gathering, within the British version of freedom, new thongs with which to lash it when they return home.

More importantly, Mr. Green does seem seriously to underestimate the surviving traces in English life of what used to be called the Nonconformist conscience. Has he compared the queue habits of London and Hamburg? Does he remember the war, when the London Tube stations were crammed with suffering wretches who behaved with a patient valour that still brings tears to the eyes for the very memory of it? And most 'gentlemen', phoney as well as genuine, can take some pride in the forbearance with which the propertied classes have surrendered their privileges without violent reaction. The notion of Fascist reprisals has never entered their heads. It has not been in this country, since the Great Divide of 1914, that strikes have been quelled by tear-gas and machine-guns, or innocent civil servants hounded from office by the boorish excesses of a muck-stained 'guilt by association'.

So one could go on. But it should be clear by now that *A Mirror for Anglo-Saxons* is a book that no lover of England should neglect to read. It is not only that the author's heart is in the right place. He is also a vivid and intelligent writer. There is, of course, only one thing for Mr. Green to do now. It is not clear where he was at the time of the publication of his book. But if he should desert England for good he will be falling into the worst kind of error. It is not so much a matter of 'decency' as of need. Writers of Mr. Green's quality are needed here, just at the moment when a vogue of pretentious, statistical navel-staring—American-inspired but devoid of Mr. Green's own native moral fervour—is coming into fashion. He is needed here—and now.

II

Scholars and Sometime Scholars

6

THE ILLUSION OF INVOLVEMENT

Reflections of a Novel Reviewer

To start reading any book is to commit an act of faith. A reader who tackles a novel must contain himself in patience, as he picks his way through a crowd of characters and notes one event after another hopefully in his memory, trusting that soon, or some time, the author—his own interpreter—will make it plain. The serious student of the novel certainly cannot complain of lack of practice in this art of trustful continence: *War and Peace* is hardly simple in design; Proust's vast novel does not reveal its pattern until the very end. But in these, as in all satisfying long novels, the reader is not gratuitously bewildered as he plods on to the final summit. Each lap of the journey has its own rewards at the time, however much more significant they may appear in retrospect. A grievance against much otherwise worthy fiction is that the reader is so exasperated *en route* that at the end of the book he feels not so much like a successful mountaineer as a cheated visitor emerging from the far end of a maze. Invited, at length, to climb up to join the author on his high maze-keeper's seat, he feels no joy at having accomplished a feat made up of innumerable 'one-step-enough-for-me' changes of direction, but only an annoyance at having been sent hither and thither to so little purpose.

'I can't seem to get *into* this novel.' It may be a dull book or a fascinating book, but once these words have been said a reader will throw it aside. All other merits will be wasted if the novelist has not learnt how to draw the reader gently into an illusion of involvement, equally necessary whether the subject-matter be simple entertainment or a new vision of life.

An analogy drawn from the cinema may offer a short cut to the theme of involvement as it affects a reader's readiness (or reluctance) to waive his consciousness of the discrepancies between life as he knows it to be and life as the novelists describe it. Two or three times a year, Hollywood presents the world with a film incomparably above its own average and better than all but a few of the productions of the French and Italian studios. This type of American film pleases for many reasons: it is technically efficient, it has wide scope and a full list of talented actors, it has a good-tempered and mainly optimistic view of the world, even when prepared to face unpalatable facts. Nevertheless, there is usually something lacking; and we do not know precisely what that something is until we see it, perhaps only for five minutes at a time, in the best French films and in Italy's contribution to the post-war screen. Then we know. Instead of a version of life—pleasant, logical, intelligent—we get life itself, or something so like life that it can only be the product of exquisite and controlled art. The beggar in such a film *is* a beggar, and not, as in the high-grade product of a popular entertainment industry, a well-known character actor at the top of his form; the soldier *is* tired, not the triumphant creation of the world's best-paid make-up artist; the girl *is* happy, not merely highly skilled in the technique of making the audience itself feel happy.

An unpretentious American best-seller, *The Great Snow*, by Henry Morton Robinson, may illustrate how an otherwise blatant 'novelist's trick' can be made acceptable because the author has first achieved the reader's willing suspension of disbelief. This novel tells a story of an intelligent, prosperous New Yorker who finds himself compelled, by the de-civilizing isolation forced upon his country house-party by a freak blizzard, to defend his life and happiness. An unpractised novelist would no doubt have made this hero a modern Robinson Crusoe, battling with pristine vigour against an over-complicated way of life: the hero would then have been as freakish as the blizzard itself, and the reader would approach his story partly in a relaxed dream-world, partly as the recipient of a crude elbow-nudging symbolism. The secret of Mr. Robinson's success is that he first introduces his hero in normal *moyen sensuel* guise—the competent town-dweller who enjoys creating a life for himself in the metropolis, who is open to impressions and prepared for an efficient Turkish bath or a week-end of artistic conversation as the case may be. Such a man, balancing brain and heart in all the nervous tension of New York, is likely enough to be able to adapt himself to the frightening change of circumstances when his country house is buried in snow for twenty days. In short, since the reader has believed in the hero from the start, he can go on to believe in his wife and his children, and even in emotional conflicts which might otherwise lack the authentic tang of a reader's shared experience. Only when all this involvement has been competently established is the novelist on safe ground when he makes it clear that these marooned human beings embody the mingled sickness and valour of everyday life as it is lived by decent, well-groomed, perplexed, unsatisfied—and non-symbolic—New Yorkers. Because in the earlier reels of the film, so to say, the man himself was made acceptably credible, his subsequent actions are allowed to pass muster simply because he, whom the reader now knows, is performing them.

The fuller illusion of real life achieved in certain moments of quite another kind of film and in certain passages of quite another kind of novel usually derives, strangely enough, from a direct impact owing little or nothing to that careful grooming of credibility noted in films starring Miss Bette Davis or in the novels, say, of Mr. A. J. Cronin. It may be helpful to select an example from a non-British novelist, Signor Giuseppe Berto, for the very reason that when reading his *The Works of God* one is no more fore-armed by local objective correlatives than when watching, say, the Italian film *Bicycle Thieves.* Yet in such a novel, as in such a film, although the setting of time and place is crystal clear it is also in a sense as unlocalized as the landscape of the moon, and although the human figures are painfully alive their passions go so far beneath the level of historical accuracy that they might well divide the globe with dinosaurs, so basic are their needs. Signor Berto's peasants can be comic and tragic at the same time; against the background of the European war their own uncomplicated role is to happen to be soldiers or to live in the cottage on which the bomb drops. The author's 'reality' is the reward of that deft economy with which he presents courage and sensibility burning obscurely in these dim lives. In the contemplation of the miseries of the humble a reader of *The Works of God* can feel again that strange pride in humanity which remains untouched by success stories, by the competence of visual or aural accuracy, or by tales which merely echo the squeals of individuals who are cheated of emotional domination. To watch human fear and human valour flowering in these paltry vessels of the human spirit is to learn that although Signor Berto, like the great film directors, can convince by means of small details of portraiture, his real achievement is to explore, without fuss and without self-conscious cunning, those levels at which national characteristics cease to matter.

Such deliberate attempts to reach down to levels of universal experience are not, of course, the only way in which a novelist can achieve a fuller illusion of reality than that considered necessary to gain the bare minimum of his reader's attention. Sometimes the illumination can come from the quality of a comment conveying the writer's own garnered experience of life; a comment presented with no special attempt at mimetic accuracy. A handy example of this curiously direct force of realism, felt when a novelist is confident enough to speak *ex cathedra*, occurs in a couple of sentences from *The Philistines* by Miss Pamela Hansford Johnson:

'They wandered up the slopes into the formal park, paused for a few moments to watch a father and daughter, strongly resembling each other in plainness and red hair, playing tennis with a kind of frantic, intimate professionalism that was somehow embarrassing to watch. It was a private expression of ambitious love, concentrated and passionate.'

Such force is curious only because it achieves the full impact of realism by means of a highly conventional off-stage observation. Yet any writer who can throw off observations of that calibre has demonstrated three qualities essential for the sustained illusion of involvement. First, energy. It is often possible to judge a novel more accurately by its asides than by its main theme, and energy is so indispensable a part of the novelist's equipment that it may be joyfully greeted whenever it reveals itself, raw and unadjusted, in by-products and odd phrases. Secondly, that strenuous concern for truth that sometimes looks like simple curiosity. Thirdly, compassion—or, to put it in less highly charged terms, a tendency to be emotionally positive towards one's characters and hence on the whole to like them, as opposed to the tendency to hate and despise human beings in general and to describe peculiarly repulsive specimens in particular. That one aside shows this particular novelist to be an energetic, truthful and sympathetic writer.

Some types of fiction call for a more than usual effort, on the part of author and reader alike, before any of these varied yet essential prerequisites of involvement can be achieved. Many readers, for example, find historical novels difficult to swallow—not because of the exertion of thinking themselves back into a past age, but because of the jolts they receive when they are called upon to switch suddenly from chapters which summarize the passage of years or fill in historical background to other chapters which concentrate on a few chosen sample days when the unrolling panorama is suddenly brought to a close-up focus. Characters who in the last chapter were names from a history-book suddenly start eating, talking, sensing the passing moment—until such time as the author is once again obliged to bowl his reader along in a spanking long-term narrative.

All this makes for uneven reading and a dislocation of interest. One contributory difficulty is that historical novelists, seeking to capture the atmosphere of the past, usually rely more on the eye than on the ear. Their readers are readily made to feel at home in unfamiliar surroundings, but can rarely believe that the voices they hear are those of living people. Very strong characterization is needed to sustain a reader's sense of implication throughout the span of time and the network of characters to be found in most historical novels—and powerful characterization is less often the result of description than of first-class dialogue. Awkwardness in the handling of tushery and gadzooksery can ruin all the credit built up by brilliant reconstructions of the Field of the Cloth of Gold or the building of the Pyramids. Given the difficulties, it is surprising how many historical novelists still succeed. Oddly enough, writers who tackle far-distant ages have been more successful in recent years than those who select for treatment more modern periods of history. Miss Selinko was less successful in enlivening the Napoleonic background of *Désirée* than Mlle. Zoë Oldenbourg who produced in *The World is Not Enough* and *The Corner-*

Stone an astonishingly vivid re-creation of medieval France. There has been, too, some brilliant new fiction based on classical history: Mme. Yourcenar's *Memoirs of Hadrian*, Mr. Peter Green's *Achilles his Armour* and *The Sword of Pleasure*, Miss Mary Renault's *The Last of the Wine* and *The King Must Die*.

The special difficulties faced by historical novelists are matched by a compensating advantage: the reader's curiosity about life as it has been lived in other ages. Simple curiosity, indeed, is one inestimable (but often strangely neglected) aid to any novelist who would suck us into the illusion of full involvement, introduce us to aspects of life far removed from our daily pre-occupation. He may deal with people geographically remote, historically distant or psychologically unfamiliar. The treatment of an unexplored scene, period or mental state can add to a good novel a bonus dose of acceptable information. A practising novelist is wise to note how many times people refer to the odd items of factual information (rather, alas, than to the odd passages of verbal beauty) they have picked up from their fiction. This curiosity can range from a simple interest in unfamiliar objects to a willingness to share fantastic states of mind and soul. The remarkable 'grip' of Mr. James Kennaway's first novel *Tunes of Glory*, for example, owes as much to the reader's interest in life within barracks and the officers' mess as to his interest in the mental aberrations of a couple of colonels.

At the first level of curiosity, Norman Douglas will never lack readers who love facts and are distressed by the sloppiness of most -isms and -ologies, who enjoy listening to the gossip of a man sharp, inquisitive and full of fun. To a writer like Douglas the world is not so much an oyster as a toyshop; he strolls from counter to counter, finding out how *this* works, admiring the bright colours of *that* thing over there. (If you begin to theorize about these pretty toys he will bark at you and call you a crooked-thinking ruffian.) And so it comes about that *South Wind*, which might have been expected to please a few readers because it hits out in all directions at our Anglo-Saxon attitudes, has nevertheless won wide popularity among thousands of readers who may not share, or even much notice, the author's point of view, but who can share his insatiable curiosity (expressed elsewhere in his notes on lizards or London street games) and his fastidious delight in the world of here and now.

(Much of the attraction of the comic novels of Mr. Aubrey Menen, who has some claim to be a post-war Norman Douglas, springs from the same source of high-spirited, alert curiosity.)

A more strenuous exercise of the same zest for information can be won from readers of 'serious' novels by writers who know how to treat complex themes in uncorrugated language. That novelist is lucky who, while failing to win our immediate emotional involvement in some strange peripheral state of mind, yet has enough narrative talent to gain our assent to the proposition that *some* people (not, as he hopes, we ourselves) do think thus and thus. A novelist who can win credence at points where the average reader *can* check fictional behaviour against his own experience, has the power to extend the boundaries of that reader's experience by coaxing him to become curious about, even if not fully involved in, the state of mind of such unlikely heroes as a madman or a dirty old tramp. One example must serve: *The Journey of Simon McKeever* by the American novelist Albert Maltz, which makes unattractive old age a theme for sympathetic study—sympathetic not in the sense of 'being sorry for' but in the much more unlikely sense of human compatibility. The hero is Simon McKeever, aged seventy-two and owning to sixty-three, who lives in a drab Californian Rest Home for the aged. The novel describes his escape, his dogged hitch-hiking, his disappointment and return to his broken-down friends of the Home. The author's feat is that slowly, as the novel proceeds, our own viewpoint, coaxed at first only by an odd curiosity, changes with it. What first sounds like tiresome babbling becomes, as we shift our interest *inside* the old man, the legitimate expression of his personal memory. What formerly looked like the slow shuffling of an old dotard becomes a grim and even enjoyable battle to move forward against the barriers set up by physical pain. What we had at first taken to be a normal disinclination to talk to a dirty old man becomes, as we read, an exasperating and incomprehensible rudeness on the part of young fools. In such a novel, the mechanism of compassion is moved but never assaulted; and, unlikely as it may at first appear, the author's fifth-column ally within his reader's breast is not so much pity ('How awful for him') as simple curiosity (' So *that* is how they feel, is it?').

It is a fair guess that many post-war novelists, desiring to reclaim the attention of readers who turned aside from the fiction shelves during the period when experiments in sensitive awareness and the stream of consciousness were in vogue, have deliberately set themselves to win an audience by striving after surface realism and a naked style of writing. This laudable intention often fails of its purpose. Realistic language is not enough, and the careful reproduction of modern speech in a popular novel can sometimes give a less clear impression of people talking than the most elaborate paragraphs of, say, Henry James. Some writers have been so determined to rid their narrative prose of excess fat that they have whittled it down to an appearance not so much muscular as gaunt. A curt accumulation of pointless detail, spat out in bleak jerky sentences, can often haze about a scene or character as cloudily as the most whimsical prose. To snatch at a handy example, it is doubtful whether that strangely gripping novel *The Victim*, by Saul Bellow, gained anything from such incidental rat-tat-tat fusillades of impartial terse reportage as the following:

'Expressionless, Leventhal put on his raincoat. His arm caught in the sleeve, and he pushed it through violently. He walked out of the office with his rather hulking stride, halting in the anteroom to draw a drink from the glass cooler. While waiting for the elevator, he discovered that he was still holding the paper cup. Crumpling it, he threw it with an energetic swing between the bars into the shaft.'

There is a difference between nervous prose and nervy prose. Clean unvarnished truth too often emerges as a maddening prolixity, whether of plain facts or an endless babble of pointless conversation. To be faithful to observed facts it is not necessary to record every observed fact in an uncorruptible pedantry of exactitude or to hop along in a *Chick's Own* style with an *ingénue* patter of 'And' and 'Then' and 'Time went on' and 'After that'. These bleak elisions, coyly clipped in short sentences from which all cargo of informed commentary has been tossed overboard, can give a hateful impression that any one thing is of equal importance with any other thing. To adopt the chipmunk rhythm for a moment—this is not true. It is not true in life. It is not true in books.

The more simple the subject-matter, the more mature and

controlled must be the novelist's touch if he wishes to lure his reader into a willing involvement. We always *know*, after all, that we are reading a novel. It may sound paradoxical, but we are most likely to assent to illusion when we are convinced, by the evidence of the 'unrealistic' commentary interlarded with his observations, that the mind of the narrator has a quality distinctive enough to make the external world *significantly* real to him—and hence to us. Moving always from the particular to the general, such a mind can release deep feeling by an observation seemingly trivial:

'The pinkish-grey stockings had a curious dead chalkiness about them. Below the calf they trembled a little and were empty. She had not enough flesh on her legs to fill them out. I was pierced by the little empty trembling spaces in her stockings. They seemed to spell all sadness and privation to me.'

Those short sentences from *A Voice Through a Cloud* may point the argument and remind us yet again of the loss suffered by lovers of the novel when Denton Welch died at the age of thirty-one.

There are still, to be sure, hopeful signs. Essays on the theme 'Is the Novel doomed?' are being displaced in the critical weeklies by the by-product scribblings of energetic young novelists. 'The dog it was that died.' But the novel still demands highly personal gifts and a flowing realistic pen will never be enough—not even for realism. Even old hands at the game of fiction have recently been turning for aid to elemental catastrophe or half-hearted symbolism or frank infatuation with life as lived centuries ago before they can display their gifts of heart and head and their narrative skill. Unless the youngsters can display a fecundity equal to their freshness, the fiction review columns no less than the front-page headlines will continue to teach our future historians something about the neuroses of this intelligent and humanitarian age.

7

COMEDY OF THE POETIC PRESENT

William Gerhardi

I

There are a few of us who, when we meet and talk about contemporary novels, always come round to the subject of William Gerhardi; and after we have reminded one another (almost like Proust-lovers and James-fanciers) of this scene and that joke and the other little touch of sad poetry, we then end up with our perennial wonder: 'Why isn't Gerhardi a more popular novelist? Why don't the library-subscribers find him much funnier than X? Why do the critics not find his style more attractive than that of Y? Why is he not acclaimed as in every way superior to that trickster Z?' We shake our heads in real puzzlement, and estimate the date when the Gerhardi boom will set in and our long-held shares be realizable at top prices. Meanwhile, we comfort ourselves with the knowledge that he has never for a moment been in any doubt about his own qualities. When a friend asked Mr. Gerhardi, in the course of a conversation about the cinema, what great novel should be the next to be filmed, he replied affably, brightly, seriously, and without one instant's hesitation: '*Of Mortal Love*!'

Mr. Gerhardi is a peculiarly difficult writer to introduce. He is an original novelist and stands in a one-man category in modern English fiction. The writers to whom he has been most indebted, Chehov and Proust, are themselves foreign to the main stream of English novels. His originality would be a useful starting-point for an appraisal were it not for the fact that his entire output is an expression of this highly original standpoint, so that in order to illustrate it adequately it would be necessary to quote not sentences but whole chapters. At this point I can adduce Mr. Gerhardi as witness. During the course of a lecture tour in Sweden, I gave one or two talks on the English novel and spoke of *The Polyglots* and *Of Mortal Love*, with suitable quotations. On my return I telephoned Mr. Gerhardi and told him of my talks—for although he is now almost an Invisible Man, he is prepared to talk exuberantly, and at great length, on the telephone. He wished to know which passages I had quoted. I told him: the sea-burial of Natasha from *The Polyglots*, some love scenes from *Of Mortal Love*, and the death of Dinah in the same novel. He listened patiently. 'Yes, yes; but what about Aunt Teresa? And that scene on the next page where . . .' Before I rang off I had to explain that my fifty-minute lecture had been on the English novel in general and not on Mr. Gerhardi's works in particular. He thought this a mistake.

Another difficulty in introducing this writer is that he has already, to those willing to listen, brilliantly introduced himself. As novelist, critic and telephonist he is of a piece: self-expository, irrepressible, propounding with serious exuberance a comic view of life, and of himself. He is not (though his early critics praised him for being one) a satirist. 'I am serious,' he writes, 'but not earnest; humour, I need hardly say, being the most serious quality in literature.' And again: 'Critics feel uneasy when a writer is not solemn. Who is he laughing *at*? who *with*? Warily they trot out the stupid word "satire", or the silliest word of all "sophistication".'

In *Memoirs of a Polyglot* (1931), one of the most entertaining autobiographies of the times, Mr. Gerhardi has shown how his long determination to be a writer was fostered by a childhood spent in pre-Revolutionary Russia and by his bizarre adventures during and after the 1914–18 war. At that time he could hardly complain of lack of attention. His early books had been acclaimed and his impudent association with Lord Beaverbrook brought him to the notice of the social and literary lion-hunters of the 1920's. As for his literary views, he has set them forth with an exasperated candour in the general Introduction (1947) to his Collected Edition, printed as a preface to *Futility*. It is here that he takes occasion to deliver some deft, graceful smacks at the book-reviewers. And so, with shy directness, Mr. Gerhardi has told the truth about himself as a man and as an artist. Perhaps because it is so difficult to bracket him with other writers, so impossible to recruit him to a school or probe him as an influence, his novels have given pleasure to individual readers without earning for him a generally recognized place among the writers of popular fiction.

Candour and tenderness are the guardian angels of this novelist—and frivolity is, I suppose, his attendant imp. At its best, his humorous writing is so candid and so tender that we accept all the poetry without recognizing its rare value. It looks so easy. It is, in fact, the result of an unusual literary tact. His best prose has the humility of works of art; it does not point or gesticulate, still less does it display a label. His characters can remain candid and tender in situations where they figure as unheroic, ridiculous and sometimes shamelessly self-seeking. For them, there is always a sense of wonder in the immediate present. Their creator has stripped them of pretence and decked them in no borrowed finery; yet he has a poet's, and not a satirist's, eye; his judgement is that of an artist, not a moralist. The best pages of *The Polyglots* and *Of Mortal Love* are the products of a poetic sensibility, wary, humorous, yet in love with the present.

'I stand before you naked and unashamed—yes, *quite* unashamed,' Mr. Gerhardi seems to say in his apologia. 'I have even been driven to the inartistic expedient of pointing out just where you should laugh, and where you should draw a gentle metaphysical sigh. It is strange that you should still not understand.' In a way, it *is* strange. For Mr. Gerhardi's poetic 'criticism of life' can be subtle and heart-searching. He is a writer of direct and sensuous simplicity who can, in the course of a few pages, make his readers laugh aloud and sigh over the gentle cruelties of life. This simplicity may deceive the pretentious reader but it ought to have warmed the heart of that ultimate arbiter, the Common Reader. It is Mr. Gerhardi's peculiar gift that he can cheer us with a smile of kinship even when his characters are downcast by their own folly, and sharpen our awareness, in the midst of sudden pleasures (listening to the voices of children, say, or feeling the warmth of a summer evening), of the underlying mystery of life. He can be as funny as Charlie Chaplin, and his place among his contemporaries is about as odd as Chaplin's would be if his films had been secretly enjoyed by small Cinema Societies and never shown in the local Odeons and Empires.

Yet when all this has been said, there remain reasons for the failure of Mr. Gerhardi's works to secure for him the place for which his artistic equipment would seem to give him title. The essence of his originality and the reason why he has not made a more decisive impact on the contemporary novel are one and the same: he cannot see that he is in any way different from other people. Thus his undeniable lack of interest in ordinary narrative construction is, to him, a virtue: he simply believes that other writers have failed to shake themselves quite free from what he calls 'evil suspense'. It is as if a giant panda, enjoying its own tricks and conscious of the admiration of the nearest audience, were not only unaware of its own unlikeness to most other animals, but were prepared to claim, when this hard truth was pointed out, that elephants and tigers were Nature's imperfect attempts to create the panda, and were miserably conscious of their own poor progress along the evolutionary road towards panda-hood.

Thus has come about the sad, faintly comic—indeed Gerhardi-like—predicament: a master of one neglected vein in English fiction has remained unappreciated largely because he himself thinks this vein to be not only the most valuable source of literature but the *sole* source. He has repeated his characters, his jokes, his frail amusing cosmic observations, and if you happen to enjoy that particular line of goods, rare, semi-precious and not very useful, you will not complain. Meanwhile the novelist himself, increasingly baffled, can never see that gross men and women mainly visit the fiction market for some quite different commodity, and have to be submitted to a far more thorough course of 'sales conditioning' than he is prepared to give them.

One feels that Mr. Gerhardi has a quick insight into the human heart and an innocent relish in unveiling his own, but that he probably does not read the newspaper regularly and has only a rudimentary notion of what busy people do when they are not just being sad, or jealous, or gay. This child-like wide-eyed irrelevance can become an irritation. It has probably lost him many otherwise sympathetic readers. It will have lost him all the staid readers. (One such disappointed sampler returned a Gerhardi novel to me with the comment: ' Not my writer.'

On hearing this, the author's response was characteristic: 'Not my reader.') His heroes have an attitude to women at once affectionate and predatory, and their shamelessness is so obtrusively unrebuked that many women readers must find his sense of humour hard to share. When his characters are childlike their perceptions are clear and delightful, but at other times his heroes become childish and say, in effect, 'Look at me!' When this happens, some readers will want to reply 'Stop it!' or 'Don't you know there's a war on?' or 'I have work to do', or give vent to similar expressions of moral superiority. At such times the Gerhardi humour, divested of its tenderness, can become facetious and over-extravagant. As for the author, he will say, with his narrator of *The Polyglots*: 'Now this sort of thing puzzles me. What am I to make of it?'

II

'One of the chief delights of reading Chehov is the discovery that our vaguely apprehended, half-suspected thoughts concerning the fluidness, complexity and elusiveness of life have been confirmed articulately and in print.

'And it is because there is in Chehov's works that fluid undercurrent by which we recognize existence, because we see that he at least did not simplify life in order to round off his picture (the loose-end nature of it being just the picture he has set out to portray), and because in a complex version there are necessarily more points of affinity than in a simplified and stripped account of human life, that we recognize ourselves in mental and emotional experiences in point of fact unknown to us.'

These quotations from the biographical and critical study *Anton Chehov* (1923) prompt the explanation that when originality is claimed for Mr. Gerhardi's novels it is not suggested that his subject-matter is startlingly new, nor even that his attitude to life is historically unparalleled. His novels are original in the sense that his recognizable models, Chehov and Proust, evidently gave him confidence to explore and expound a view of life native to himself and not hitherto specifically expressed in English fiction. *Futility* (1922) and *The Polyglots* (1925) were published at a time when the English novel was being subjected to a number of experiments, some of which have extended the scope of subsequent writers and some of which have caused many Common Readers to turn in despair to detective stories. It is to Mr. Gerhardi's great credit that, equipped as he was with sufficient cleverness to join or even lead one of the fashionable 'satirical' or 'precious moment' or 'symbolic' groups for which the descriptive terms *avant-garde* and *vieux jeu* are simply a matter of rapid chronology, he steadfastly developed his comic-poetic apprehension of our 'spiritual riches subsisting under the surface of Time'. Irreverent to the point of frivolity, he refused to see in human relationships much more than the alternating sorrows and jests of 'tender sympathy deepened by humorous discernment'. A quarter of a century later, he remained impenitent:

'The more deeply rooted in life, the more steeped in humorous tragedy . . . , the more serious in a real sense will be the work of the heavenly forces released in implication. And the more highfalutin' the subject, the more grandiloquent the manner and dead-earnest the aim, the more nebulous, windy, dogmatic, flat, inaccurate, woolly, lifeless, trivial, shallow and worthless will be the result: because the writer has seen fit to use his own foolish tongue to state that which a wiser man would have left implied.'

In all of which, whether in 1922 or in 1947, the debt to Chehov and the sturdy independence are about equally balanced.

Futility was published when the author was twenty-six. Fresh, candid, impudent, it showed already almost all the Gerhardi characteristics—which may be a way of saying either that he has been true to his genius or that he has never developed. (On this point, as on all others concerning himself, Mr. Gerhardi spoke early and has not retracted. In the short story *A Bad End*, published in 1926, he has a writer of whom the critics say, alternately, 'one wishes that the author would break new ground, express life from a new angle', and 'get you back to the simple delights of your earlier books and we will listen to you till the crack of doom'.) Here for the first time he introduces his readers, in a spirit of resigned comedy, to 'the prevailing Russian atmosphere—chronic uncertainty'. Here are the thin trickles of Gerhardi dialogue, deceptively simple; the repeated use of catch-phrases ('Ach! Andrei Andreievich') to animate a caricature through the aural sense; the influence of Chehov; the incidental felicities of phrasing whether of passing comments on life ('that stupid scepticism that comes from too much happiness') or his own miscalculations ('My passionate explanations of my own aloofness began to anger her').

Futility light-heartedly displays domestic chaos against a larger political chaos viewed with equal shoulder-shrugging indifference. Nikolai Bursanov, whose wife refuses to divorce him, lives with Fanny Ivanovna who mothers his three daughters Sonia, Nina, and Vera. The arrival of the narrator, the Gerhardi-figure who philanders with the daughters, coincides with Nikolai's discovery that he himself, already owning one absent legal wife and one all-present and highly respectable mistress, desires to marry Zina, a girl of seventeen. The young narrator views this tangle in a spirit of sympathetic non-interference and with an eye to the main chance:

'I wrote down their names in two columns. Then I perceived that the two columns did not serve my purpose; so I drew arrows and circles round the names and endeavoured to arrange them in sets and groups according to my own ideas of how they should be mated. I began with mating Nina with myself. This was easy enough: it was obvious.'

Into this feckless turmoil are flung other farcical ingredients: the financial unsoundness of Nikolai's Siberian gold-mines, the family of Zina who swell the list of the dependants of this gallant impecunious *paterfamilias*, and finally—for they are treated simply as farcical adjuncts—the changing fortunes of the Russian Revolution and the Allied Intervention. The families wait, observing the Vladivostock weather and talking of life and death like characters from a Chehov play. The narrator is vain, serious, and watchful: ' "How awfully funnily your mouth moves when you speak," said Nina, who had been listening to me attentively.' At length Nikolai and all his dependants ('We are inseparable—financially') board a train and their tangled hopes and fears are submitted to the scrutiny and resourcefulness of other passengers, such as the English Admiral who 'combines the manner of Napoleon I with the mind of Napoleon III' and Sir Hugo with his 'masterly grasp of the inessential'. Outside, the winter misery of Siberia, the fighting and the confusion; inside, the maddening re-examination of hopeless causes and the dizzy disequilibrium of true actions and false attitudes, so that Nikolai can be humble in his generosity and Uncle Kostia arrogant in his dependence:

' "Remember, we are all behind you; we shall follow you, if need be, to the end of the earth. Courage, Nikolai Vasilievich! Keep hard at it! Keep hard at it!" '

In all this, then, there is little room for moralizing. Yet a curious and tender truthfulness flickers across these mad inconsequent pages, a truthfulness sometimes voiced by the narrator in sudden wide-eyed seriousness ('Perhaps there is nothing that brings home so clearly the conviction of the temporary nature of things as the sight of a dead body'), but more illuminating when it lights up for a moment the comic sorrows and pathetic joys of life when people act not as they *should* act or as we should prefer them to act, but with self-absorbed irrelevance:

' "I chuck Oxford, come all the way to Vladivostok, spend three months on the journey because—because I love you, and you——"

' "You have a speck of soot on your nose," she remarked.

' "Nina!" I cried laughing, my heart all weeping tears. "Nina!" '

The Polygots, like *Futility*, stems from the author's family ties in Russia and his unmartial duties as liaison officer during the muddled period of Intervention. Again the domestic scene and the outside world are chaotic, and again the freshness of communication is the result of the narrator's single-minded concentration on his own comfort, modified by a lively curiosity about the behaviour (never, significantly, the motives) of his friends, all viewed in the spirit of comedy even when their predicament, like his own, verges on tragedy. There is another set of Gerhardi characters: Uncle Emmanuel Vanderflint with his catch-phrases ('*Que voulez-vous? Courage, courage!*'); Aunt Teresa, 'the incarnation of delicate health', a more flippant version of Proust's Tante Léonie; and, in the Nina role, the sixteen-year-old cousin Sylvia Ninon. The narrator is again unashamedly vain, his eyes for ever turning to the looking-glass, and again he pursues the young girl with an infantile and uncomplicated directness, much like one of the Marx Brothers loping off after a passing wench. The narrator's love is serious enough; he suffers jealousy and pique like the most romantic heroes. But he refuses to be solemn about it:

'While I read aloud, Sylvia "prepared" an expression of wonderment on her face, to show that she was sensitive to what I read. But she began to fret as I read on, absorbed. . . .

'There is something soft about my nose and mouth, like a rabbit's. I forget whether I told you I'm good-looking? Sleek black hair brushed back from the forehead—and all the rest of it.

' "You're so clever—and yet you're nothing much to look at,' she said. This, I must confess, astonished me. I have no shallow vanity—but this astonished me. Sleek black hair and all that sort of thing. It astonished me.

' "Never mind, darling. I don't like handsome men," she added. Now this sort of thing puzzles me. What am I to make of it?'

Mr. Gerhardi was at once, we felt, too lazy to think out his psychological problems to a solution, and too honest to strike poses and invent a bogus apparatus of attitudes to explain emotions he never felt. A novelist who employs this latter method only too often mimics emotions that neither he nor anybody else has ever felt. The author of *The Polyglots* can be maddeningly frivolous in his habit of switching from 'major' to 'minor' matters, but although one can be aghast at his irreverence, one is never embarrassed, in his company, by a disregard for truth. Doubtless, it is this *gamin* irreverence that has caused him to be esteemed a cynic, a satirist. 'Who is he laughing *at*? Who *with*?' But he is no more a satirist than the child in Hans Andersen's tale who observed, without malice or intent to improve the social scene by ridicule, 'But the Emperor *has* no clothes!' The nearest he comes to social indignation is when his narrator chides Aunt Teresa for wanting wars 'conducted in good taste, outside in the yard, but please not on the drawing-room carpet!'—and suggests that 'soldiers should begin at home with the civilian population, particularly with the old ladies'. There is no rancour, nor is there a sense of high-minded outrage. We feel that the narrator is thinking only of himself as being, technically at least, a soldier who, as wars were then conducted, was in greater danger than his aunt. Yet this cowardly common-sense is less unattractive than the false heroics of the aunt who would whip other people towards gallant death. And similarly, the narrator's lecture to his aunt about worry, 'the failure to control imagination,' is eminently sensible, unheroic, unsentimental, childish.

At the end of the novel, the moving description of a child's burial at sea is followed by a mood not of theatrical grief but of a far more piercing 'acute resignation' which is only an intensification of the same mood in which are observed the antics of children, the helpless folly of Major Beastly with his 'What *I* always say is: one man's as good as another and a damned sight better!' and the beauty of the tropical sea. Here is the passage:

'Once more we looked back at the sea, and went down to breakfast. But the table where the girl with the sea-green eyes had sat showed empty, and we avoided looking at it as we ate. They talked of a mishap to one of the boilers, of the ensuing delay in our voyage, and that we might have to drift to Bombay to replenish our vanishing coal supply; but I did not care whither we steamed or whither we drifted, and if we were destined to drift for the rest of our lives and never reach England, or stop drifting, or drift straight into hell, it was to me, in my mood of acute resignation, a matter of welcome indifference. After breakfast Aunt Molly came out on deck with a bottle and tablespoon, and gave Nora her codliver oil. Perhaps the burial had wrecked her nerves a little, but she said impatiently, "Get on, Nora, don't waste half an hour over it."

' "*Wait*—but I like to *taste* it," Nora pleaded, as she licked the spoon.

' "Now go and fetch Harry."

' "Harry: your wi*me*!" came Nora's voice as she ran off down the slippery deck.'

If the manner was learnt from Chehov, the master had done no more than encourage the pupil to describe life as he himself, without prompting, saw it and felt it.

III

Before he was thirty, then, Mr. Gerhardi had published a short critical study which is one of the most sensitive interpretations of the creative processes of a major artist, and a couple of novels expressing his view (later defined in the Letter to a Reader forming a preface to *My Wife's the Least of It*) that 'humour does not express hate, but a clairvoyant view of the maladjustments of our life which, like a traffic block from one end of Oxford Street to another, can best be dispersed, not by shouting and shoving, but by recourse to an autogyro for a just appreciation of the situation'. There were no doubt readers who, exasperated by his refusal to identify himself with a faction, could find 'nothing *in* his books'. To them, too, he has given an answer (in the same letter):

'The romantic writer identifies himself with a faction of sinful humanity which he whitewashes, to make it stand out in relief against a background of other factions, which he unavoidably colours. If the classic tradition means anything, it means the suspension of sentence till the Day of Judgement and an underlying gaiety of spirit rooted in our irrepressible belief in the divine balance of things.'

Alas, during the next decade he failed to practise as well as he had preached, or has preached and practised again since. In *Pretty Creatures* (1927) he collected his short stories, amusing pieces sometimes betraying a disquieting impression of Sterne-like frustration, not indeed absent from the novels, but here made more apparent by the shorter form. A year later came *Jazz and Jasper* (rechristened *My Sinful Earth* in the new edition), introducing Lord Ottercove and—to my mind disastrously—a taste for fantasy. *The Memoirs of Satan* (1932), written in collaboration with Brian Lunn, is another essay in the fantastic. It is sad to have to record these lapses. The fall from grace can be forgiven in the light of Mr. Gerhardi's later return to what he would call his own genius—and particularly in the light of *Of Mortal Love*, which would redeem almost anything. For it is clear that in concentrating his interest on 'that residuum of happiness, barely noticed in the stress of living, perhaps best defined as the poetry of life', and expressing his belief that 'the novel, the newest, the most fluid, plastic, malleable and commodious of the arts, is the rightful heir of the poem', the author had sacrificed everything to sensibility, candour and a wonderful flair for atmosphere. In *Jazz and Jasper* he first tossed these assets aside. The result is a chaos of clever high spirits; a concoction of caricature, snippets of satire, and at times an excruciating facetiousness. This book, and to a lesser extent *The Memoirs of Satan*, was more modish, more 'wickedly' funny than its predecessors; it represents the author's attempt to obtain recognition in a more readily identifiable field.

Midway between *Jazz and Jasper* and *The Memoirs of Satan* came *Pending Heaven* (1930). It is as 'shocking' as the one and as 'original' as the other, but it recaptures the impudent tenderness of *Futility* and *The Polyglots,* and with it the authentic Gerhardi note. Max Fisher, an amiable buccaneer of hearts, ambles through the plot collecting lovers and failing to discard old ones, so that he ends up like an unsuccessful player of rummy. A London *vie à trois* swells to a Saharan *vie à six,* and there are a couple of enchanting exasperating Gerhardi children. It is a light, frivolous and highly entertaining novel, irrational in all conscience, but never self-consciously or 'wickedly' so; the impudence is once more a matter of candour, not of striking clever and in the end boring poses. And in this gay pavilion there are, now and again, those clear panes through which can be seen the white radiance, if not of eternity, then of the inescapable human predicament—'a revelation', to quote the General Introduction again, 'of our common being moved to obey the unknown laws of the kingdom of heaven within us.' Here is one such passing comment:

'This depending entirely on his love, this devotion to him, disconcerted him. It was as if his soul were a room and somebody was looking into it, but he was standing there looking out through another window.'

The next novel was *Resurrection* (1934). It is a long book, with rather more narrative vigour than Mr. Gerhardi had hitherto troubled to put forth. It can be read and enjoyed for different reasons by different kinds of reader. There is an 'astral body' theme leading to discussions on immortality: we are assured by the author that this experience, complete with a tape of light connecting, like an umbilical cord, the sleeping body and its floating, luminous and sentient counterpart, was genuine. I am inclined to believe the formal protestation, if only because Mr. Gerhardi has always been at his best when telling the truth about his own life as he has lived it, and at his weakest when caprice or experiment led him to be 'inventive' as well as imaginative. But what is more interesting, in this uneven but accomplished novel, is the technical skill of a very high order that enabled the author to introduce so esoteric an experience into the world of social comedy—to keep subdued, this time, an element dangerously irrelevant to his own special mode of amused tolerant observation.

The narrator has his first gingerly astral flight shortly before attending a debutante ball. However much he may protest at the incredulity of his fellow-guests when he comes to them all aglow with intimations of immortality, the scene of his disappointment, as his friends in turn show themselves unwilling to pursue so frivolous a topic on so important a social occasion, or else treat his confidences as an excuse for exchanging tales of psychic experiences they themselves have had or heard about—this scene is one in which Mr. Gerhardi's peculiar virtues as a novelist have full play. We are the more persuaded of the truth of the poor narrator's story as we are made the more certain of the equal truth that no man's experiences, however revealing, are likely to be of much interest to his fellow-men when they themselves are wrapped up in the small affairs of the moment.

Meanwhile, the 'straight' description shows the author at his best. There are passages in the early chapters that recall the happier observations of Proust at a Guermantes reception—though here again, as earlier with Chehov, one feels glad to be reminded that Proust too was a great *comic* writer, and that a partial similarity of temperament should have guided Mr. Gerhardi to so apt a model. One paragraph must serve to illustrate the fortunate influence of Proust's vivid, flowing, and image-decked narrative sweep:

'Suddenly a fat old butler in knee-breeches ran across the whole length of the ballroom with a preoccupied air on his face, stopping the band and automatically as the music stopped clearing a centre path all the length of the ballroom. There appeared, as if to justify the working of cause and effect, though, as in the case of other natural phenomena, such as thunder and lightning, we had seen the effect before the cause—there appeared on the threshold a royal pair. Indeed, there appeared two couples walking through the opening thus made for them: the host leading the royal lady, followed by the royal spouse with the hostess on his arm. The transformation of the scene was instantaneous. The host who, despite his white gloves, had been a man among men, suddenly looked like his own lackey. A strange expression came on his face—a sugary one, as if he were anxious to register that he was sensible of the honour, and one of stiffened alarm, as if he would stand no affront from the crowd through which he was leading his precious visitors. The guests, who had a moment before danced light-heartedly, drew themselves up a little stiffly and awkwardly, because stiffness does not come naturally to the free-born Briton. The ladies, conscious of the womanly grace of submission and, moreover, eager to parade their training which marked them as having been presented at Court, curtsied with ready grace as the royal guests, with that trained eye of theirs for recognizing a face, quickly spotted a few for special greeting as they moved on. Then, as suddenly as the music had stopped, it resumed, the sea which had parted for the passage of Moses rushed together once more, the dancing continued, and so excellent and discreet are English manners that no one betrayed even by a look the slightest interest in the royal pair, whose advent had caused such commotion, and who were now lost in the dancing crowd.'

It vexes Mr. Gerhardi when the astral body theme of *Resurrection* is not taken seriously. There are, after all, plenty of parallel experiences, from the Flying Carpet of The Arabian Nights to the more technical disquisitions of J. W. Dunne. Nor need one accept the charge of 'Incredible!' on the score of immortality and the various types of Other Worlds, except from those who are foolish enough to consider our own 'normal' life to be unmysterious. Yet Mr. Gerhardi is less good as a prophet than as a humorist. I have had the advantage of hearing him expound his astral experiences to a group of eager listeners, and it was interesting to note, then as in reading the novel, that one's chief entertainment was not in the story but in the ill-concealed impatience of most of the company to express either a brusque cynicism or a competitive list of bigger and better astral flights. A man with Mr. Gerhardi's gift of social comedy could be entertaining with a less original theme; a narrator not thus endowed could be a bore though he himself had just risen from the dead.

IV

Here is Mr. Gerhardi's own description of his finest novel, *Of Mortal Love* (1936): 'a novel containing fresh love-lore and treating of the succeeding stages of transmutation of love erotic into love imaginative; of love entrancing into love unselfish; of love tender into love transfigured.' In it are concentrated all his tender poetic qualities and from it he has excluded the imitative weaknesses of some of his other works. Lord Ottercove is rescued from the world of *My Sinful Earth* and reappears in fiction with the winning vitality of Lord Beaverbrook in *Memoirs of a Polyglot*. Dinah, recipient of the various loves described above, is the most engaging and life-like of all the 'silly, enchanting girls, rootless and wayward' (to quote from an appreciation of this novel by C. P. Snow) who people the Gerhardi world. Walter, feckless, sensitive, self-centred and passionate, is more solid than the preceding Gerhardi-like heroes but never hardens to an attitudinizing lay figure. And here, more than anywhere else, the fun and the poetry of life combine in a smile now mysteriously sad, now outrageously high-spirited. This book, as the author himself so rightly insists, calls aloud for long quotation. There are snippets enough to display most of the Gerhardi moods, and the title of the Third Part of the novel, 'The Tender Friends', sums up pretty well the half-shy half-sensuous quality of his 'love-lore'.

Here, then, in Walter, is the hero unheroic:

'He rarely, if ever, returned hospitality. He considered that by accepting he had already given up of himself, of his energy, of his time, of his appetite, to requite the debt. With casual dinner companions he would throw himself into conversation with a devotion, a whole-heartedness, which exhausted him. Had he been invited to dine out by himself he would have enjoyed concentrating on the food and the wine. But what pleasure was there in ordering haphazardly from a bewildering list of courses a chicken which he had to eat while conscientiously talking, risking every minute to swallow a bone, or leaving the chicken while dutifully dancing with some woman not in her first youth? Nor did he lightly accept an invitation to dinner, weighing carefully the probable quality of the food against his own intellectual expenditure and delaying his reply to the last. "Mr. Walter Smith," he wrote, "thanks Lady de Jones for her kind invitation but is unable to come to a decision as the arguments for and against appear to him overwhelming." Latterly he rarely accepted invitations at all unless allowed to bring several of his friends, whose atmosphere, he urged and argued, was indispensable for his well-being, but to whom in reality he was returning hospitality at the expense of his host.'

Here is Dinah, plying busily between lover and husband:

'When Dinah came home in the early hours of the morning Jim was usually fast asleep. He asked few questions. If he did ask—he emphasized that it was a point of interest—what she had been doing the night before, she said she had been meeting interesting people in Walter's flat, and she quickly added, "Walter says——" and transmitted some mystical reference to music that Walter had made, to which she had been too bored to listen in his presence, but that now clearly came back to her. Jim, very interested, contributed to it out of his well-stored knowledge, so that Dinah next day was greeting Walter gaily with, "Oh yes, Jim says——". Such messages were taken backwards and forwards by Dinah who, though she took no interest in them, transmitted them with an accuracy born of sheer zest in transmission.'

Dinah's oft-repeated line 'Oh, darling, I do love you because you are so funny' represents at its simplest Mr. Gerhardi's view of love and of comedy. The absurd characters from earlier novels reappear (Bonzo and Aunt Minnie and the others) either under the same names or thinly disguised: Mr. Gerhardi certainly loves his own characters too well ever to tire of them. And with the absurdity goes the poetry of life, with the meanness goes the resignation to sorrow and to beauty. After Dinah's death, Walter recalls their ludicrous appearance at a Ball:

'But when they got there, there was only a buffet with sandwiches, no champagne or wine, only coffee and tea and lemonade, and the party was commonplace and dull in the extreme—not a face you had ever seen anywhere before. They were back almost as soon as they had started and she sat down in the dress it had taken her three weeks to make, and cried. And now that she was dead he thought of that dinner he had not given her and it was as if she had died hungry. He saw her lying on her dark-blue divan in a sort of daze, trying to understand why her life was unhappy, why there were so many nights in her life when the one man she wanted to be with did not want her, and how to step into that other life where you loved and were loved, every sensible woman's life, which was happy. His gathering distress was hovering over some rising lamentation which, could they brush wings, would speak to him, say what it was. She had died with too much life in her: it was this, this.'

Mr. Gerhardi's last novel, *My Wife's The Least Of It* (1938), comes nearest to expressing, with rueful patience, his own bemusement at his status in the critical lists of English novelists. The grotesque hopes and dismal downfalls of Mr. Baldridge as he tries to sell his film scripts reflect, in their very tone of farce, this novelist's sturdy belief in himself. The plight of Mr. Baldridge, baffled by the enthusiastic indifference of the film moguls to the fate of his scripts, might seem too close a parallel to Mr. Gerhardi's own case, if it were not for the presence throughout the novel of other exasperating, and funnier, instances of the bemusement of Innocence in Society. The innocent at large is not always, of course, as innocent as Mr. Gerhardi would have us suppose: there is a repeated note of special pleading in many of the passages in which he claims for his Gerhardi-like characters a remission of the dues normally exacted by society. 'There is no measuring rod for genius,' he seems to be saying over and over again: 'you must accept it on its own terms.' The trouble is that few readers share Mr. Gerhardi's recognition of genius; the narrators of the earlier novels and Dinah of *Of Mortal Love* sometimes ask to be forgiven rather more than seventy times seven by other characters who are insufficiently persuaded of the validity of their claimed exemption from customary law.

Yet Mr. Baldridge, for all his eccentricities, is nearer the conception of the Common Man, misled and misunderstood, dodging to accidental triumph like a Charlie Chaplin personification of Mr. Gerhardi's general view that life is tragic but people are comic. This much granted, the comedy need only be mild; satire is unnecessary, malice out of the question:

'Having made Mr. Baldridge now stand up, now sit down, now kneel with her on the concrete floor of the balcony, according to whether they were singing a hymn or listening to a lesson or praying in Westminster Abbey, Aunt Minnie all at once declared her wish to leave the balcony and climb back through the window. There was a plate with a plover's egg and some salt on it which she had been vainly offering to people and now said it was a waste to leave behind and suggested that Mr. Baldridge should bring the egg in. Mr. Baldridge did as he was told but, finding no table on which to set the plate, he entered the dining-room with it while the other guests in a stillness of awe were just tensely listening to the King taking the holy sacrament.

'Bess looked at Mr. Baldridge, shaking her head. "You would!" she murmured. "You would!" And Mr. Baldridge stood there holding the plate with the plover's egg under looks denoting the whole gamut of disapproval, running from mild derision to shock and suppressed indignation.'

This scene is developed with the highest of spirits and becomes farcical as the unhappy man, missing the first round of various delicious foodstuffs, always attracts the malevolent eye of his hostess when, picking at his eventual scraps, he is judged to be devouring a second or third huge plateful. The comic sense here is best expressed in the host's 'confused dual look denoting compassion for the poor old boy who was too shy to ask for food but, given half the chance, would eat him out of the house'. Here, the claimed innocence and the open suspicion merge into that tolerant observation, missing nothing and judging nothing, which is basis of this author's theory and practice of comedy.

Even Aunt Minnie, one of a gay party who sat on Captain Devonshire's balcony to watch the Coronation procession, is treated as a figure of fun but is not made inhumanly comic. Resisting the snigger, Mr. Gerhardi has been true to his own precepts: 'The notion that the humorist is malevolent has always struck me as comic. One might as soon eat one's dinner with contempt, or listen to music in indignation, as laugh maliciously'—and again: 'You cannot have a penetrating and impartially charitable representation of human, and therefore sinful, beings except in terms of humour.' The alteration of 'charitable' to 'uncharitable' and 'humour' to 'malice' would describe only too accurately the kind of humour (*not* satire, which is quite another matter) now in vogue. Aunt Minnie is ridiculous enough, *in* herself, perched on the balcony. Mr. Waugh, to make her funny, might have put a parrot on her shoulder or dropped her off the balcony. I am sure that other more recent humorists, seeking to outdo Mr. Waugh in hilarity, would have caused the parrot to *push* her off the balcony. Perhaps this is only to say that Mr. Gerhardi's more gentle sense of humour, nurtured on the Russian novelists, is nevertheless well within the older English tradition and has shown no sign of adjusting itself to more grisly fun.

V

There must be some reasons why Mr. Gerhardi has not yet caught the wide popular vote. There is sometimes an irritating propensity to be diverted from the development of his own undoubted gift. The reintroduction of characters and incidents and jokes, tolerable once one has acquired a taste for his work, may be a symptom of a certain failure of creative robustness that the ordinary reader is quick to detect, even in the lightest novel and even if he does not consciously define the missing quality.

On the other hand, it is strange that students of fiction, turning aside from the larger animals in search of more specialized game, have overlooked this enchanting disrespectful panda and discovered with joyous cries of comic sensibility the toad or the porcupine. For all his 'human' qualities, Mr. Gerhardi's comic view of life is also a poetic view, and readers on the look-out for the 'extra something' should find, with the late Sir Desmond MacCarthy, the 'silvery vein of genius' running through the novels. My guess is that when many 'significant' symbols have become meaningless and much glum hatred of life has been exposed as the shallow thing it is, the poetic comedy of these novels will attract readers who want to be entertained but who also know, though they may not be too good at articulating their knowledge, that to laugh and be tender at the same time is one good way of coping with this world of flesh and time. Mr. Gerhardi omits much; too much. But as he says of Chehov, 'Progression means a succession of lost opportunities. And that is where Chehov grips us'.

8

WORLD WITHOUT END

Upton Sinclair and Lanny Budd

I

By the year 1938, according to figures supplied by his British publishers (T. Werner Laurie Ltd.), some 690 editions of the books of Upton Sinclair had been issued in European countries and a further 67 in India, China and Japan. In Great Britain, Germany and the Soviet Union alone, over seven million copies had been sold by the same year. During the years 1940–53, eleven volumes have been published in this country in Upton Sinclair's series of novels with the collective title *The World's End*, concerning the adventures of an American hero, Lanny Budd, on the world's political stage in our twentieth century. In the British edition they run to an average length of well over 600 pages; all obtainable paper was used during the post-war years of short supply, and although an offer by a Book Club to take 140,000 copies of one volume had to be turned down because of the paper shortage, the average sale of the whole series was about 35,000 per volume. It would therefore seem that a large and loyal public in this country, and countless thousands of readers elsewhere, are prepared to read an exceedingly long and depressing account of contemporary history served up in a form of semi-fiction. I have rarely met a member of the literary intelligentsia who had read even one of these books. I have followed Upton Sinclair as he pursued his prodigious task and have read his eleven volumes (and will read a twelfth, if he writes one) with marked distaste on all literary and aesthetic counts, but with a dogged and sustained interest. Why?

Wherever my speculations may lead me, they can bring no possible annoyance to the novelist himself, who tells us, in a note appended to the tenth (and, as he then thought, last) volume of the series, that 'The critics really do not matter; they are a small group which writes for a small audience.' One must admit that a novelist whose books are advertised on billboards and in street-cars in 'the small islands of Japan', who is conscious that his work has given 'pleasure and instruction to millions of people', must feel singularly invulnerable. Yet he seems to hanker after posthumous fame too: 'name an American author,' he asks us with hectoring and possibly aggrieved tone, 'who achieved world fame during his lifetime and whose reputation has not held up since his death.'

In simple terms, the *World's End* series exemplifies the triumph of an immense human goodwill over an inadequate style, of a high degree of sympathetic invention over a very low degree of individual characterization, and—in the reader—of curiosity over tedium. Yet the resounding success of these books cannot be accounted for by any normal popularity of theme. The emotional temperature is low; there is plenty of adventure but nothing in the nature of romance; when 'love interest' is injected it is so tepid as to invite the reader to skip these paragraphs and get on with the politics. Of 'sex' in the sense accepted by readers of popular fiction there is absolutely none. There is little here to attract the careless day-dreaming reader who is supposed to be the mainstay of fiction libraries. On the contrary, the subject is deadly serious (no less than an international survey of politics between 1913 and 1950); the treatment, though stagey at times to the point of melodrama, is never superficially attractive. The hero of the book converses with international figures in highly incredible circumstances, but when they speak these lay figures usually have nothing more sensational to utter than a flat political commentary. Of the author of this unpalatable pabulum, Bernard Shaw wrote:

'When people ask me what has happened in my long lifetime, I do not refer them to the newspaper files and to the authorities, but to Sinclair's novels.'

This high praise is in line with the view of H. G. Wells that the novels present 'the completest and most faithful picture of [the] period that has been done, or is likely to be done'.

II

It is common knowledge that children love hearing certain stories re-told indefinitely. 'Tell me a story,' they may say; but they are more likely to clamour 'Tell me the story of Jack the Giant-Killer,' and to be incensed at the minutest divergence from the accepted convention. There can be few nannies who do not pause at significant points in their narrative, allowing their charges to supply by rote the unvarying adjectives: 'great big', 'ever so small', and so on. Throughout the long history of the epic the device of recurrent epithets has been maintained, following upon Homer's 'godlike' princes, 'noisy' dogs, 'fast' ships and, of course, 'wine-dark' sea. Upton Sinclair's habit of repetition is not fully operative until after we have read his first volume, where its place is taken by the complementary quality of freshness: the reader's interest in discovering a hero, Lanny Budd, and his complicated family of comfortable human beings who are significant only in their relation to the central figure. In the place of epic gods and goddesses and allegorical personifications we meet the first batch of a recurring set of public characters as familiar to the modern novel-reader as were the dwellers on Olympus to a Greek audience.

In *World's End*, covering the years 1913–19, Lanny Budd is introduced in his thirteenth year. (It is a convenience to remember, over the forty-year stretch covered by eleven volumes, that the hero is as old as the century.) A speedy survey of this first volume will 'place' him adequately enough: we are all set to follow his life from the age of thirteen, into contemporary history. New Olympians will appear, but old ones will recur, either on earth or through the medium of the spirit world. New members of the family circle will also emerge in the ensuing volumes, but only to fill gaps in the existing ranks.

Lanny is the son of Robbie Budd, American arms manufacturer, by his former mistress 'Beauty' Blackless, who in the course of the first novel marries and becomes the widow of a French painter, Marcel Detaze. Robbie remains on excellent terms with Beauty and visits her from time to time at her Riviera home. Beauty's brother, Jesse Blackless, is a doctrinaire Socialist (later Communist); although a member of Lanny's inner circle, it is his function to remain in the wings, awaiting any cue calling for the appearance of the Party line or a direct contact with Party figures. Lanny is shown as a favoured and attractive product of pre-war society: he loves music, plays the piano, and is trained at the Dalcroze school of dancing. He has two special school friends: Kurt Meissner, a German from Silesia, and Rick Pomeroy-Nielson, son of an English baronet. By reason of the genial admixture of his own young friends and those of his parents—the influential Robbie for ever popping in *en route* for another shady arms deal, the social Beauty maintaining her court at Juan-les-Pins—Lanny is able to take an early survey of the world of leisure so soon to be interrupted. He spends Christmas with his friend Kurt at Schloss Stubendorf, learning the disciplined life of the German nobility; he is taken on an Aegean pleasure cruise in the yacht of Ezra Hackenbury, soap-manufacturer from Indiana, and watches the behaviour of the uncultivated rich; he visits England, seeing the sights of the 1914 season and the country house of Rick's father; he returns by way of a French château owned by Mrs. Emily Chattersworth, widow of a New York banker. (Here we have passing glimpses of Anatole France and Isadora Duncan, minor Olympians who will figure again reminiscently but not in any active role: like incidental gods in earlier epics, or like the strolling 'extras' in a modern film, they serve to remind us that there are other beings, moving about their lawful occasions, unconnected—oddly as they may strike the reader of all eleven volumes—with Lanny Budd.) On one of his periodical trips to Europe, Robbie explains to his son the political background of the arms business: 'Politicians of Rumania sell out to France and get a supply of French money and arms; so then the Germans hire a new set of Rumanian politicians, and when these get into power you hear reports that Rumania is buying Krupp guns.' Lanny learns about Vickers, Skoda, Schneider-Creusot, and particularly about Basil Zaharoff, king of the arms merchants. They meet, and the old brigand takes a fancy to him. So far, all has been agreeably domestic; this is the first meeting with a significant Olympian.

War breaks out. Lanny watches its progress from the Riviera and from Paris. He listens to the talk of his elders. He fishes (and, of course, spots a submarine) off the Côte d'Azur with Jerry Pendleton, a genial American tutor-cum-handyman who will figure later as one of the splendidly reliable right-hand men, willing at any moment to drop their private lives to spring to the aid of the boss, who are so plentiful in novels and films and so very hard to find in real life. In his sixteenth year Lanny has his first love affair with an English girl, Rosemary Codwilliger ('pronounced Culliver'—this is one of the minor recurring jokes). Robbie is at hand to give periodical behind-the-scenes views of the war:

'The great source of steel for both France and Germany is in Lorraine, called the Briey basin; get your map and look it up, and you will see that the battle line runs right through it. On one side the Germans are getting twenty to thirty million tons of ore every year and smelting it into steel, and on the other side the French are doing the same. On the French side the profits are going to François de Wendel, President of the Comité des Forges and member of the Chamber of Deputies; on the other side they are going to his brother Charles Wendel, naturalized German subject and member of the Reichstag. These huge blast furnaces and smelters are in plain sight; but no aviators even tried to bomb them until recently. Then one single attempt was made, and the lieutenant who had charge of it was an employee of the Comité des Forges. Surprisingly, the attempt was a failure.

'They're building big industry, and they'll own it and run it. Whatever government comes in will have to have money, and will make terms with them, and business will go on as it's always done. It's a steam roller; and what I'm telling my son is, be on it and not under it!'

Meanwhile, on the plane of the suffering mortals, Marcel Detaze is horribly wounded. He goes on painting during convalescence. From him, Lanny learns his first lessons in art criticism, gaining the basis for a profession which, in the succeeding volumes, will keep him in touch both with the mortals who produce art and the Olympians who collect it.

After the entry of America into the war, Lanny for the first time accompanies his father to the United States. At Newcastle, Connecticut, he inspects the factories of Budd Gunmakers and meets another batch of relations who will all be groomed as handy symbols for another set of attitudes to modern life: stepmother Esther Budd, stepsister Bess, grandfather Budd who is

President of the firm and also the leader of a weekly Bible class, and great-great-uncle Eli who feebly represents a more cultured New England and bequeaths to Lanny his excellent library. During his absence in America, continuity is guaranteed by the appearance of members of the next generation: Beauty bears Marcel a daughter, Marceline, and Rick's wife Nina produces a grandson for the English baronet. Lanny himself, who is now attending an American school (the reader recalls with embarrassment the age of this worldly-wise young hero), has a second unsuccessful love affair with a young actress who seems destined for a major role, but is dropped after exhibiting, expertly enough, a further aspect of the hard-boiled. Of more importance to the unrolling epic is the introduction of a significant new theme: the spirit world. One morning, Lanny is startled by the appearance of a ghostly figure in his bedroom:

'. . . it seemed to be shaping itself into a mass at the foot of his bed, and the mass began to move, and suddenly Lanny realized it was Rick. A pale grey figure, just luminous enough so that it could be clearly seen; Rick in his flier's uniform, all stained with mud. On his face was a grave, rather mournful expression, and across his forehead a large red gash.'

A cable from Nina confirms that her husband has narrowly escaped death in a flying accident. Lanny has a new problem to ponder, a problem beyond the scope of Robbie's canny cynicism.

After the Armistice Lanny returns to Europe with his father and becomes an unofficial secretary at the Peace Conference. He busies himself with the Georgian question, leading his principal to Uncle Jesse for a sidelight on popular opinion:

'Lanny explained to his chief that Uncle Jesse didn't have to live in such a place, for he enjoyed a modest income from an inheritance. Apparently he wanted to be close to the people. Alston said there were men like that; sometimes they were saints, and sometimes a bit crazy, and sometimes both.'

Zaharoff swims into view again, ticketed once again by Robbie, this time as the power behind Clemenceau: 'Robbie said that "the Tiger" had been Zaharoff's friend for years, and both his brother and his son were directors in Zaharoff's companies.' We learn to become expectant for Zaharoff's epic epithet—'the Grand Officer of the Legion of Honour', a title soon to be matched by his K.C.B.

The volume ends with some personal excitement for the hero arising from circumstances which demonstrate two of his friends acting parts predetermined by their political aims. Lanny stumbles upon Kurt, who is working in Paris as a German secret agent trying, ostensibly, to influence French opinion against the continuing Allied blockade of his country. Lanny passes money from Kurt to Uncle Jesse for anti-blockade agitation among the workers. Jesse's comrades are involved in the attempted assassination of Clemenceau. Kurt, trailed by the Sûreté, seeks refuge with Beauty and quickly becomes the lover of his friend's mother. Lanny is arrested by the Sûreté when he is found in possession of Red leaflets printed by Jesse's organization with money provided by Kurt; Jesse is sent packing from the open political scene and, momentarily, from Lanny's immediate circle. Wiser after his escapade, Lanny rejoins his father.

III

Already in the first volume thus sketchily summarized, Upton Sinclair's methods are those fitted for the epic rather than for the novel. We are hurried along by an unobtrusive narrative skill. There are six Books, thirty-eight chapters and innumerable sub-sections, none longer than a couple of pages, serving the function of the stanzas of a Canto—'There's time to read just one more short section; oh, well, I may as well go on to the end of the chapter; only two more chapters and I shall have come to the end of this Book.' Descriptive passages are perfunctory, and there is almost no attempt to 'get inside' even the chief characters. We do not share their thoughts or feelings, we are not invited to examine their motives. We soon learn that in addition to the horizontal line dividing Olympians from mortals, there is an equally simple vertical line dividing good Olympians and good mortals from bad Olympians and bad mortals: the former are progressive, humanitarian, politically conscious; the latter are reactionary, selfish, lacking in ideals. We are *informed* of their thoughts and feelings in much the same manner as we are informed of their actions; whatever effect is produced will be cumulative. A sympathetic reader may at this point invoke Matthew Arnold (*Preface to Poems*, 1853), applying to Upton Sinclair his remarks on Greek drama:

'The terrible old mythic story on which the drama was founded stood, before he entered the theatre, traced in its bare outlines upon the spectator's mind; it stood in his memory, as a group of statuary, faintly seen, at the end of a long and dark vista . . . stroke upon stroke, the drama proceeded: the light deepened upon the group; more and more it revealed itself to the riveted gaze of the spectator. . . .'

It is admittedly preposterous to compare this cycle of novels to Greek tragedy; the Arnold quotation serves to indicate just where a modern reader is disposed to criticize the novels, and acts as a reminder that structural advantages may accompany the manifest defects. For the narrative is at times so slipshod that a boy and his mother can be thus described: 'and they would experiment and argue, and have a very good time,' so flat that natural description can be disposed of by an insertion beginning: 'New England was beautiful at that time of year,' so platitudinous that an encounter between Beauty and Lanny can be introduced with the cliché: 'Such a myriad of things they had to talk about!'—and so wooden that a boy talking in private with his father can be made to say: 'Everybody's been kind to me, and I'm glad I came. I had to know your people, and I wouldn't have missed the experience. But I have to see my mother, too. And she needs me right now.'

It is strange that after being fobbed off time and again with this sort of slapdash patter, a reader can still look forward to the reappearance of characters, pleased to recognize their external traits, patiently awaiting the set-piece jokes—such as Beauty's fear of *embonpoint* and her addiction to the cream jug. The truth is that just as in a genuine epic we are prepared to accept stagey gestures and indifferent dialogue so long as we can be sure of being borne along with the flood of a well-known story abounding in larger-than-life figures, so we have come to accept the youthful Lanny, smug and preposterous as we may think him, as a hero who will reintroduce us to figures of contemporary history and lead us back through tangled mazes of public affairs certain to interest us because we too, like the hero but without his larger-than-life advantages, have travelled the same path.

When confronted by the fluctuating balance between the public and the private life of Lanny Budd, the reader is disposed to indulge that 'willing suspension of disbelief' of which

Coleridge speaks. When the two worlds come together, the artifice is too obvious to bear for long. Because Lanny is a picaresque hero, we are prepared to follow him from one European country to another, accept his unusual luck in being always at the right place at the right time, meeting the interesting people and getting them to talk to him as to a brother. We do not 'believe' in him as a normal human being. And so, in the second volume *Between Two Worlds*, covering the years 1919–1929, we watch through his eyes the international conferences at San Remo and Cannes, we are in Geneva for League of Nations sessions, we see the advent of Mussolini in Italy and watch Hitler's 'Beerhall Putsch' in Munich in 1923; nor are we surprised that, after a few years given over to personal pursuits at a time when the international scene is comparatively placid, he should be in America in time to see at close quarters the Wall Street crash of October, 1929.

Similarly, although we are not concerned to participate in the inner motives of the private circle, the habit of repetition has made us feel reasonably acquainted with the family, and we can follow Lanny's no less picaresque private life without too strong a feeling of unreality, simply because he himself, as a living soul, is as unreal and as colourless as the hero of a Western film or a detective story. He matches his mother's love affair with his friend Kurt by forming a liaison with Marie de Bruynes, a married Frenchwoman as old as Beauty. We are *told* that they are very much in love, and we see them together often enough to pretend to believe it. Yet when Marie dies, Lanny rapidly takes up his former relationship with Rosemary, now Countess of Sandhaven with an equally complaisant husband. She, like Marie, can live acceptably enough under Beauty's tolerant roof; the reader is interested in the epic hero's private life but has no desire to peer behind the surface narrative. Only when a passing attempt is made to display the heart does the narrative wander into the habitual region of contemporary fiction, and, finding itself in the wrong place, begin to look ridiculous. Thus, when Rosemary in turn passes from the active scene, Lanny's broken heart is revealed in a passage reading remarkably like a parody:

'Lanny went down to his studio and played all the eighteen nocturnes, one after another, and imagined that Rosemary was in the room and sorrowing with him. He played other Chopin pieces, not forgetting the very sombre funeral march. In the course of days and nights he played Ballades and polonaises and mazurkas, fiery and tempestuous, yet freighted with a burden of bitter pain; he played études which were studies in emotionality even more than in piano technique. Before he got through he had played some two hundred compositions and got a fine lot of exercise, a workout both physical and spiritual. After it he was ready for some new kind of life.'

For the most part, Upton Sinclair the popular historian is content to eschew such embarrassments. Lanny's next adventure is with Irma Barnes, a twenty-three-million-dollar heiress who becomes his first legitimate wife: her character is sketched in the acceptable epic style, and we can suspend our disbelief in her as readily as we suspend our disbelief in Lanny's growing intimacy with Zaharoff, his meeting with Mussolini (epic label: 'Blessed Little Pouter Pigeon'), Matteotti, Balbo and the like. He tries to educate his wife in liberal politics:

'She knew the names of the leading screen stars, of the singers heard at the opera, the leaders of jazz bands who were announced over the ever more popular radio; but literary names, except for a few bestsellers, were unknown to her. The names of statesmen were also vague in her mind; she had no idea what they stood for, except that her father had approved of certain ones at home and disapproved violently of certain others.'

It was this kind of quiz that distinguished Lanny from Irma's playboy suitors and endeared him to her, we are to understand, during their strange courtship: she played a very temporary Desdemona to his Othello:

'Many of the things he said were over her head; she told him so, and he explained what he meant. He didn't make love to her; hadn't even tried to take her hand. She wondered why. He had made love to other women. Didn't he care for her that way? Was it because of her money? Hang the money!—so she would think, but not for long.'

One should not complain of marionettes that they move like marionettes. Only when we are asked to take a close-up view of their strings and take the jerks for thought or emotion does the convention become awkward. Irma is not compatible; we can believe as much without burden of proof. But when, in the seventh volume (*A World to Win*, covering the years 1940–42), Lanny takes unto himself, at the mature age of forty-two, his latest wife (to date), the author is at great pains to point out that Laurel Creston is selected after long trial and error as the hero's perfect soul-mate. She has a fine mind, a fine conscience; he can talk with her as well as make stilted love to her. Intimacy of this quality brings us perilously close to the marionette strings. By this time, Lanny has had so many exciting adventures, has shown so consistent a high-mindedness, has rejected so many wives, mistresses and supplicants, that we are led to expect something pretty rare when we are invited to overhear the private communion of the hero and his favourite consort. Alas, the broad epic pen is blunt indeed for domestic lyricism. All the foregoing narrative passages about Lanny's hard choice of a partner, valid enough in the epic context, come under suspicion when we hear the happy pair conversing in a mixture of flat Mr.-and-Mrs.-Everyman dialogue and blood-curdling archness:

'Lanny and Laurel took turns reading the book aloud; and when they finished, the bride said: "We ought to go and see those things, Lanny; it would be a crime to be so near and pass them by."

' "It sounds near, but it isn't, darling. It's as far from New York to Chicago, and there are no railways for a good part of the way. . . ."

' "It seems a dubious sort of way to start a baby, darling."

' "It would only be a question of the first months. We wouldn't have to stay long—I am quick at getting impressions and making notes of what I need. . . ."

' "If we go by the north," he suggested, "we might get a plane to Russia."

' "The Moscow-Heaven Axis in reverse," smiled Laurel.

'The husband, swapping wisecracks, remarked: "I have a title for your first book, *The Red Honeymoon*!" '

IV

A synopsis makes poor reading. Yet only by rapid summary along the private and public lines already indicated is it possible to attempt an evaluation of the author's unfashionable but demonstrably successful qualities. In *Dragon's Teeth* (1929–34) we are taken inside Germany and become eye-witnesses of the terrible and at times moving story of the rise of the Nazis. The private story concerns the disasters overtaking the Jewish Robin family, the father a jovial business associate of Robbie's, the son Hansi a virtuoso violinist who has married Bessie Budd, the younger son Freddi who is tortured at Dachau. During the course of his rescue operations, Lanny becomes an intimate pal of Goering, Goebbels and Hitler himself, posing as a playboy American concerned only to buy old masters for the picture galleries of his rich friends, and to carry to the outside world stories of the wonderful achievements of National Socialism. The Olympians are allotted their customary epithets; we shall learn to anticipate Hitler's thigh-rubbing, Goering's ever-increasing bulk, and so on. As before, the private-public links are produced with equal dexterity and incredibility. Everybody who lives at or calls at the convenient Riviera hide-out will sooner or later lead Lanny to more headline personalities. Beauty's new husband is Parsifal Dingle, a simple-minded faith-healer who dabbles with the spirit world; the entourage now includes Madame Zyszynski [*sic*], an elderly Pole who possesses strange power as a medium: she is destined to deliver messages to Zaharoff from his dead duquesa, and for Hess and eventually Hitler. Rick and Nina still pop in for left-wing love-feasts; the place in Lanny's admiration vacated by the anti-Fascist Barbara Pugliese ('Poll-yay-say') is taken by the anti-Nazi Trudi Schultz, who will oust Irma in his affections and through whose eyes he shares in the terror and valour of the German underground.

Lanny's Scarlet Pimpernel activities are repeated in *Wide is the Gate* (1934–37). He smuggles Trudi out of Germany, stopping by at Berchtesgaden on the way for an intimate conference with the Führer. With Goering he is now on Hermann-Lanny terms. Still acting under cover of his art purchases, which earn him a comfortable living with a generous margin for left-wing charities, Lanny travels in Spain for the Civil War, guided by his old friend Raoul Parma, first known to the reader as the organizer of a Socialist Sunday School at Cannes. By this time the author is handling his epic theme with great skill; we accept the Lanny conventions and are moved to excitement and indignation by the slow unrolling of the agony of Europe. The fact that we know the outcome, that we have already seen the consequences of each new folly, each new betrayal, each successful gamble of the diabolical forces, only adds to our suspense. Our wooden hero becomes almost human as he drives his car hither and thither about Western Europe or nips across the Atlantic for a passing view of the New Deal and the growing resentment of America's would-be Fascists. During the course of this fourth volume Lanny changes partners again: Irma tires of her role as fellow-traveller and marries the Earl of Wickthorpe—and we are less troubled for Lanny's domestic peace of mind than pleased with the knowledge that the new link with the Wickthorpe family will stand him in good stead when the time comes for him to worm secrets from the Foreign Office. Meanwhile, Trudi will serve as mate and *confidante*; we value her for her heroism and as a source of information, but any private satisfaction she may give her man is hardly sufficient to impede the accelerating pace of the narrative or trouble us with irrelevant domesticity:

'Lanny knew that the lady of his latest choice was a predominantly ethical being. She was guided by her intellect and moral sense. He had taken a long time to think of what he was going to say to her; in fact, he had been over it so often that, without meaning to, he had learned it pretty well by heart. . . . He pointed out to her that love-making is an extremely ancient practice, which nature has established for purposes of her own. . . .'

Wooing of this quality is of far less moment than the real excitement of Lanny's adventures in Spain, and the warmth of our friendly interest in the family circle is aroused less by Trudi than by the fact that the young Loyalist aviator smuggled away from Franco's prison should be none other than Alfy, son of our hero's old friend Rick.

In *Presidential Agent* (1937–38) Lanny achieves professional status as collector of information and finds in President Roosevelt the first public figure to whom he can devote himself with admiration. His interviews always take place after the President has retired to his bed, and the epic label in this instance is the President's habit of wearing blue striped pongee pyjamas: in this and the following volumes the reader confidently (and in a strange bogus way, affectionately) expects a reference to the pongee pyjamas on the occasion of every interview; he is never disappointed. The rescue scene in this volume is even more exciting than the escape of Freddi from Germany or Alfy from Spain: Lanny and his fellow conspirators penetrate to the dungeon of a château near Paris occupied by a Nazi diplomat, in which Lanny the 'Nazi sympathizer' has been entertained as a guest. The solid historical scenes are concerned with the growth of Fascist appeasement in France (link: Denys de Bruyne) and the triumphant incorporation of Austria within the Reich (link: Lanny's 'friend' Hitler himself, with Hess, Schuschnigg and others thrown in for good value, all seen from within Berchtesgaden). The narrative pace has been speeded up, the broad scope of the public theme taken for granted, and by this time the reader enjoys the assurance that the pleasing recurrence of epic lay figures and their conventional attributes will not now be interrupted even by death. 'Dipping into the subconscious mind of a dull old Polish woman, Lanny had discovered fragments of the minds of other people, mostly dead, but now and then a living one.' The illusion of intimacy fostered by Grandfather Budd's Biblical homilies or Zaharoff's label 'Grand Officer of the Legion of Honour and Knight Commander of the Bath', and the odd goodwill aroused in the reader by that illusory intimacy, need never be wasted while the series of novels continues.

Dragon Harvest (1938–40) and *A World to Win* (1940–42) have rather less behind-the-scenes interest, for war has a way of stripping off diplomatic pretences and making the intentions of one's enemy painfully clear. The only thing smuggled out of Germany this time is a secret aircraft supercharger; the routine of secret meetings, careful attention to make sure that the car is not being followed, notes in harmless-looking art-dealer's code, all keep up the atmosphere of a high-grade serial film. The scion of Budd-Erling aircraft is still *persona grata* to Hermann at Karinhall and Adi at the Berghof.

'Lanny Budd's life had settled into more or less of a routine. He stayed a while on the Riviera and then in Paris; he went to Germany, and then to England. In each place he put on the proper clothes and made himself interesting to the wealthy and powerful, told them what they wanted to know, and used his tact to steer the conversation where he wanted it to go. After each effort he would make out a report—unless it was in Germany, where he never put anything on paper. There were some things he wouldn't write anywhere, and when he had enough of these he would take a trip to the land of his fathers, make sure that the Big Boss had duly received the reports, hear his comments and questions, and take on board a fresh load of courage and determination.'

The courage and determination issuing from behind the pongee pyjamas propel Lanny, in *Dragon Harvest*, to Hitler's mountain retreat on the very brink of the invasion of Poland (he bears with him his latest lady, the intelligent bore Laurel Creston, who reveals unsuspected powers as a medium and utters words of warning disapproval from Bismarck to an exasperated Führer); to the cautious cells of American Fascists; to the beaches of Dunkirk; to No. 10 Downing Street; to Les Invalides, where Hitler stood contemplating the tomb of Napoleon. *A World to Win* (1940–42) whisks Lanny from France (chats with Pétain, Darlan, Laval) to England (Battle of Britain), America (Hearst's stronghold San Simeon), and back to France again, where the 'friend' of the Pétainists is captured by the *maquis* and is wholly occupied, this time, in rescuing himself. Returning to America, he is told the secret of the atomic bomb, masters the elements of atomic physics (from Einstein, of course), and is only prevented from a further mission to Europe (to discover the state of German atomic research) by the crash of his transport plane into the waters of the North Atlantic. Broken bones and convalescence earn the Presidential agent a holiday—we leave the world-stage for a moment and at once our hero is entangled, after what for him is a longish absence, in the toils of female candidates. But it seems that the author's invention is beginning to flag when he has to hew out another wooden dummy in female shape: we wonder if we are reading earlier Cantos by mistake, or seeing the same film twice. Another millionaire's daughter, another yacht, another toss-up between beauty plus wealth and brains plus social conscience. A glance at the calendar tells us that by December, 1941, it will be necessary for Lanny to be in the Far East, and we are not surprised that the final surrender to Laurel Creston's dim charms should take place in Hong Kong. The yacht, with millionaire's daughter on board, is conveniently sunk by the Japanese. Lanny, with his seventh lady-love and third Mrs. Budd, investigates China, is inspired by the Chinese Communists, and takes leave of us in 1942, chatting agreeably in the Kremlin with Stalin—who has, it seems, the conventional Olympian notion of the right kind of gossip for the evening of a busy day:

'The capitalist state, in the Marxist-Leninist interpretation, is an agency of class repression. In a classless society there would be no function for it. As fast as people get education, they will assert themselves, and a democratic society will come automatically . . . . . But we do not use the name democracy as a camouflage for the continuation of wage slavery.'

V

As World War II hots up, Lanny's civilian exploits increase in speed and variety, but he is no longer a lonely agent of light in a dark passive world. As he moves into the recent past his to-and-fro progress becomes less impressive to readers who were themselves, during those years, not unoccupied with political and military affairs. In *Presidential Mission* (1942–43) the author is content to ramble on with a sequence of 'then he did this' and 'then he did that' episodes. For once, our Lanny is pushed to the fringe of affairs simply because several million other people had managed to push their way to the centre. We rely more and more on the pleasure of remembered associations. Lanny goes to Algiers, but calls at Bienvenu on the way and we are more pleased to see the family again than to be involved in remembered troubles of Allied strategy. He dines with Winston Churchill and Roosevelt, but the most sympathetic and devoted follower of the Budd fortunes cannot help feeling that those gentlemen had other and more pressing matters on their minds. And so it is to the long-suffering Laurel, rather than to contemporary Olympians, that the Budd observations on the passing scene are now revealed:

'He told her the details of his trip; the aspects of Vichy, the elderly roués being taken to the baths in wheel-chairs, the half-starved poor standing patiently in front of half-empty food-shops—etc., etc.'

The secret agent still has, of course, the confidence—and the private ear—of the Olympians on both sides. Allied plans? 'Roosevelt had mentioned to Lanny that the expeditions to the Mediterranean ports were sailing from Scotland, while those to the Atlantic ports were sailing from America.' Axis troubles? 'Hermann set himself against my policies in a way that I considered presumptuous,' confides Adi Hitler to his American friend Herr Budd; 'but even so, he is the Commander of the Luftwaffe, and in that capacity he is indispensable to me.' To those who have plodded through the epic thus far, Larry's war situation is made more credible by such personal touches as the fact the two de Bruyne sons are fighting on opposite sides, one for de Gaulle and the other for Pétain, or that Lanny's horrifying experience of a Berlin air-raid should take place in the ruins of Hilde Donnerstein's palace. There is so much to tell, so much journeying to do in order that our omnipresent hero may be in the right place at the right time (in America with the Nazi-sympathizers, in Morocco, in England for chats with Rudi Hess, in Stockholm with reports for the diplomatic bag, and so on), that successive sections or 'cantos' open with flat tired statements of fact: 'Lanny sent the code letter to Jerry'; 'Lanny received a note from Jerry'; 'Lanny prepared another report for F.D.R.'; 'Lanny handed his report to Murphy'. We snatch with relief at every contact with the old pre-war world where progressives (Bernard Monck) and reactionaries (Kurt Meissner) were lined up more neatly in rows of white and black.

One Clear Call (1943–44) opens with Lanny and Laurel on holiday in Florida, sharing a Paradise to which Upton Sinclair's omnivorous reading has brought not the serpent but an even less lovable creature, the chigger or red flea. Our hero expatiates on the natural habits of the chigger, what time his complaisant Eve ('He for God only, she for God in him') plies the busy question:

'Laurel listened to all this, and was amused to observe her husband's interest in entomological details. She asked him why, and he said he was fascinated by the problem of what nature could have meant by creating so many strange forms of life, each struggling desperately to survive at the expense of others.

'When the couple had exhausted this subject, they turned to the sponge industry of the Florida west coast——'

From the light relief of such horrifying domestic naïveté the reader is only too willing to be whirled away, for the ninth time, with Lanny on another 700-odd pages of improbable adventures. It is true that as the war gathers momentum our hero's ability to shuttle to and fro between Berchtesgaden and the White House, Karinhall and Westminster, grows less and less plausible—but the long-accepted convention of Lanny's debonair resourcefulness and the credulity of all Nazis is now so thoroughly established that we can believe in it all far more readily than we can brace ourselves to lend credence to his home-life with Laurel, that nefarious incarnation of the female Inquiring Layman. Sooner, by far, would we follow him to wartime Berlin, where his Mr. Everyman observations are offered without the assumption that they make suitable badinage for the boudoir: 'for walking at night in blacked-out Berlin you carried, if you could afford the price, a tiny electric torch.' Better still to blunder with him into the middle of the Battle of the Bulge, where the narrative pace accelerates and we suffer, for a few pages, no solemn reminders of shower-baths and suit-pressings.

O Shepherd, Speak! finds Lanny coping with the aftermath of war. Musso and Adi are dead; the great man of The White House is dead too, and the reader is embarrassed by the suspicion that Roosevelt himself will soon be uttering platitudes through the lips of Laurel, the unprofessional medium. Lanny the art-expert still moves freely amid the ruins, visiting Dachau, chatting with Goering in prison, taking delivery of the wrecked body of his sister Marceline and restoring her to the Riviera to be nursed back to mental and physical health by the invincible lovingkindness of Parsifal Dingle. There is, we feel, more for him to do than leave tactful boxes of chocolates in the shattered homes of his European friends, and soon the peace-time activities of our hero are unfolded: he sets up, in America, a new radio Peace Programme, using for expenses a fortune left him in the will of our old Riviera friend, Emily Chattersworth.

Here, if ever, is the chance to show us how far Lanny and his friends have developed from the amiable left-wing humanitarians of the pre-war volumes. After so much experience, human and superhuman, will they still be content to believe that a few pink catch-phrases (slightly bowdlerized now that

Soviet Russia is seen to be not only anti-Fascist but also anti-democratic) will do the trick? Alas, it seems so. At the launching of the new venture, Rick (now Sir Eric) informs us that 'a profit economy cannot market all its products at home, for it does not pay its workers enough . . . it is a drive to expansion, and so it becomes a drive to war'. Laurel, adding her blow for the cause, has a few well-chosen words on the subject of birth-control, 'or what they are now calling planned parenthood'. With the rightness or wrongness of these and similar beliefs I am not at the moment concerned; but faithful followers of Lanny and his circle can hardly avoid distress, after two world wars and a few atomic explosions, at finding the old gramophones still playing, somewhat sourly but with hardly a scratch from a hundred blitzes, the same old records.

But there will soon be some new records, too. We expect to be told (via fan-mail for the Peace Programme) the solemn news: 'Yes, the American people didn't want another war!' But it is not long before—in the last volume to date, *The Return of Lanny Budd*—we are hearing the voice of a new America, an America one might have expected the Upton Sinclair of the earlier volumes to take with just one grain of salt. Alas, it is a hook-line-and-sinker swallowing: 'The more you watched affairs in the old world the more glad you were to be living in the new. Johannes declared that half the people in Europe and Asia would come to the United States if they were able to gain admission.' Our author had been quick to spot, in earlier volumes, the English tendency to lump all foreigners together as interchangeable norms and assume special superiority for themselves; he ends by falling foul himself of the only very slightly different American belief—that America is the norm and that other cultures may be graded according to the degree to which they have succeeded in coming within recognizable distance of it.

In this last volume, the Olympians are scaled down and the members of the Lanny circle, older and better established, are scaled up. Of President Truman, for example, Lanny 'had said that he was a man of peace and this was a consolation to Laurel. . . .' A somewhat more distant view is taken, too, of world conditions, as if the author and his readers could no longer summon up surprise at lapses from democratic grace. We learn that in post-war Poland there were 'swarms of half-starved people on the roads', which was 'very depressing, and also very insanitary'. Even the Mr. and Mrs. Everyman tête-à-tête sessions of the Budds at home have lost something of their devastating sprightliness:

' "Dialectical materialism," said Lanny. "Diamat" is what they're calling it now in Europe."

' "It hypnotizes people's minds. It's like that hypnotized hen we saw: the man pressed her beak down to a chalk line and she couldn't move from that line."

' "The party line," said Lanny, permitting himself a smile. "The capitalists build up their power and fight to protect it. The rising proletariat opposes them, seizes the power, and takes it away from them, and out of the struggle a new society is born. Thesis, antithesis, and synthesis!" He said it every now and then.

' "And out of it has come the blackest tyranny ever dreamed in modern times.' It was strophe and antistrophe with the pair.'

Interest in *The Return of Lanny Budd* is divided between a skilful retelling of the fascinating story of Sonderkommando Himmler and its forgery factory in which our old friend and enemy Kurt Meissner (*en route* for the hangman and—one supposes—further revelations from the spirit world) plays his sinister role, and the progressive entanglement of Lanny's half-sister Bess (the wife-half of our musical couple 'Hansibess') in Communist spy activities in the United States. Lanny's liberal conscience, bruised already by the ancient tendency of so many of his friends to favour the Fascists, is now more sharply twinged when his own sister, involved in an elaborate espionage plot (named after 'the boilerplate papers' and so hinting broadly at a notorious trial in recent American history), must be exposed and handed over to the authorities. The broken-hearted Hansi, his marriage shattered and his early crusading zeal baffled, is delivered into the sustaining hands of a hideously facetious authoress named Rose Pippin, who will, we are to understand, lead him gently back into the best of all possible worlds.

As for Lanny, his reluctant distaste for Russian methods is confirmed when he himself, engaged in Allied radio propaganda in Berlin, is kidnapped by the Reds and subjected to torture before escaping—oh, it must be for the twentieth time.

But the attentive reader will shake his head sadly when he finds his hero over-aweing his Soviet captors by easy references to his chatty friend Stalin, as once he walked the tightrope in Nazi German with a genial *laisser-passer* from Adi Hitler in his pocket. When we finally take leave of the now middle-aged Budds, we find them sadder but only a little wiser, having 'brought back from Europe the dreadful conviction that we were failing in our propaganda against the Reds', and bravely pitting themselves, yet again, against the foe.

VI

It has been useful to sketch the progress of the *World's End* series at some length only because the astonishing size and loyalty of the author's audience may shed light on certain basic habits and requirements of some readers of fiction. However we may judge Upton Sinclair as a literary craftsman, he is a scholar of the human heart to this extent at least: he knows what a large number of obviously intelligent readers are looking for, and he knows how to supply their demand.

I say 'obviously intelligent', and I am prepared to defend that assertion. I do *not* say 'obviously intellectual'—that would be an absurd claim. At almost any point where the author's forays into intellectual or cultural fields may be checked by readers with special interests, their reaction is likely to vary between an unsurprised shrug at a platitude and stupefaction at some more than usually naïve judgement. Similar reactions may well be experienced from time to time by readers with special qualifications in politics or sociology. It is likely, then, that an 'intellectual' browsing through the series will scoff at a passage of art criticism beginning with the sentence: 'Anyhow, there were the paintings, and many of them were really grand'—or wince at the banality of this essay in social psychology: 'It is well known that in the great world people frequently practise such arts of masquerade; they maintain a surface of friendship while in their hearts are raging storms of hatred, contempt, jealousy, spite'—or raise an eyebrows at any one of scores of dead-pan pronouncements of political truisms. Yet any such reader who implied that devotees of Lanny Budd must be lovers of trashy novels would be sadly wide of the mark.

The *World's End* novels are sometimes exciting, sometimes tedious, always superficial, always wide in scope—but never trashy. Lovers of sensation may be pleased at first to identify themselves with Lanny Budd and chat with Hitler and Stalin: they will find that the revelations of these and other Olympians can be matched from old newspapers. Lovers of sensation who, still in the person of Lanny Budd, catch seven successive women in their arms, will soon discover that they are embracing dummies. Psychological motive is sometimes falsified, but always in the interest of black-and-white simplicity, never in terms of glamour or day-dreams. There is adventure galore—in each of the novels Lanny or one of his associates makes an exciting escape from captivity or danger—but it is embedded in close wads of political history and would never be reached by the half-baked reader who had a single-minded passion for 'sensation'. No; the subject-matter is difficult throughout, and although the author has nothing to offer the reader who wants sensitive writing or subtle appraisals, his style is equally barren of all attraction for lovers of sexy stories or thrilling mystery.

It is often difficult for literary people to realize how much the common reader values *information* in his library novels. The *World's End* series is crammed full of information of every sort. Do you want to know what the Wall Street crash was like, who was Goering's wife, or the name of the man who forged the 'Vermeer' pictures? If you have patience, Lanny Budd will tell you. 'I saw it in a novel,' people say. The cumulative information about world history contained in these eleven books is accepted by many readers in much the same way that their grandparents accepted moral uplift from novels—willingly, and without too close attention to detail. When Upton Sinclair provides this department-store information for readers who have neither the time nor the patience to visit, so to say, the better-class shops stocked by specialists, he may seem crude but he is remembering one important fact about the human make-up that is forgotten by many of his fellow novelists.

He is showing himself to be still more of a scholar of the heart when he makes unashamed use of all the old epic tricks of repetition, narrative sweep, and a collection of large clearly-labelled figures with large well-labelled attributes. Such conclusions may be depressing. One could perhaps prefer to discover that lyrical tricks, as once accepted by readers of, say, Tennyson, could be accepted by readers of contemporary novels. It may be a pity, too, that a public which will tolerate comic verbal tricks in television programmes nevertheless dislikes solemn verbal tricks in its novels. Yet it is certain that many more talented and self-conscious novelists have underrated in their readers a steady compassionate interest in public affairs rather than in stylistic problems, in chunks of experience however large and raw and inaccurate rather than selections of sensitive moments. If the strange success of Lanny Budd and his creator have reminded us of these ancient truths, known to simple minstrels but forgotten by Mr. A. and Miss B., then this hodge-podge epic may, for all its ineptitudes, have a claim on the literary critic no less than on the seeker of sugared pills of information.

9

THE PRISONER OF *THE PRISONER OF ZENDA*

Anthony Hope

I

One day in November, 1893, a young barrister of thirty was walking from Westminster County Court to his chambers in the Temple, when the idea of Ruritania came into his head. He smoked a pipe on it, and the next day wrote the first chapter of *The Prisoner of Zenda*. This young man had already published five novels with only moderate success; a sixth novel was about to appear, and he was meditating a seventh. He was torn (as many were before and have been since) between the safety of his profession and the nagging itch to make more time for his writing. He made time. Within one calendar month the new novel was finished. It appeared inApril 1894—for in those unenlightened days it was possible to see your book on sale within three months of completing the manuscript.*

The creation of Ruritania made one reputation and has ruined another. Both reputations belonged to Ruritania's creator, Anthony Hope Hawkins (he used a ready-made *nom de plume* by docking his surname). The first, a reputation for a 'rattling good story', for romance larger than life and refreshingly unlike life, has had a sturdy survival. (Sixty years after its publication, a Hollywood film company found it worth while spending a fortune on the fifth film version of *The Prisoner of Zenda*—a Technicolor version in which, to the distress of purists, the Elphberg red hair was overlooked.) The second, a reputation for social and political comedy of a high order, barely survived the author's death in 1933. Its duration may be gauged by the

* For biographical material I have relied solely on Anthony Hope's *Memories and Notes* (1927) and the authorized life by Sir Charles Mallet: *Anthony Hope and his Books* (1935).

ease with which it is possible to collect a library of Anthony Hope novels by scouring the less-favoured shelves of second-hand bookshops, at an average price of perhaps one shilling and sixpence per volume.

II

Zenda or no *Zenda*, it would have been difficult for the critics of the 1890s to forecast Anthony Hope's future as a novelist. All they could learn from the pre-*Zenda* books was that the young writer was remarkably versatile and productive. His first novel, *A Man of Mark* (1890), was published at the author's expense. It is a carefully contrived unambitious little tale of Aureataland, a South American republic—and the first step towards Ruritania. The plot includes a small-scale revolution with stagey late-Victorian 'effects' of horses' hoof-beats and presidential yachts; the dialogue is in the main stiff, with only occasional gleams from the future author of *The Dolly Dialogues*, such as the reference to 'a sum of money too small to mention but too large to pay'. The second novel, *Father Stafford* (1891), ushers in Hope's long series of novels of courtship, the common quality of which is a combination of quite astonishing naïveté of motivation (as we say nowadays) and a singular aptness in conveying observed behaviour. Here, for example, is a sample of his commentary on Lady Julia: 'She had a considerable, if untrained and erratic, instinct towards religion, and exhibited that leaning towards the mysterious and visionary which is the common mark of an acute mind that has not been presented with any methodical course of training worthy of its abilities.' The jolt from this sort of urbanity to horrible fustian must strike a modern reader with an almost physical shock and remind us of Anthony Hope's divided view of himself, his art and his public. 'Be it good or evil, she was his! Who forbade his joy? Though all the world, aye, and all heaven, were against him, nothing should stop him.' It is hardly possible to believe that the man who wrote the two passages could, when he sat down to dash off this sort of thing, wilfully mistake fustian for emotion, tale-telling for art, day-dreaming for psychology.

The plot of *Father Stafford* is equally bedevilled. At first, all is pleasantly witty in the leisured world in which Eugene Lane, a wealthy young M.P., happily engaged to one damsel and mildly flirting with another, turns aside for a moment to entertain his old friend Stafford, an ascetic but fashionable Anglo-Catholic priest. Stafford is charmed by the flirtatious Lady Julia, but only recognizes his own feelings when he sees them staring from the portrait of himself painted by an artist, another of Lane's house-guests. Horrified, he flies to the embrace of the Church of Rome, leaving Lady Julia to that of Lane. The amiable old cynic who in so many of Hope's novels stands aside in the wings muttering the author's own commentary, ends the novel with the observation: 'I think, Lady Julia, you have spoilt a Saint and made a Cardinal.' *Father Stafford* had grace and wit in plenty, but the young novelist was still willing, sometimes with insulting abruptness, to fob off his readers with archness, melodrama, or (as in the absurd revelation of Stafford's true passion *via* the portrait) downright drivel.

Mr. Witt's Widow (1892), the third pre-*Zenda* novel, offered a simple 'reversal of fortune' theme, an easy familiarity with the world of fashion, and a more consistent tone of light intrigue. Gerald, son and heir of Lord Tottlebury, is engaged to marry the widow of Mr. Witt. His cousin George recognizes her as a pauper whom he had defended years ago in an obscure courtroom—her crime being the theft of a pair of shoes. George must save the family honour, but his reluctant mud will not stick because he cannot bring himself to substantiate his hints and charges. He himself, of course, falls in love with Mrs. Witt. When, by another hand, Mrs. Witt's past history is confirmed and Gerald dutifully drops her, the reversed championship now undertaken by George brings him in turn into the social shadow. The whole enterprise is competent, novelette-ish, readable; once again the reader is kept firmly in his place, and wonders quite what to do, in the contrived pantomime, with such bonus gems as this: 'It was Mr. Blodwell's practice to inveigle people into long gossip, and then abuse them for wasting his time.'

Here is a sentence from the first page of *A Change of Air* (1893), the most successful of the pre-*Zenda* novels: 'Manners and etiquette are first the shadowed expression of facts and then the survival of them, the reverence once paid to power, and now accorded, in a strange mixture of chivalry and calculation, to mere place whence power has fled.' This is the world of Henry James—and it is true that in their shocking lapses into melodrama no less than in their set-pieces of social and moral 'placing', Hope's novels do remind us that his writing career overlaps, for much of its course, that of The Master. Yet two other qualities, one to Hope's advantage and the other sadly hampering, were already present in these early tales to indicate how widely separated—how almost opposite—were the developments of the two writers; so widely separated, indeed, that the discovery that as men and artists they had something in common comes almost as oddly as the disclosure of Mr. T. S. Eliot's affinity with Kipling. The first quality, an inestimable arrow in Hope's quiver, was his fine ear for dialogue. (Henry James had a witty turn for social exchanges, but anyone who turns to his plays can see at once how far that talent was from the ability to point and polish actual talk.) The second quality, setting Hope at the opposite pole from James, was his modest concern to be a 'professional' seller of stories, always ready to disclaim the higher reaches of fiction, always ready to stoop to 'tricks of the trade'. Those very passages of social comment that a present-day admirer would most readily quote are often found in the opening paragraphs of his chapters, where they serve as neat exercises in suspense, interrupting and thus sharpening the reader's desire to know 'what happens next'—a trick less characteristic of James than of Dr. P. G. Wodehouse.

A Change of Air concerns an *avant-garde* poet, Dale Bannister, who rents a house at Market Denborough, thus transferring—in the eyes of most of its inhabitants—Bohemia to Arcadia. He quickly becomes involved in local life and politics, scales the county ladder, and when the local Radical quotes one of his own more revolutionary verses in the local press, hastens to disclaim his earlier opinions. There is an oddly distant 'period flavour' about the details of these conflicts between county snobbery and Radicalism, between literary Republicans and the entrenched gentry. But the human situation is both fresh and universal: it is not the prerogative of any one age or political faith to discover that flesh-pots are not over-stuffed with principles. It is all the more distressing when the young author, having set his lively characters in a situation at once entertaining and serious, urbane and symbolic, suddenly remembers the claims of the readers of 'tales' and introduces melodrama: Dale writes an ode to grace the visit of a Royal Duke and the aggrieved Radical, aiming an assassin's pistol at his Lost Leader, hits and kills by mistake the poet's jilted Nellie. Nellie is not the only victim. The novel's poise is shattered, the outmoded mechanics creak like pantomime trapdoors, and at the approach of the larger-than-life, all the carefully observed real life has fled.

A second political novel, *Half a Hero,* was published in the same year, 1893. It has a strong main subject, the rise of the new Labour movement and the shuddering rings caused in the social pond when a great stone, in the shape of a Labour Prime Minister, is plopped into its midst. The scene is New Lindsey, a British colony as remote as Aureataland or Ruritania, but peopled by a recognizable London society; one can hardly stroll in the Park of its capital city without bumping into Cabinet Ministers, the Chief Justice, or the Governor's Lady. Social and political strands are interwoven; the emotional and political temperatures rise together. Quite enough matter, one would have supposed, for a deck-chair novel designed to catch one's interest without insulting one's intelligence. But no: the demand for melodrama, whether from within Hope's own nature or (more likely) his view of the reader's expectations, will not be denied. The Labour Prime Minister must needs be blackmailed by the husband of his ex-mistress, fall into a squalid public brawl, and be killed in a riot. Amused attendance at Government House and the Chief Justice's ball have hardly prepared us for such drastic goings-on, and once again the accumulated interest is scattered.

However sad it may be to contemplate the damage wrought to Hope's reputation by his over-production (a risk which in his case provoked the full ferocity of Gresham's Law), his early fecundity was certainly impressive. The year of the birth of *Zenda,* 1894, saw the publication of four new novels, and each is a prototype of many later books. Of *The Prisoner of Zenda* itself there is no present need to speak—indeed, Hope's own literary reputation has been for too long a prisoner in that crowned and gilded cage. Enough to say that it has added a word—Ruritania—to the English language and crystallized, like a fly in amber, that inescapable magic of royalty which has long outlived the tinsel pageantry of vanished Balkan kingdoms. *The Indiscretion of the Duchess* is a piece of tedious triviality cluttered with duels, honour and diamond necklaces—and there were to be several repetitions of this formula, which may be shelved midway between Restoration Tragedy and the clockwork productions of Science Fiction: competent riggings of a conditioned reflex for which automatic responses would click as readily as chocolates from a machine, full of 'smothered oaths and 'cold steel' and gadzooksery. *The Dolly Dialogues* show the master of cynical repartee at his most scintillating—and there is not one of his thirty-odd books without the saving grace of wit. *The God in the Car* proves with what effect Anthony Hope could combine his strongest talents—dialogue and a knowledge of the world of affairs—when he set his mind to it.

The instant popularity of *The Dolly Dialogues* can be attributed to the sharp yet mellow note of their social satire: sharp because the wit has a pointed verve, mellow because the satirist, speaking from within the circle, throws his barbs with a smile of amused toleration and does not hate the objects of his passing ridicule. And so, although the badinage concerns itself mainly with such mild social misdemeanours as philandering, the epigrams scattered through the talk are not so much tart exposures as, in a sense, 'useful' observations delivered with a sly straight face. 'Economy is going without something you do want in case you should, some day, want something which you probably won't want.' No savagery there! Nor is there more than a shrug in the presence of social dishonesty—as when the narrator is surprised that Mrs. Hilary Musgrave should express moral disapproval of Lady Mickelham, because after all 'Mrs. Hilary is quite good-looking herself'. The exact quality of Hope's implicated amusement may be illustrated by the typical theme of one dialogue: a fashionable wife, piqued to hear that her husband has helped a young scapegrace to emigrate after embezzling money in order to live up to the social standard of the lady he was 'cultivating', relents with a smile on learning that the lady was herself. The extent of Hope's participation in the world he exposes is everywhere apparent; his wit played well within the limits of late-Victorian social assumptions:

' "She has a north-country accent."

' "It might have been Scotch," said I.

' "She plays the piano a good deal."

' "It might have been the fiddle," said I.

' "She's very fond of Browning."

' "It might have been Ibsen," said I.'

No entrenched order is likely to turn to rend so urbane a critic; among the chorus of praise there was grave commendation from Mr. George Meredith.

The God in the Car, the novel that is said to have caused Cecil Rhodes to exclaim, 'I'm not such a brute as all that,' was the book Hope finished a month before he smoked his pipe over the notion of *Zenda*. Here, the political and the social comfortably cohabit: the political actions of the aggressive hero Ruston may flutter social dovecotes, but it is action based upon the world of the doves and is not, this time, a matter of swords and pistols hired from a theatrical costumier. Ruston is like one of the more dashing Elizabethan privateers who cut a poor figure at court, but whose shady frigates were financed by courtiers and by the Queen herself. But the significant quality of this novel is not Hope's ability to set our sympathy veering between the 'buccaneer modernized' and his more squeamish stay-at-home backers, but in the fact that Ruston's Empire-building enterprise is unfolded in outspoken talk among well-informed equals. The plot demands that the standards of society shall be violated by society's licensed Juggernaut, but those standards are taken for granted throughout and were shared by Hope's intended readers. Behind the surface tensions of a serene social group sniffing after glory and riches but, on the whole, daring not to snap, the theme is that of an intelligent woman, accustomed to act through her less gifted menfolk, suddenly confronted with a chance to act for herself—to sail away with the pirate instead of sitting at home with the shareholders. It was, in 1894, a sufficiently daring subject. It demanded a rare degree of 'handling'. It was handling of the kind Hope could best organize. There was no James-like hesitancy as to the nature of the enterprise or the price to be paid for full collaboration. The long struggle between Maggie Dennison's duty to her own personality and her duty to her circle was fought out in the open in passages of fine dialogue only occasionally marred by Hope's distressing 'ays' and 'nays' and 'recking of naught elses'. The climax (and this *is* a James 'situation') comes at a relatively low point, where Ruston confronts Maggie with the intention of sending her away but blurts out that he wants her, while Maggie—whose intention it was to translate love into action by eloping with her pirate—finds her best qualities pulling with rather than against the social magnet, and returns to her husband.

'I am very nervous about it,' Hope wrote in his diary. *The God in the Car* had caused him more labour than any other book to date. It was well received. Personal tributes came from such ill-assorted readers as Field-Marshal Sir Evelyn Wood and H. G. Wells. The former as a man of affairs had known many people like the tempted hostess and her ruthless champion, but 'had never thought to have seen their inward minds so clearly set forth'. The praise is significant; its source is more so. Since Hope's day, there has been a marked decline in the chances of a Field-Marshal being enthralled by the work of a fashionable well-reviewed young novelist. The fault is not wholly with the Field-Marshals. Since 1894 the novel has broken new ground and Hope himself, writing today, would probably have had courage to give his imagination freer rein. But there has been loss, too—the loss of a cultured but not specifically 'literary' body of readers, who must now search far on the fiction shelves for an intelligent treatment of the sort of problems they, as men and women in society rather than as experts in new modes of expressing niceties of guilt or frustration, know and understand.

By this time, Hope had turned his back on the law and was to be for the rest of his life a doggedly 'professional' writer. His constant awareness of the reader was to lead him to squander his gifts on inferior melodramas, but those same gifts also informed his best work. His subtleties were to be subtleties of presentation, and his notable phrases would be valued for their sense rather than their poetry: they were never subtleties of expression rearing up a barrier between writer and reader. He wrote to be read.

III

At the end of 1896 Anthony Hope surveyed a profitable year of writing and then wrote in his diary: 'I have not been very happy. The writing does not, as a life, altogether content me and I grow more and more despondent as to my chance of doing anything really good.' Brought up as a Liberal and Broad

Churchman, he had listened to the conversation at his father's dinner-table, had read the *Spectator* and *The Times* from the age of twelve, had followed a steady enjoyable course through Marlborough and Balliol to the Bar, had acquitted himself without disgrace as a Parliamentary candidate, had seemed all set for a public career. At the end of his life Sir Anthony Hope Hawkins, of whom Barrie was soon to write: 'He made more people happy than any other author of our time,' showed no disposition to be faithless to his first love:

'For the political life is in its higher grades a great one, and to be immersed in great affairs makes a man bigger. I have a strong liking and admiration for public men, and I have small patience with people who sneer at them; thinking to be superior, they are merely silly. One sometimes hears a tenth-rate writer, or artist, sneer at Cabinet Ministers, and the least gifted of them had ten times the brains possessed by such critics as these.'

The division of loyalty implied by these extracts from Hope' diary in the first flush of literary success and from *Memories and Notes*, the considered summary of his life, is the clue to his status as a novelist. On the one hand, a sense of the dignity of public place and his ability to keep in step, both as man and writer, with the world of responsible affairs, did preserve him in the long post-*Zenda* period from the temptation to produce nothing but a series of trumpery cloak-and-dagger imitations of that *succès fou*. On the other hand, he was content to leave unexplored, even in his most ambitious work, those compelling below the-surface areas of human personality which were exerting, throughout his career, an ever-increasing fascination over his fellow-novelists. Nor could he ignore bread-and-butter considerations; to maintain himself and his family in the higher ranks of comfortable officialdom he set himself to earn as much by his pen as he would have earned at the Bar or in public life. To this need, and to his own undoubted enjoyment in spinning an exciting yarn, may be attributed such 'tuppence-coloured' stories as *The Chronicles of Count Antonio* (1895) with its 'damned lot of "Ands" and "Nows" and "Buts"—pseudo-Scriptural' (Hope's own description, when he re-read the novel in 1913); *The Heart of Princess Osra* (1896), compounded of coy homilies and gadzooksery; *Phroso* (1897), chock-full of sieges, secret passages and smothered oaths; *Rupert of Hentzau* (1898), sequel to *Zenda*, in which Rudolph Rassendyll confronts again his engaging adversary against a background of high-souled cavaliers, high-falutin loyalties and the involuntary charm of a period when an English milord could lightly order a 'special' on a Balkan railway; and *Simon Dale* (1898), an intricate historical romance starring Charles II and Nell Gwyn. Taken at a gulp, these amiable rigmaroles are still readable, once one has grown accustomed to the abominable peppering of 'ays' and 'nays' and 'what befells'; and *Simon Dale*, for all its swagger, comes very near to being a plausible historical novel of real worth. Several of Hope's romances were adapted for the stage (and some, later, for the films). He had always loved the theatre: financially, if in no more lasting manner, the theatre repaid his ardour.

The King's Mirror (1899), considered by Hope himself and by some distinguished contemporaries to be his best novel, owes its distinction to the blending in one volume of the ineluctable romance surrounding kings with that mellower more intelligent attitude to life hitherto reserved by the author for his commentaries on the English social scene. For the first time, inhabitants of a Ruritania are allowed as much wit as the frivolous ladies of *The Dolly Dialogues*. The courtiers, still gaudy with Teutonic titles, utter aphorisms no longer restricted entirely to the themes of love and loyalty: much latitude was permissible at the court of a young king who could admit that 'the history of my private life is . . . the record of the reaction of my public capacity on my personal position; the effect of this reaction has been almost uniformly unfortunate'. Real politics and a genuine conflict between love and duty allow King Augustin to speak and write with a sureness of touch unwarranted in the overcharged atmosphere of Strelsau.

IV

Between the publication of *Zenda* and the end of the century Hope had published ten books, was busy with drafts or dramatized versions of several others, had seen his industry rewarded by a growing volume of critical acclaim and was collecting an annual income large enough to make a modern author pop-eyed with envy. Before 1900, when Hope reached his thirty-seventh year, the diary quoted in Sir Charles Mallet's biography includes such end-of-year entries as 'In money all right: £8500 about (about £3000 from plays, I think)—much less than last year, but much more than it will be and more than I need.' No wonder he felt able, towards the close of his life, to advise young authors to invest half their earnings! Firmly established with a growing public, well equipped by upbringing and income to cut a respectable figure in social London, he could congratulate himself that neither financially nor professionally had he lost by the sacrifice of his legal career.

Yet he could never have become so skilled in the observation and exposition of the world of affairs had he not still hankered after a more active role. It may be thought that any English Liberal Duke who died, ripe with years and honours, round about the year 1900, must be envied as perhaps the last serene exponent of the art of having one's cake and eating it. Certainly, for a prosperous Radical, 'bliss was it in that dawn to be alive.' Anthony Hope Hawkins had been offered several chances to renew his bid for a seat in Parliament; in 1900 he accepted a Liberal candidacy but had to withdraw, on medical advice. He had come within a hair's breadth of active political experience—and it can be guessed that a man of his gifts would not have languished for long on the back benches, but would have played his part in the great Liberal administrations of the early years of the new century. It was his good fortune that at the time when a political career was finally barred to him, he could feel secure enough in the esteem of the reading public to turn his attention to the mellow 'inside' treatment of the English governing classes in their last autumnal glory.

The germ of *Quisanté* (1900) was a conversation with Lord Chaplin who described how the Bentinck brothers had 'taken up' the young Disraeli. In certain superficialities of manner, gesture and social origins the ambitious Alexander Quisanté bears a resemblance to Benjamin Disraeli, but it needs no Jamesian utterance on the process of artistic creation to lend credence to Hope's statement that his development of the character and career of Quisanté 'was in no way meant to represent or reflect Disraeli's'. There is a wonderful assurance in the writing of *Quisanté*, never previously attained (nor, I think, later surpassed) by Hope. He had begun work on it in

1897—and, for once, it *was* hard work. He took to heart the criticism of his friend the Duchess of Sutherland—'concentrate it!'—and produced the best-constructed of his books. In narrative deployment, literary tact, in the exposition of his major character first through the conversation of the privileged group he was soon to dominate and then in direct presentation of a complex personality—in all these aspects *Quisanté* displays Hope in full mastery over all the resources he had hitherto tried out in varying proportions. The opening chapters may be recommended to the attention of any would-be novelist who wishes to learn how to 'place' a character by deft alternation of narrative and dialogue, each paragraph witty in its own right and only slowly revealing a structure more significant than the sum of its parts:

' "I think hands and brains are better than manners."

' "I'll agree, but I don't like his hands or his brains either."

' "He'll mount high."

' "As high as Haman. I shouldn't be the least surprised to see it."

' "Well, I'm not going to give him up because he doesn't shake hands at the latest fashionable angle."

' "All right, Dick. And I'm not going to take him up because he's a dab at rhodomontade." '

The general observations, too sensible for epigrams and more genial than biting, are no longer tricks to create suspense but have an organic relation to the book like that of imagery to a poem: 'Most girls are bred in a cage, most girls expect to escape therefrom by marriage, most girls find that they have only walked into another cage'—or again: 'As soon as the ultimate came on the scene, the Dean felt that the game was up; the Crusade depended on an appeal to classes which must be reached, if they could be reached at all, by something far short of ultimates.' In many asides, as when the Dean notes that for many men 'good form' acts as a substitute for conscience, Hope touches that moral-cum-aesthetic nerve already identified by Henry James as so significantly characteristic of the upper reaches of English life at the turn of the century. All in all, Hope now seemed to be in full command of his faculties and less eager to throw sops to Cerberus. His set-piece presentation of minor characters began to show an exuberance of confident enjoyment in the writing:

'It was impossible not to admire the wealth of experience which Mrs. Baxter had gathered from a singularly quiet life; many men have gone half a dozen times round the world for less. Whatever the situation, whatever the actions, she could supply a parallel and thereby forecast the issue. Superficial differences did not hinder her; she pierced to the underlying likeness. When all the world was piteously crying out that never in its life had it heard of such an affair as this of May Gaston's, Mrs. Baxter dived into her treasure-chest and serenely produced the case of the Nonconformist Minister's daughter and the Circus Proprietor. Set this affair side by side with the Quisanté business, and a complete sum in double proportion at once made its appearance. The audacity of the man, the headlong folly of the girl, the hopeless mixing of incompatibles were common to the two cases; the issue of the earlier clearly indicated the fate that must attend the later. Lady Richard could do nothing but gasp out, "And what happened, Mrs. Baxter?"

'Mrs. Baxter told her, punctuating the story with stitches on a June petticoat.

' "She ran away from him twice; but he brought her back, and, they said, beat her well. At any rate she ended by settling down to her new life. They had seven children, all brought up to the circus; only the other day one was sent to prison for ill-treating the dancing bear. He's dead, but she still keeps the circus under his name. Of course all her old friends have dropped her; indeed I hear she drinks. Her father still preaches once on Sundays." '

Within five years of the appearance of *Quisanté*, four more novels of society were published, all characterized by a broad-fronted narrative sweep and an exhilarating brilliance of dialogue which in combination are the mark of a more than competent novelist at the height of his powers. Closely related as these novels are to the exact social rules of the period, there is in them a vividness of individual portraiture, a fresh gaiety of commentary, preserving the colour of life well beyond the validity of its social setting. All we have to remember, turning to Hope's best novels today, is that high social comedy demands the existence of a class system rigidly enforced: only thus can spontaneity of revolt be measured, personal freedom be illuminated against social restraints, magnanimous or eccentric behaviour gain its proper effect of surprise. We have only to recognize the pre-1914 distance between Mayfair and Bohemia to enjoy, as Hope and his readers enjoyed, the busy unconcealed traffic between them:

' "There are believed to be Bohemians still in Kensington, and Chelsea," observed Tommy Trent. "They will think any thing you please, but they don't dine out without their husbands."

' "If that's the criterion, we can manage it nearer than Chelsea," said Trix. "This side of Park Lane, I think."

' "You've got to have the thinking too, though," smiled Airey.'

The Intrusions of Peggy (1902), from which this quotation is taken, has an extraordinary liveliness: it is as though Oscar Wilde had written the dialogue and Henry James the narrative, and the collaboration had corrected the faults of each partner with the unlikely merits of the other. When Trix Trevella is launched into society, the denizens of the different *quartiers* of Vanity Fair commingle in happy intimacy without losing their separate characteristics—good or bad, high or low, gentle or vulgar. This cross-fertilization, so to say, produces a vitality quite unimpaired by the intervening changes which might otherwise cause a modern reader, accustomed to view his social map in all its post-blitz uncertainty of outline, to ask what all the fuss is about. The early chapters of *The Intrusions of Peggy* have a marked (but independent) similarity to the organization and handling of *The Bostonians* and *The Princess Casamassima*—a quality made most explicit in that amused deliberate inflation of language employed by an author who is entertained by the parallel development of private and public lives. When Hope writes 'obligations' for 'unpaid bills' in the sentence:

'The freshness of delicacy is rubbed off, the appeal of shyness silenced, by a hand-to-mouth existence, by a habit of regarding the leavings of the first-floor lodger in the light of windfalls, by constant flittings unmarked by the discharge of obligations incurred in the abandoned locality. . . .'

—he is akin to James describing with affectionate distaste the milieu of little Hyacinth Robinson in *The Princess Casamassima*. When Hope, a few pages later, invests squalid violence with a mock-heroic objectivity, he is at precisely the same distance from the subject as James sketching the Tarrant family in *The Bostonians*:

'When her husband was sober, she never referred to what had happened when he was drunk; if he threw a plate at her then, she dodged the plate: she seemed in a sense to have been dodging plates and such-like missiles all her life.'

Other parallels, in the lighter air of Hope's Mayfair, suggest themselves. There is something of Merton Densher of *The Wings of the Dove* in the character of Airey Newton; Mrs. Bonfill, considered as a social midwife, is sister to Kate Croy's aunt, Mrs. Lowther, and her brilliant set-piece presentation is worthy of a place beside that of Mrs. Farrinder in *The Bostonians*:

'At the age of forty (a point now passed by some half-dozen years) Mrs. Bonfill had become motherly. The change was sudden, complete and eminently wise. It was accomplished during a summer's retirement; she disappeared a queen regnant, she reappeared a dowager—all by her own act, for none had yet ventured to call her passée. She was a big woman, and she recognized facts. She had her reward. She gained power instead of losing it; she had always loved power, and had the shrewdness to discern that there was more than one form of it. The obvious form she had never, as a young and handsome woman, misused or over-used; she had no temptations that way, or, as her friend Lady Blixworth preferred to put it, "In that respect dearest Sarah was always *bourgeoise* to the core." The new form she now attained—influence—was more to her taste. She liked to shape people's lives; if they were submissive and obedient she would make their fortunes. She needed some natural capacities in her protégés, of course; but, since she chose cleverly, these were seldom lacking. Mrs. Bonfill did the rest. She could open doors that obeyed no common key; she could smoothe difficulties; she had in two or three cases blotted out a past, and once had reformed a gambler. But she liked best to make marriages and Ministers. Her own daughter, of course, she married immediately—that was nothing. She had married Nellie Towler to Sir James Quinby Lee—the betting had been ten to one against it—and Lady Mildred Haughton to Frank Cleveland—flat in the face of both the families. . . . It was not small achievement for a woman bred in, born at, and married from an unpretentious villa at Streatham. *La carrière ouverte*—but perhaps that is doing some injustice to Mr. Bonfill. After all, he and the big house in Grosvenor Square had made everything possible.

Mrs. Bonfill loved her husband, and she never tried to make him a Minister: it was a well-balanced mind, save for that foible of power. He was very proud of her, though he rather wondered why she took so much trouble about other people's affairs. He owned a brewery, and was Chairman of a railway-company.'

If Mrs. Bonfill suggests Mrs. Farrinder, Mr. Bonfill is surely the literary blood-brother of Mr. Farrinder. (It will be remembered how *that* unhappy man was introduced—and dismissed—at the end of a similar paragraph with even shorter shrift: 'She had a husband, and his name was Amariah.')

V

Alongside *Peggy*, three novels varied the social theme by the addition of one new ingredient apiece. *Tristram of Blent* (1901) turns on legitimacy and the prize of an ancient peerage; *Double Harness* (1904) seeks, by studying a number of particular marriages, to arrive at a general view of that institution; *A Servant of the Public*, Hope's *Tragic Muse*, draws to the centre of the stage from its usual position in the wings his own abiding interest in all matters concerning the theatre—and especially actresses. Each novel is a solid achievement, but a certain failure of confidence, reflected in a reduced exhilaration of narrative power, allows more of Hope's native melancholy to affect the tone of his writing. *Tristram*, 'set in reality, but tinged with romance,' suffers a little from that illogical irritation that afflicts the reader who, identifying himself with a hero, is offended rather than uplifted by that hero's tendency to self-sacrificing altruism. *Double Harness*, brilliantly sustained though it is, appeals to a reader's acquired experience rather than to his untutored instincts, and so gains approval rather than assent. The stoical author comes as near as ever he did to revealing his own nature in passages where fortitude is accepted as substitute for adventure and forbearance for passion. *A Servant of the Public* hovers round the theme of the attraction exerted by an actress, selfish, irresolute and fascinating, over an inhibited young man with twice her decency and half her vitality.

'He is sad without being sour,' said *The Times Literary Supplement* of the author of *Double Harness*. The underlying melancholy running through Hope's diary, toning down his triumphs and blunting the edge of disappointments, was leading him—now that he had won the security to write as he himself wished—to dwell more and more on tendencies to withdrawal and renunciation. In *Double Harness*, Grantley Imason's spirited canter on the downs with his Sibylla mounted behind him like a captive princess may give a rare hint of lyrical passion: but it is quickly reduced by both participants to a more manageable level of affectionate independence. 'Between idle praisers and idle blamers, and one's own *inevitable* lack of a balance,' Hope asked himself at about this time, 'where is judgement of one's self?' The writer's life still failed to satisfy him wholly. (A writer who *is* wholly satisfied with his life is unlikely to become a good novelist.) A few years earlier he had noted: 'As I became a young man early from boyhood, so I am becoming middle-aged rather early from youth.' He hated and feared idleness: 'it lets the mind so loose for speculation and review.' Similar instances of an ingrained melancholy may be found in the Mallet biography and in Hope's own autobiographical notes. What distinguishes Hope from some other writers who nurse such temperaments is that he did not consider this attitude to life to be, in itself, sufficient equipment for a novelist.

A below-standard Ruritanian exercise, *Sophy of Kravonia* (1906), and another collection of short stories, *Tales of Two People* (1907), kept the pot boiling before the publication in 1908 of *The Great Miss Driver*, a full-scale study of a *nouveau riche* heiress, possessed of great wealth and greater energy, who fights to extend her empire over the territories, conventions and hearts of the county gentry. Plot and treatment come very near to the Henry James method; all the apparatus is there even to the detached observer who tells the tale. It is more expository and explanatory than any previous Hope novel, thicker in texture and more sustained in its organization of what Henry James called, so comically for his own immense elaboration, an 'ado'. (Once again one has to rub one's eyes at the knowledge that bouncing Sophy of Kravonia and the minutely observed Jenny Driver sprang from the same pen at much the same time.) In *The Great Miss Driver*, Hope waded in deep. He was not quite out of his depth in all the reiterated subtlety of analysis, but he sometimes gave the appearance of being out of his depth. His characteristic modesty as a writer did extrude, in this new vein, as a real flaw. The failure of confidence shows in such a passage as this:

'Well, they were the joy of her life—it would have needed a dull man not to see that. The real joy, I mean—not what at that moment—nay, nor perhaps at any moment—she would herself have named as her delight. Her joy in the sense in which we creatures—and the wisest of us long ago—come nearest to being able to understand and define the innermost engine or instinct whose working is most truly ourselves—the temptation to live and life itself, which pair nature has so cunningly coupled together.'

In other respects the book is well within the Hope compass. Jenny Driver, torn between the attraction of ennobled privilege and the more virile claims of a roughshod man of action, is a typical Hope heroine; Leonard Octon figures as a Ruston or a Quisanté who leaves behind him a more turbulent wake. And the aphorisms, subdued to a thoughtful unbrilliant narrative, hardly stand out at all as clever remarks, but are barely noted with a sad acceptance of their literal truth: 'A mind that thought for itself in worldly matters . . . would very likely think for itself in moral and religious ones too—and such thought was apt to issue in suspending general obligations in a man's own case.'

Mrs. Paxon Protests (1911) returns to the theme of the price paid by those who rebel against the rules of society; once again Hope feels impelled to point out that retribution comes not so much from the world's outraged opposition as from the rapidly declining currency of liberty: 'social liberty might, it seemed, be more exacting than social bondage.' A lighter note had been struck in *Second String* (1910), a reversion to personalities and politics. It is the fable of a tortoise, Andy Hayes, and a hare, Harry Belfield. Andy, devoted to the gilded Harry, eventually wins both his girl and his seat in Parliament. There is a Jamesian mixed foursome; Harry is engaged to Vivien Wellgood but flirts with Isobel, her companion, with whom father Wellgood is secretly in love—a circumstance reinforcing his anxiety to defend his daughter's honour when he catches Harry making love to Isobel. A sub-plot or 'sub-atmosphere' made up rather implausibly of denizens of the London stage throws into relief the county setting—the whole complicated quadrille once again made possible only by considerations, now obsolescent, of marrying 'above' or 'below' one's station: 'The more definite a line, the more graciousness lies in stepping over it.' For all the comings and goings, the elections and excursions, there is a leisurely Edwardian pace about *Second String* allowing clever talk and witty commentary to flower more readily than in the laboured 'placing' of Jenny Driver: 'Harry's feelings passed a retrospective Act by which the love-making and passion became and were deemed always to have been, flirtation and attention.' The hare-tortoise situation is pointed in a phrase echoing the Hope of ten or fifteen years earlier: 'Neither of them is the ideal man, you know. Andy wants an occasional hour of Harry . . . and Harry ought to have seven years' penal servitude of Andy.'

The Great War of 1914–18 dealt Anthony Hope's world its death blow. The last pre-war novel, *A Young Man's Year*, came out in 1915; by accident but appropriately it harked back to the days of his own first steps on the stage now overshadowed—his young hero, presented by a mellower Hope, fumbles his way to a discovery of the ways of the world and of himself. During the war Hope buried himself in work for the Ministry of Information (for which, rather than for his novels, he received his knighthood). He was growing exhausted, and when he hankered after his non-propagandist pen it was for the old adventure stories and not the more demanding effort to cope with the ways of the battered new world. 'If ever I can write again,' he confided to his diary in 1917, 'it shall be a *yarn*, and not why Mrs. Smith proposed to Mr. Brown.' The yarn, when it did arrive (late in 1918), added little to Hope's laurels: it was a re-hash of an earlier 'love and honour' plot, *Captain Dieppe*, which bore no trace of reality or the old knack of dialogue, descended in dispirited fashion from Kings to Counts, and unwisely wore in the new world its 20-year-old tinsel.

In 1919, when all the Ruritanias of Europe were toppling to their fate and a new tangle of ethnically correct republics were taking their place on the map, the creator of Ruritania wrote a strange little-known pot-boiler, *Beaumaroy Home from the Wars*, which includes a gruesome scene where a crazed old man, sitting on a make-believe throne, gives audience under the pathetic delusion that he is the Kaiser. It is as if the mature Anthony Hope, having written in such novels as *Quisanté* and

The Great Miss Driver a far more ambitious treatment of the private and public world of here and now, came near to disowning the phenomenal popular success attending *The Prisoner of Zenda* and its sequel, *Rupert of Hentzau.* As the old besotted Kaiser grimaces at us from his hallucination, it is as if the creator of Ruritania is teasing us with the ignoble pleasure we feel when, fancying ourselves in the shoes of the gallant red-headed Englishman Rudolf Rassendyll, we too parade for a few intoxicating hours with the crown of Ruritania in our keeping, the faithful Colonel Sapt at our side, and Black Michael and his dare-devil henchman young Rupert of Hentzau held at bay:

'I wore a silver helmet with gilt ornaments, and the broad ribbon of the Rose looked well across my chest. I should be paying a poor compliment to the king if I did not set modesty aside and admit that I made a very fine figure. So the people thought; for when I, riding alone, entered the dingy, sparsely-decorated, sombre streets of the Old Town, there was first a murmur, then a cheer, and a woman, from a window above a cookshop, cried the old local saying:

' "If he's red, he's right!" whereat I laughed and took off my helmet that she might see that I was of the right colour, and they cheered me again at that.'

Two last novels, numbers 31 and 32 in his long output of fiction, were gallant tokens from the man who could write: 'I believe I am so much of a craftsman . . . that, if I were to live again, I would ask only to write better.' *Lucinda* (1920) and *Little Tiger* (1925) are readable reversions to his old interest in women bold enough to defy convention. They would be significant only if he had not done the thing better before. There remained only, before his death, the 'slight and reticent' *Memories and Notes* (1927) to present, not so much a clearer picture of Sir Anthony Hope Hawkins as a confirmation that the temper of his best writing was the temper of the man himself—competent, stoical, never unaware of the profundities underlying life's surface but determined, as a good citizen of the world, not to add insult to injury by facing tragedy in a spirit of resentment or contemplating the common human predicament with undignified fuss. When he *did* complain, it was in rueful professional privacy:

'It is rather hard to keep heart writing when once you know

thoroughly your own limitations. Through my really productive years from 29 to 43 or thereabouts, the *next one* was always going to be *great*. But now! Oh, Anthony, Anthony!'

VI

Anthony Hope's achievement, no less than his limitations, sprang naturally from his consciousness of his own place in a world where private motive and public behaviour were afforded equal attention, where aspects of life could be illuminated not only in terms of blood and glands but also in terms of legal or political imagery. An estimation of that place is only possible after a glance at what, over a 35-year span too recent to be 'history' and too distant to be a memory for most novel-readers, he set himself, as a professional man among professional men, to achieve.

Sir Anthony Hope Hawkins was the most 'clubbable' of men. For years he occupied a two-way embassy between the world of affairs and the world of letters. On many public occasions he was the spokesman for contemporary writers; his whole writing career proclaimed that public life was a fit theme for novelists. Nowadays, for all the lowering of ancient barriers, the two worlds mingle less freely. One rarely sees the young novelist Mr. X at political parties, and if the Rt. Hon. Sir A. B. should figure in his stories, it will probably be as a none too well observed caricature. There is much to be said, of course, for diving deep below the surface of social life if a novelist has a gift for it (and precious few *have*), and some advantage doubtless accrues to a novelist from moving within strictly literary circles (though what the advantage is, I would not care to guess). In his early twenties, Hope made a character in his first novel throw off an observation that may be relevant to the mingling of his two worlds: 'Wine is better without smoke, and smoke is better without wine, but the combination is better than either separately.'

There is at present no lack of exponents of a type of fiction Hope never attempted—the art of sensitive awareness. Stories now abound in which the reader is invited to share the hero's self-absorption as, scrutinizing with ungovernable fascination the black hairs on the back of his hand, he is filled with a sense of significance so overwhelming that only a quiet vomit in some convenient corner, or perhaps the contemplation of the death-throes of a crushed stoat, will serve to reduce the pressure. Such writing can be good or bad. Ruritanian romances can be good or bad. Ruritania has long figured as a crowned and gilded cage wherein lovers of romance have been pleased, for a spell, to dwell. Anthony Hope needed no painstaking modern psychologist to point out to him, and to us his entranced readers, just why we love to think ourselves into the thrilling predicaments of Rudolf the Fifth in 'his good city of Strelsau'. In 1919 there was perhaps some excuse for a disillusioned anti-masque to the comedy of Ruritania. Forty years later, we are no longer so enamoured of the unadorned versions of European democracy. Sir Anthony Hope Hawkins lived to see the decline of European royalty; he was fortunate to be spared the days when enlightened nations which had pushed aside the baubles of crowns and sceptres found themselves rushing to worship, instead, a group of unspeakable thugs in dirty raincoats. *The Prisoner of Zenda* may yet capture the imagination of a new generation of seekers after romance. Weary of space-suits and the unchivalrous menace of intercontinental missiles, they may taste afresh the innocent thrills of swordplay and the glitter of courtly derring-do.

Social comedy, too, can be good or bad—with the added quality of rarity, nowadays, in the publishers' lists. Anthony Hope produced some of the most intelligent social comedies of a period when, in England, a few classical virtues of proportion and high competence were briefly flowering. He had not a poet's equipment, but he did possess, among many more 'civic' qualities, one bright technical skill which flashed, in his hands, with all the delight of imagery: a mastery of the art of dialogue. His interest in behaviour is still shared not only by club diners but by anyone who gossips in a queue, speculates in a bus on the character of his neighbour, or finds pleasure in plucking from experience one or two general observations with an applicability to more than one set of troubled nerves. It would be pleasant to think that a rediscovery of the urbanity and witty fortitude of the author of *Quisanté* or *The Intrusions of Peggy* or *The Dolly Dialogues* might even yet release from ironic bondage the prisoner of *The Prisoner of Zenda*.

10

MORALS AND MORALITIES

Maria Edgeworth

'At six o'clock on Thursday morning your excellent mother expired in my arms. She now lies dead beside me. . . . Continue, my dear daughter, the desire which you feel of becoming amiable, prudent, and of USE.' Maria Edgeworth, the daughter to whom this information and this advice were conveyed, was then, in 1773, in her sixth year. The little girl was to be given ample opportunity to exercise these and other, more difficult, virtues. Her first stepmother appeared on the scene four months later, her second in 1780, her third in 1798; the fourth Mrs. Edgeworth was young enough to be at the bedside when Maria herself died in 1849, in her eighty-third year. While Maria was amiable enough to sustain the complicated loyalties of domesticity (her father's seventeenth child was born when she herself, his eldest daughter, was thirty-three), she was never prudent enough to free herself completely from that *triste utilité* (to use Madame de Staël's phrase) for which her father's literary productions are so justly, and her own so unhappily, famous.

The life of Maria Edgeworth in the 'English Men of Letters' series—a collection catholic enough to include Anglo-Irish women—is peppered with exclamations, or 'marks of admiration' as she herself would have called them, each one an eye-brow raised, in 1904, at the platitudes of Richard Lovell Edgeworth or the sad traces of his influence in the works of his spirited daughter. And it would be idle to pretend that the author of *Moral Tales*, *The Parent's Assistant* and *Belinda* was not in all her writings a handmaid to morality. But today morality is no longer a word to make critics shy and readers bolt—perhaps because critics and readers alike have had the advantage of seeing something of what happens when immorality in the guise of amorality has flourished unchecked even by hypocrisy.

Indeed, by facing the word bravely, magnifying the very initial letter into a capital, it may be possible to claim for Maria Edgeworth some share of that sympathetic understanding we now bring to the pre-Shakespearian Moralities—provided always that the personifications mingle freely with recognizable human beings so that we may speak of 'double vision', 'direct and patterned speech', or whatever phrase be popular at the moment; and provided also that certain phenomena outside the human sphere may be interpreted as symbolism. The first characteristic is present throughout Maria Edgeworth's novels, but fails to be effective because the two 'levels' are so frequently employed by the same speaker that direct and conventional speech come out in accidental alternation, without significance. Even Master Charles Percival, of *Belinda*, can prattle like a lively boy one minute and like Richard Lovell Edgeworth the next. As for symbolism, it is only 'significant' in the late novel *Helen*, and then only at minor points: in the hawking scene where Helen saves a dove by sacrificing a heron (which may be read as a symbol of her own relationship to Cecilia, though the applicability of the symbols is, to say the least, doubtful), and again on the evening when, falsely accused.' Helen breaks the strings of her harp, and the words 'Miss Stanley's harp is unstrung' are bandied about among the company of friends who maintain silence on the subject of her unstrung reputation.

The effect on Maria Edgeworth's early works of an overt morality appearing simply as a sequence of adages is plain enough, and damaging enough: she herself, in later years, could write of *Belinda* with something like distaste. If her first efforts, those children's tales with titles like *Forget and Forgive*, *Waste Not, Want Not*, and *Simple Susan*, have something of the vigour that is never quite absent from her writing, it is the vigour of a small steam-roller pursuing a perfectly straight course. So it is not surprising that all commentators agree that *Castle Rackrent* is her first real achievement and in some respects her most original. This novel appeared anonymously in 1800. Its success was immediate; Walter Scott was among its admirers.

The secret of its success? The novel was written without any interference by her father. This seems plausible enough, but it raises the question how she managed to elude his vigilance, and how, having done so, she could ever again allow him to poke his admonitory finger into her later books. There is something not quite convincing in these accounts. It had been one of Richard Lovell Edgeworth's principles to 'allow his children to participate in his own occupations', and from what is known of the man it seems unlikely that he was one to waive the rights of reciprocity.

The notion of a repressed Maria bounding upwards like a released balloon after her father's death in 1817 may commend itself to opponents of his educational theories. But it does not account for the long gap between his death and the appearance of her last and greatest novel. Three volumes of the *Tales of Fashionable Life* appeared in 1809, three more in 1812; her mammoth novel *Patronage* in 1814, and in 1817 both *Harrington* and *Ormond*. *Helen* did not appear until 1834; work on the book began in 1830, when the author was well into her sixties. Even more to the point is the question why, if joyous escape from Papa's moral influence was the secret of Maria's later happy years, *Helen* should be, of all her novels, the most mature in moral and social judgement, the strictest in standards, the most inflexible in integrity. The answer, surely, is that a steadily increasing literary competence permitted her finally to knead her own principles more closely into the substance of her story. 'In economy, as in morals, false principles are far more dangerous than any one single error.' Substitute 'fiction' for 'economy', and this sentence from *Helen* can stand to shield Miss Edgeworth from the worst effects of her several 'single errors'.

' "There is Helen in the limewalk." ' The opening words of *Helen* are fresh, lively. It is not only the most 'modern' but also the most readable of her novels—and for reasons not confined to the modernity. Maria Edgeworth's narrative sweep (by no means a modern quality) is as vigorous as ever; the momentum is necessary to carry the reader over some sluggish chapters. Told in a few words, the plot sounds more like Restoration comedy than nineteenth-century fiction. Helen Stanley, the very embodiment of straight dealing, is ensnared in a tangled web of deception when she shields her friend, Lady Cecilia

Clarendon, from the displeasure of her unbending husband, the General. Helen refrains from denying that she was herself the authoress of certain damaging letters actually written by Cecilia before marriage. For a time suspicion, attracted to Helen by her own self-sacrificial posture, endangers her own romance with Granville Beauclere. To complete the circle of influences playing upon the heroine, there is a villain, Lord Beltravers; a wise old woman, Lady Davenant, Cecilia's mother; a slanderous wit, Horace Churchill; and a selection of backbiters, candid friends and the like. The double utility of these characters, both as *dramatis personae* and spokesmen of certain Humours, Moralities or well-defined attitudes to life, is more apparent here than in any of the other novels.

Lady Davenant is a figure from the high comedy of manners; even the least dramatic of her aphorisms contain in themselves a certain power of propulsion, so that they never impede the action and sometimes push it forward a little:

'I was very romantic, not in the modern fashionable young-lady sense of the word, with the mixed ideas of a shepherdess's hat and the paraphernalia of a peeress—love in a cottage, and a fashionable house in town——'

or, again, 'What right has he to have enemies as if he were a great man?—a person of whom nobody ever heard, setting up to have enemies!' But it soon becomes apparent that Lady Davenant's social position not only gives her judgements authority and a respectable circulation; the kind of training she represents (duty, loyalty, sense of proportion) is itself the basis for aesthetic judgements no less than social decisions. Good taste and good breeding predispose her towards a simple symmetry of style in art and life alike, and her straightforward snobbery is transferred to non-social spheres with an effect as startlingly apt as that of some of the most admired great ladies in the pages of Henry James. Moral outrage and artistic judgements come together, in some of Lady Davenant's sentences, with all the force of a well-rooted confidence:

'But this cowardly, negative sin, *not* honouring his father and mother!—so commonplace, too, neutral tint—no effect.'

Maria Edgeworth's wholehearted approval of these sensible judgements of the gentry is made clear enough in the attitude of her heroine. Helen is no Belinda; she can assess very creditably the characters of the diplomatists and politicians who visit Lord Davenant and sit at the table of his son-in-law, General Clarendon. At the same time she is pleased to observe 'the manner in which [the conversation] went on and off without leading to any unpleasant consequences, notwithstanding the various shades of opinion between the parties'—a state of affairs for which credit is given not so much to 'good sense and talents' as to 'good breeding and temper'. And lest this complacency on the score of manners should cause the participants to shrink from major issues, there is Lady Davenant always at hand to point out that frivolity is of all things the most ill-bred, and that 'the common namby-pamby little missy phrase "ladies have nothing to do with politics" ' will never be countenanced in *her* house.

No; the more closely a reader examines *Helen* the more clearly he sees that the reason for its superiority over Maria Edgeworth's other novels is not that her besetting morality was driven out after her father's death, but that it was more firmly driven *in*. Self-conscious rectitude ruins the effect of her earlier heroes and heroines. Here it spreads out, a little beneath the surface, to give consistency to their reactions to a life simplified by 'group-assumptions' and complicated by the slow intricacies of 'plot'. This consistency once established, the characters are then at liberty to be inconsistent, to act at times 'out of human nature', as it is indeed the privilege of human nature to behave. And it is at this point, when we see the contradictions behind the Humours, when we see Moralities breathe and move a little to right or left of centre, that we say 'Ha! Maria Edgeworth has come to life at last.' Thus, when Cecilia's innocent deception of her husband succeeds, she 'can hardly believe it—it seems out of nature' to discover that her love for him decreases and that he is lowered in her estimation as he straightforwardly believes her lies.

Once it is perceived, then, that the statues are human beings standing very still, it is possible to praise the novelist's art in keeping them so steady and at the same time to share the pleased surprise when each one spots another stirring slightly. The following passage between General Clarendon and Helen is a case in point:

' "My mind, Miss Stanley, is made up, and once made up, is not to be changed."

' "I am certain of that," said Helen, "but I am not clear that your mind is made up."

'The General looked at her with astonishment.

' "You do not know me, Miss Stanley."

' "I think I do."

' "Better than I know myself!"

' "Yes, better, if you do yourself the injustice to think that you would not yield, if it were right to do so. At this very instant," pursued Helen, disregarding his increasing astonishment, "you would yield if you could reasonably, honourably—would you not?" '

The General's astonishment is shared by the reader, but if Helen's tribute to Truth normally takes the form of quiet suffering, yet the consistency of her identification with Truth should have warned us that at other times the same devotion will make her bold, even inconsistently bold. Alas! She is insufficiently so. Like the long-suffering hero of Howard Sturgis's *Belchamber*—perhaps the last of a long line of works of fiction in which Maria Edgeworth's take their place—Helen's virtues are of the exasperating self-sacrificing kind. The author's own irritation is voiced sometimes in direct comments ('she felt a sort of triumphant pleasure in the courage of sacrificing herself') and sometimes through Lady Davenant. Morality, tempered by good judgement, requires that morality itself be reasonable.

It is hardly necessary at this date to call attention to the qualities of Maria Edgeworth's Irish novels. Her 'Irishness' has indeed caused her to be esteemed too narrowly in terms of the regional novel. *Castle Rackrent* is a delightfully racy book; Sir Condy, Sir Kit and Sir Murtagh and, above all, Old Thady are all figures of real comic stature. Lord Colambre, hero of *The Absentee*, comes to vigorous life only when he is redressing the wrongs of his neglected Irish tenants; as for *Ormond*, it is still a heartening book for the presence of the eccentric King Corny, a petty chieftain lording it over his independent island and training young Ormond in all those older courtesies and obligations neglected by his more sophisticated relations. Moral indignation is present in the lightest of these stories, and far from destroying the reader's pleasure it can often keep him in warm sympathy with the author—a figure strangely self-effacing behind all her precepts and hortatory excursions. Sir Walter

Scott wept for *Simple Susan* and Macaulay was impressed with the missionary zeal of *The Absentee*. Modern readers will be singularly self-conscious if they cannot, from the Tuscan ranks, raise faintly the cheer they so readily bestow upon propaganda films much nearer the nursery in moral simplicity and much more likely to raise a yawn a century hence.

Miss Edgeworth had no cause to complain of the reception afforded to her books during her lifetime. Nor did she. Totting up her receipts, she produced a total of well over £11,000 (the list may be found in the biography by Emily Lawless); enough, as she admits, to provide presents for the family and still leave a little over for Continental jaunts. Pilgrims to Edgeworthstown found her, in her seventies and eighties, still 'busy as a bee'. Right-minded but never thin-lipped, she said what she had to say and was content to watch the manifestations of the reforming spirit; she died before that zeal sank into doubt. No gentleman of fashion who read *The Dun* could go on thinking it clever to defraud his tradesmen; no absentee landlord who read the life of Lord Colambre could think it clever to fritter away his patrimony.

Yet this wagging finger could also probe deep into personal problems quite divorced from social obligations. 'I have no belief in sudden reformations,' says Lady Davenant. 'This change in Cecilia's mind has been some time working out.' Witty and boring, didactic and human, Maria Edgeworth was one of our first novelists who saw that in England aesthetic and moral nerves twitch in sympathy, and that in fiction 'characters' are not more important than character.

III

Professor Emeritus

11

CHER MAÎTRE AND *MON BON*

Henry James, Man and Legend

I

There is an unpublished letter by Henry James—a plain refusal of a dinner invitation—in which occurs the characteristic phrase: 'for I shrink from the brutality of a telegram'. That is the note of the legendary James, the James who is made out, by his admirers no less than by his detractors, to be a wincing spinsterish humbug. The true James, present in that same unremarkable scrap of writing paper, lies in the humorous cruelty of his administered snub—for it is plain enough in the social sigh 'I am, to my great regret, so utterly taken up this evening', that he resented (as all properly constituted diners-out must resent) a last-minute invitation. Offences against good taste, whether in life or literature, Henry James deprecated by the deceptively mild application of a standard anything but mild. Over and over again in Mr. Nowell-Smith's compilation of biographical notes and records of 'The Master',* there are reminders that an immense regard for his own personality led Henry James to shrink from the brutality of the telegrammatic in all his dealings with other people, for whose personalities he had an equal regard. That famous 'later style', whether in speech or in writing, displays not only a controlled sensibility but also a quality still rarer in contemporary life—consideration.

Speaking of telegrams, there is that prodigious wire—anything but brutal—in which Henry James refused another invitation: 'Impossible impossible impossible if you knew what it costs me to say so you can count however at the regular rates

* *The Legend of the Master.* Compiled by Simon Nowell-Smith (1948).

ask Miss Robins to share your regret I mean mine.' Anyone who misses the self-parody here must be stone deaf to the Comic Muse. Indeed, pretending not to understand the minor practical things of life seems to have been one of James's recurring comic themes. 'How do you suppose they know?' he is said to have mused, when the cashier at a café estimated in advance how many cakes had been eaten by his party—'They always do!' Such stories, and they are legion, suggest that some of the more exasperating reticences in James's later novels are due quite simply to a gleefully elaborated teasing. The absurd screening of 'the little nameless object' on the manufacture of which was based the Newsome family fortune in *The Ambassadors*, and which is variously guessed by the curious in the same novel as 'Clothes-pins? Salertus? Shoe-polish?' is surely a case in point. There is nothing strange in this self-parodying humour, for Proust, that other master of the meticulous oblique, is full of it too. George Moore noted that in his normal conversation Henry James was anxious that 'every sentence, or if not all, then at least every third or fourth, should send forth a beam of humour', and to J. M. Barrie it was worth missing a train to watch 'his disarming smile . . . while he rummaged for the right word'.

After talking with Holman Hunt while searching for 'an obscure street in Chelsea', James related to Sir Edward Marsh that even on the 'not unattractive subject of Ruskin's marriage' the painter had proved 'not otherwise than DULL'. James himself, on whatever subject, was often perplexing but never dull, to credit the testimony of the dozens of witnesses called by Mr. Nowell-Smith. T. A. Guthrie (F. Anstey) reported that however long it took James to arrive at his point it was always worth waiting for, and Alfred Sutro stated that in spite of his mannerisms and hesitations 'Henry James never came even near to being a bore'. His physical presence seems to have been equally impressive—so impressive indeed that he is described in a bewildering variety of terms: as an Elizabethan (by Violet Hunt), as a sea-captain, as a French prelate (by Edmund Gosse), as an eminent cardinal in mufti or a benevolent Napoleon (by Theodora Bosanquet), as profoundly sad-looking (by Ella H. Dixon), and by Borys Conrad, aged four, in the pleasant tribute 'Oh, Mamma dear! isn't he an elegant fowl!' It is inevitable that such a man and such a writer should have given rise to legendary stories, repolished and retold by competing memoirists. The compiler of *The Legend of the Master* conducted a searching examination, from which Ford Madox Ford emerges with little credit and E. F. Benson with rapped knuckles; and others are convicted of faulty memory or exuberant credulity.

II

James the man can best be distinguished from James the legend by a study of his surviving letters and notebooks. Those who hesitate before the bulk of the two-volume edition* of his letters may be recommended to sample the short printed correspondence† between James and Robert Louis Stevenson, whose warm mutual regard became personal only after they had detected in each other a common concern for the craft of fiction.

To many readers—and especially to those who have swallowed too hastily the legend of James as a frigid prig—it will come as a surprise to note that it is the roving, playful 'romantic' R.L.S. who is the cooler in correspondence. He writes always to 'James' or 'Henry James'; to the master of reticence he is 'Louis'. There is a certain pawkiness about Stevenson's letters, even at their most amiable, that shows a trifle thin beside the generous considerate periods of his affectionate colleague. 'The mere thought of you,' writes James, 'is better company than almost any that is tangible to me here, and London is more peopled to me by your living in Samoa than by the residence of almost anybody else in Kensington or Chelsea.' Again, 'missing you is always a perpetual ache,' and a thread of almost irritated deprivation runs through the letters from De Vere Gardens to those damnably distant islands: 'I want to *see* you—where you live and *how*—and the complexion of your days. But I don't even know the name of your habitat nor the date of your letter. . . .' There is something strangely revealing in James's greed for facts, his power of self-implication, his long-memoried courtesy, as he follows the truant Louis 'with an aching wing, an inadequate geography and an ineradicable hope'. And

* Edited by Percy Lubbock, 1920.

† Janet Adam Smith (Editor): *Henry James and Robert Louis Stevenson.* A Record of Friendship and Criticism. 1948.

nothing could be gentler than his sorrowful letter of condolence to Stevenson's widow—surely one of the noblest examples of that most difficult epistolary task; encompassed about by such a cloud of sponsored witnesses, the most stricken heart would be upheld:

'For myself, how shall I tell you how much poorer and shabbier the whole world seems, and how one of the closest and strongest reasons for going on, for trying and doing, for planning and dreaming of the future, has dropped in an instant out of life. . . . He lighted up one whole side of the globe, and was in himself a whole province of one's imagination. . . . More than I can say, I hope . . . that you are feeling your way in feeling all sorts of encompassing arms—all sorts of outstretched hands of friendship. Don't, my dear Fanny Stevenson, be unconscious of mine. . . .'

When, in 1899, James had the melancholy task of reviewing Colvin's edition of Stevenson's *Letters to his Family and Friends*, he was able to quote passages more personal than any contained in the letters written to himself. It was to Gosse, not to James, that Stevenson wrote, two days before his death, these self-revealing lines: 'It is all very well to talk of renunciation, and of course it has to be done. But, for my part, give me a roaring toothache! I do like to be deceived and to dream, but I have very little use for either watching or meditating.' One can understand that Henry James was not the right confessor for such an admission, and the friendship between the two men stands defined, in those few words, as the attraction of opposites. By that same definition one can measure James's occasional disappointment in his friend's choice of epistolary subject-matter—a disappointment so acute at times that on receiving from legendary Vailima a piece of spirited gossip about a trip on board H.M.S. *Curaçoa* and some jocose sketches of native life interspersed with unrevised banter ('Did you ever blow the conch shell? I presume not. . . . I have no idea what I have said, . . . and I am a total ass'), he cannot keep his chagrin to himself, but informs Gosse that 'the devilish letter is wholly about the man-of-war, not a word else', and descends, in his annoyance, to misquotation. A few months later, James is writing again to Gosse, heartbroken by the news of 'this ghastly extinction of R.L.S.' This letter (included in Mr. Percy Lubbock's edition) concentrated in two paragraphs all his feeling for Stevenson—'the loss of charm, of suspense, of "fun" is unutterable.'

It is made clear in these letters that these two novelists—can there ever have been, by the way, a gibe wider of the mark than Hardy's 'Polonius and Osric' joke?—sought one from another a critical understanding as well as personal regard. When they 'talk shop' they cherish an integrity as rare as their friendship. 'All smart journalism and cleverness,' writes Stevenson of one famous contemporary; 'shameless *industriels*,' writes James of two others; and when James sent to Samoa a copy of *The Tragic Muse* he could refer to his friend, with a sad seriousness beneath the extravagance, as 'the sole and single Anglo-Saxon capable of perceiving . . . how well it is written'.

III

It is a fair guess that Henry James was a great talker-to-himself. We know him to have been a greater talker in the social way, and readers of the Letters and still more the Prefaces will recognize his habit of fumbling through parenthesis after parenthesis towards the *mot juste*, with that exasperated patience which few people can risk in conversation but most of us practise in private soliloquy. It is no surprise that the prevailing tone of the long-awaited *Notebooks** should be that of measured self-communion, running over at times into observation of people and places, but mainly a self-colloquy on the problems of the writing career. Henry James goads himself ('But courage, courage, and forward, forward'); he argues with himself; sometimes, in a moment when ideas flow free and he thrills to a conviction of mastery over his medium, he hugs himself: 'Oh, divine old joy of the "Scenario", throbbing up and up, with its little sacred irrepressible emotion, WHENEVER I give it again the ghost of a chance!'

All these notes on the tricks of his trade, these private (and lengthy) chastisements of long-windedness, these jig-saw puzzle scenarios and unravellings of self-tied knots, all these jottings are, in melancholy truth, Henry James's diaries. His work was

* F. O. Matthiessen and Kenneth B. Murdock (Editors): *The Notebooks of Henry James*. 1947.

his life. But there is the flaw; for he was a novelist, and life—not the art of fiction—was the subject of his work. And so we find him peering into the secrets of his work when he might have been examining the springs of the emotions. Instead of talking to himself about his raw material—the nature of man's life—we find him musing on the construction of *nouvelles*, on some new way of making a fictive pattern out of withdrawals from life and refusals to feel. 'Isn't perhaps something to be made of the idea,' to make use of one of their recurrent phrases, that the study of these *Notebooks* would provide a plot for one of his own sad, valorous, inhibited later stories about authors? The tale of a novelist who, failing to 'let himself go' in a private journal, discovers that instead of laying bare his human heart he has only laid bare the mechanism of the writer?

There is, at all events, something strangely moving in this record of sensitive genius finding it so difficult to feel; there is something pathetic and eloquent in the notes of this most articulate of men who never learnt to 'speak out'.

'I have only to let myself *go*! So I have said to myself all my life—so I said to myself in the far-off days of my fermenting and passionate youth. Yet I have never fully done it. The sense of it—of the need of it—rolls over me at times with commanding force: it seems the formula of my salvation of what remains to me of a future. . . . Go on, my boy, and strike hard; have a rich and long St. Martin's summer.'

Like a diver unwilling to take the plunge into the element he knows so well, he seems to stand on the brink of life, tracing with his toe in a puddle on the side of the swimming-bath a score of knowing patterns. 'Jump!' he cries, again and again—and draws a picture of someone brilliantly caught in the act of not jumping. Perhaps the last irony is reached (the last turn of *his* screw) when James directs his unrivalled power of observation to the study of himself standing in his own light. This comes out, concisely if negatively, in his delighted appreciation of Taine's saying 'that Turgenev so perfectly cuts the umbilical cord that bound the story to himself'. His self-knowledge shows him not only his many virtues as a writer but also, with equal clarity, his own chief fault: 'a strange nervous fear of letting myself go. If I vanquish that fear, the world is mine.'

But if he rarely let himself go, no writer exemplified more

fully than Henry James the contrasting if secondary quality of holding oneself in check. If in later life he would not or could not plunge again into the main stream (for he had already done so with almost abandoned freedom in *The Bostonians* and *The Princess Casamassima*), he would at least make himself the master of the backwaters. So that although as private papers the *Notebooks* are disappointing (we learn, for example, that when he talked to himself James called himself '*mon bon*', but of the self that talked we learn little that is new), as notes on his trade they are fascinating. From the first entry (1888) about the early novel *Confidence* to the last entry in the *Notebooks* proper (a paragraph dated May 10, 1911, with the characteristic opening query: 'Can I catch hold—if it be in the least worth the effort—of a very small fantasy that came to me the other month in New York?'), they contain discussions of 'all his finished novels and all but a handful of his stories', a record of 'upwards of eighty victories in completed stories and novels, and of thirty or forty more skirmishes with themes that he abandoned for one reason or another'. As we now watch him contemplating, year after year, his work in hand, elaborating his dramatic symmetry, playing with his counters, patting and petting his themes, teasing out the last essence of some tiny *donnée*, it is difficult to resist a feeling of embarrassment, a suspicion that the whole thing, for all its maddening garrulous reticence, is too self-conscious.

The editors seem to take at his own valuation (as readers of the Prefaces have done before them) James's constant preoccupation with 'methods by which his stories might be reflected through a central consciousness'. But is there not something unhealthy about it all, something (to repeat Ford Madox Ford's unforgettable adjective) a little 'high'? It is not even as if, in the event, he could ever for long make up his own mind. The precise nature of his self-communicated ambition changes again and again. To select a random sample, we find him sighing for '*short* things' and 'something *great*' (these from the same paragraph), for 'scenic, constructive, "architectural" effects' and 'rapid, concrete action' (these, too, from the same paragraph). 'A truce to all subjects that are not superior!' he can cry, or hesitate with some trifle in the words: 'One might write a tale (very short) about. . . .'

In a writer of such swarming fecundity there is nothing necessarily inconsistent about these kaleidoscopic enthusiasms, and it is idle to complain that the three or four recurring themes are already familiar enough from the Letters and the Prefaces—the eternal struggle against overshooting the mark in the matter of length, the itch for neat symmetrical plots, the obsession with the notion of too little and too late ('*That* was what might have happened, and what *has* happened is that it didn't'). We ought to know that Henry James is the last person to whom to apply if we want the result of a lifetime's consistency in the art of fiction concentrated in two or three epigrammatic words.

IV

It is hardly surprising that only a decade or two should separate the Henry James discarded as pettifogging and unreadable from the Henry James accepted as first favourite by novelists and careful readers. To a generation growing weary of statistics and 'mass opinion' his concentration on the individual personality is so refreshing that the very tedium of much of his writing appears as a fault in the right direction. Yet it has been suggested that during the present 'boom' James is being read for the wrong reasons, that he is being deified by writers who batten on curious technique in the effort to conceal their own poverty of subject-matter, and cultivated by readers who, even before his boasted century has run its course, are tiring of the Common Man.

'Obviously,' writes Mr. Dupee in his introduction to a collection of critical essays,* 'Henry James is not an author whom it is easy to take or leave.' The twenty-six studies of the Master here collected range from 1879—an American critic beating the 'expatriate' drum with a peevish but not ineffective stick: 'To be really cosmopolitan a man must be at home even in his own country'—to a selection from the centenary tributes of 1943. 'No literary standpoint that allows for the dismissal of [*The Wings of the Dove*] as a "pretty performance" can possibly be valid,' writes Mr. Philip Rahv in 1943 (the quoted judgement is that of Mr. Van Wyck Brooks less than twenty years earlier).

* F. W. Dupee (Editor): *The Question of Henry James.* A Collection of Critical Essays. 1947.

A more temperate American critic has suggested that James's attempt to make the *tone* of speech and behaviour 'carry vastly more significance than is proper to it' comes nearer to defining a point over which the contending parties can argue without loss of manners. Another statement debatable in cool blood is Mr. Stephen Spender's view that the later heroes and heroines are called upon to suffer generously for 'being more intelligent than the other characters'. The trouble now will be, of course, that the publication of the *Notebooks* will invalidate many of the critics' theories, at least so far as James's self-confessed conscious intentions are concerned. Mr. Rahv, for example, has a pleased peroration to the effect that a combination of the 'romance and reality and civilization' of Europe and the 'spirit' residing in America is the 'secret of his irony and of his humour'. Splendid; but do writers even as self-conscious as James feel any such neat dichotomy? The vexation of the *Notebooks* for humane critics will be precisely that they contain no new revelation of the man who played so assiduously with his themes, who struggled with such half-hearted indulgence against verbosity, or jotted down, 'in the remnant of a beguiled morning, 3 or 4 things that I have noted before and may identify with a small label.'

W. D. Howells, in 1903, asks himself the question, in discussing the novelist's treatment of his characters, 'Why isn't he a sculptor?'—and answers himself thus: 'Because he is a painter'. A year later Frank Moore Colby amuses himself with jocose comments on James's reticent obscurity: 'The man's style was his sufficient fig-leaf,' he sniggers, and suggests that he was 'bent more on eluding pursuit than on making converts'. Could adverse criticism find more damaging ridicule than in Colby's version of a James plot: 'A wraith proves faithless to her marriage vow, elopes with a bogie in a cloud of words'? For the defence, Mr. Percy Lubbock, editing the Letters in 1920, beautifully elaborates the implications of the Master's submission to 'the wear and tear of discrimination', and rephrases in acceptable terms the mistrusted magniloquence: 'a kind of personal splendour'. Where the *Notebooks* chime with later opinion, they offer, as might be expected, a less confident valuation. James, in 1881, described himself as accepting experience 'as an artist and as a bachelor; as one who has the passion of observation and whose business is the study of human life', whereas Stuart Sherman's valuable essay on *The Aesthetic Idealism of Henry James* (1917) shifts the emphasis and draws a moral: 'a fastidious connoisseur of experience, an artistic celibate to whose finer sense promiscuous mixing in the gross welter of the world was wearisome and unprofitable'. That adds little. The most profitable theme for elucidation, after all, is that of communication between author and reader, as when the same critic makes the point that 'Anglo-Saxons are quite unaccustomed to having their deeps of terror and pity, their moral centres, touched through the aesthetic nerves'. I should prefer, myself, to suggest that although the Anglo-Saxon aesthetic nerve is normally well guarded, it does, when touched at all, lead straight to 'the moral centres'.

Communication! No novelist so yearned after the full articulation of the private heart. What is 'tone', for Henry James, if not the same will-o'-the-wisp that could lure another major novelist into the obscure accuracies of *Finnegans Wake*? Those who adopt the *'cher maître'* attitude to James, watchful with esoteric glee for the pathetic mannered slang or the obfuscating parentheses, are applauding the frail means and ignoring the end. *Cher maître* he certainly became, but only as a result of failure to break through the limitations of *'mon bon'*. Psychologists will pry in vain for the spiritual secret (the physical is anyone's guess) of his magnificent impotence. The notion that James himself was unaware of his own psychology has only to be stated (and it *has* been stated) to be dismissed as an absurdity. Other writers have demonstrated, imperfectly, our active impulses; he has made himself the scholar and the poet of passive states of consciousness. And the nature of this unsquandered capital, this gloriously buried talent? Let Fulke Greville speak for him:

> *My exile was not like the barren tree,*
> *Which beares his fruitlesse head up to the skye,*
> *But like the trees whose boughs o'erladen be,*
> *And with self-riches bowed downe to die.*

His 'irrepressible cries from the heart'* do indeed 'spill over'

* A phrase used by Miss Sylva Norman in a letter to *The Times Literary Supplement.*

at times into the *Notebooks.* It is when they spill over into his fiction that Henry James approaches the narrow first rank of the great novelists of the world. Something happened, I know not what, to screen from much of his fiction that undoubted warmth of heart that irradiated the early novels and is to be found again, somewhat cooled by opacity of style, in the autobiographical volumes *A Small Boy and Others* and *Notes of a Son and Brother.* Reticence is a human virtue, but rarely a prime quality among major novelists.

Other dedicated spirits have side-stepped down roads of respectable escape. James trod the lonely way—whether towards the heroism of artistic solitude in his own *Great Good Place* or to self-immolation on *The Altar of the Dead* remains still a matter for each reader to decide. But the surviving letters and notebooks of James the man show that James the author was never for an instant in doubt as to his own genius or his own aim. A superb consciousness nourished his creative powers and has set his best work, well beyond the tide-marks of fashion, among the monuments to literary integrity.

12

BENVOLIO

'Everyone was a little someone else'
THE GREAT GOOD PLACE

I

When, 'at the height of his age', Henry James laboured over the astonishing Prefaces to those of his works considered worthy of inclusion in the great New York Edition, the first novel so honoured was *Roderick Hudson*. It had been written in Florence in 1874 and published serially the following year. This first 'acknowledged' novel is a book of such mingled promise and achievement that it would stand among the really significant works of fiction even if James had never written another. It is here that the genius of Henry James first blazed out through the talent, here that his pedantic scholarship of the human heart produced poetry as well as rhetoric. Here we meet in Mary Garland the first of his long line of timorous efficient young women; in the persons of Roderick the young sculptor and Rowland Mallet, the friend with a 'constitutional tendency to magnanimous interpretations', we are introduced to a theme to which he will constantly return—the relationship between careless artist and careful consumer of art, the problem of the intellectual Mary and Martha.

The close relationship of two contrasting characters is a theme of which Henry James never tired; from his earliest to his latest work there is ever to be found a pair (or even a quartet or sextet) of figures who seem, in their fascinated complementary unlikeness, to be different expressions of the same larger character, or separate shoots of an identical parent plant. The least adulterated statement of this recurring theme was contained in a short story, *Benvolio*, which appeared in 1875,* the year of *Roderick Hudson*. A mellower version of that same diptych, representing once again the hinged and self-confronting aspects of action and contemplation, was printed a quarter of a century later in the story *The Great Good Place*, and the parts of the same unresolved problem, like exasperated Siamese twins or the warring words of an oxymoron, are clearly visible through all the elaboration of the later style.

Benvolio is a simple parable, and makes no claim to be anything else. It is fantasy at its most lucid. The young man Benvolio is the clearest possible statement of the young author's view of himself. He is as unreal, and as revealing, as a figure in a ballet. I am conscious, James seems to be saying, of two natures within me; let me see if I can construct a little marionette and make him jog to and fro to illustrate my discovery:

'It was as if the souls of two very different men had been placed together to make the voyage of life in the same boat, and had agreed for convenience' sake to take the helm in alternation. . . .

'Sometimes he looked very young—rosy, radiant, blooming, younger than his years. Then suddenly, as the light struck his head in a particular manner, you would see that his golden locks contained a surprising number of silver threads; and with your attention quickened by this discovery, you would proceed to detect something grave and discreet in his smile—something vague and ghostly, like the dim adumbration of the darker half of the lunar disc.'

This young gentleman's double nature expresses itself in the simplest possible manner in his mode of lodging. The artless metaphor of Benvolio's two rooms provides a decorous early instance of James's intense love of 'settings', his unusual power of putting on paper the 'feel' of a room or a landscape:

'At home he lived in two chambers. One was an immense room, hung with pictures, lined with books, draped with rugs and tapestries, decorated with a multitude of ingenious devices (for of all these things he was very fond); the other, his sleeping room, was almost as bare as a monastic cell. It had a meagre little strip of carpet on the floor, and a dozen well-thumbed volumes of classic poets and sages on the mantelshelf. On the

* Reprinted in *The Madonna of the Future, and Other Tales*, 1879.

wall hung three or four coarsely-engraved portraits of the most exemplary of these worthies; these were the only ornaments. But the room had the charm of a great window, in a deep embrasure, looking out upon a tangled, silent, moss-grown garden, and in the embrasure stood the little ink-blotted table at which Benvolio did most of his poetic scribbling. The windows of his sumptuous sitting-room commanded a wide public square, where people were always passing and lounging, where military music used to play on vernal nights, and half the life of the great town went forward. . . .

'His friends, coming to see him, often found the great room empty, and advancing, rapped at the door of the chamber. But he frequently kept quiet, not desiring in the least to see them, knowing exactly what they were going to say, and not thinking it worth hearing. Then, hearing them stride away, and the outer door close behind them, he would come forth and take a turn in his slippers, over his Persian carpets, and glance out of the window and see his defeated visitant stand scratching his chin in the sunny square. After this he would laugh lightly to himself—as is said to be the habit of the scribbling tribe in moments of production.'

In that last paragraph there is more than a hint that poor Benvolio was whistling to keep his courage up, for when young men adopt a 'remote' and 'aloof' pose, it is a hundred to one that something or other, whether force of circumstance or some inner check, is impeding their free social circulation. Later, in *The Princess Casamassima*, Henry James would turn to good effect the anguish of an excluded adolescent. (Nor were his excluded persons always adolescent: the observer who sees most of the game is perhaps the best-known 'type' in James's fiction.) That he saw himself in this light during the early years of his life (and perhaps even to the very end?) is more than an inference drawn from characters in his novels—always a dangerous game when played with prolific creators, as anyone will agree who has read books proving beyond a shadow of a doubt that Shakespeare was an atheist, a Roman Catholic, a woman-hater, an idolater of the fair sex, a snob, a Communist, or what you will. In those chapters of autobiography *A Small Boy and Others* (1913) and *Notes of a Son and Brother* (1914), in which he recreates—with septuagenarian meticulousness and a style elaborate to a degree sometimes well beyond the borders of mystification—his feelings as a child and a youth, Henry James admits that by contrast with his more active brothers he could at best try to be a trained observer of the sort of life *they* could live in real earnest. He was banned from active service in the American Civil War (which broke out when he was eighteen) by reason of an injury sustained when, helping to put out a small farmyard fire, he bashed himself with the pump-handle. This incident, which I have translated to the best of my ability after a reasonable acquaintance with the style of 'the later James', is narrated* with an obliquity so remarkable even in this master of the oblique that one suspects a deep inner reluctance of revelation:

'Jammed into the acute angle between two high fences, where the rhythmic play of my arms, in tune with that of several other pairs, but at a dire disadvantage of position, induced a rural, a rusty, a quasi-extemporized old engine to work and a saving stream to flow, I had done myself, in the face of a shabby conflagration, a horrid even if an obscure hurt. . . .'

It would be foolish to relate the prolixity of Henry James Senior to a similar youthful accident, yet it is certain that when his son made reference† to the father's mishap he wrote with an obscurity almost equal to that which shrouded his own: 'an accident received in early youth and which had so lamed him for life that he could circulate to any convenience but on even surfaces.'

Whatever part this accident may or may not have played in his decision, it is clear that young Henry James quite deliberately resigned himself, in the main, to the role of spectator. Like Benvolio, he seems to have accepted this role with a good grace touched with an irony which would be a sufficient preservative against self-indulgence:

'Ennui was at the end of everything that did not multiply our relations with life. To multiply his relations, therefore, Benvolio reflected, should be the wise man's aim. Poor Benvolio had to reflect on this, because, as I say, he was a poet and not a man of action. A fine fellow of the latter stamp would have solved the problem without knowing it, and bequeathed to his fellow-men not rigid formulas but vivid examples. But Benvolio had often

* *Notes of a Son and Brother*, Ch. IX. † *Notes of a Son and Brother*, Ch. VI.

said to himself that he was born to imagine great things—not to do them; and he had said this by no means sadly, for on the whole he was very well content with his position. Imagine them he determined he would, and on a magnificent scale. He would multiply his labours, at least, and they should be very serious ones.'

The rest of his story is of no significance: that Benvolio should waver between the attractions of a worldly Countess and a retiring Scholastica is but another personification of the dichotomy already symbolized in the arrangement of his rooms. What *is* noteworthy is the persistence, in Benvolio's make-up, of the love of direct impressions and the sensuous appreciation even of his somewhat artificial austerities:

'He flung himself on the grass, on the edge of the wood—not in the same place where he had lain at the Countess's feet, pulling sonnets out of his pocket and reading them one by one; a little stream flowed beside him; opposite, the sun was declining; the distant city lay before him, lifting its towers and chimneys against the reddening western sky. The twilight fell and deepened and the stars came out. Benvolio lay there thinking that he preferred them to the Countess's wax candles. He went back to town in a farmer's wagon, talking with the honest rustic who drove it.'

Viewed as a symbolic self-portrait, Benvolio figures Henry James in his early thirties as 'a tissue of contradictions' and 'a mixture of inconsistencies', but he is endowed, like his creator, with a saving grace. 'He did possess the magic ring, in a certain fashion; he possessed, in other words, the poetic imagination.' For James, the poetic imagination was to be very largely a matter of seeing things from both sides—from the early tales to the final Prefaces his writing is full of images invoking the obverse and reverse, the back and the front, the passive and the active, the efficient and the visionary, the romance and the disillusion. Even Benvolio has his youthful senilities—it seemed to him at times that 'the gustatory faculty of his mind was losing its keenness'. That is no way for a young man to talk, we may tell ourselves. Benvolio heartily agreed: 'There is a way of never being bored, and the wise man's duty is to find it out.' And yet that is the way young men at times *do* think, becoming conscious like Benvolio 'of an intellectual condition similar to that of a palate which has lost its relish'. That complete honesty of the double vision will explain much of James's work that is otherwise obscure; it elucidates his own brilliant elucidations of the young mind at odds with itself (Isabel Archer in *The Portrait of a Lady*, Hyacinth Robinson in *The Princess Casamassima*, and a score of others), it helps to explain the tortuosities of the full Jamesian style, where he makes the reader dizzy by his conscientious efforts to be fair all round, to take every possible aspect into consideration.

Before turning to the radiant exposition in *Roderick Hudson* of the 'cousin' theme ('cousin' simply because the contrasting characteristics seem to be not so much 'brothers' as the sons of brothers, to spring not from a common living progenitor but rather from a more distant and probably dead grandsire), I would glance at another treatment of the ennui which beset Benvolio in his prescient imagination, and which is but the 'other side' of an intense love of life. Like the tale printed twenty-five years earlier, *The Great Good Place* (1900)* is a parable. Again we are shown the double nature in the single breast. It is a lovely and moving rhapsody on the text 'the world is too much with us', an appeal against the tyranny of affairs, the presence of unavoidable items of secondary importance as they afflict the social life of civilized man, the desire of the harried soul to seek peace from social demands in some retreat or haven. The 'legend' is as simple as that sketched in *Benvolio*. George Dane, a successful author, one day just cannot cope any longer with the complexities of his social and literary life. He falls asleep after greeting an unknown young man. He dreams that he is in 'The Great Good Place', a lay monastery where quiet men in a spacious hostel in the country live remote from everyday life and win back their peace of mind—as Benvolio won back his by walking into his inner room. Waking from his sleep much later in the day, Dane finds the young aspirant at his desk, who greets him with the comforting phrase 'Everything's done'. He has gained the perfect secretary—and perhaps something else besides?

The quintessence of the 'cousin' theme is distilled in George Dane's discovery that 'everyone was a little someone else', but the poor harassed fellow has first to experience the conviction

* Reprinted the same year in *The Soft Side*.

that 'the real exquisite was to be without the complication of an identity'. The following description of Dane's plight reveals, in addition to a significant enrichment of imagery, a full understanding that it is only the world-sated who grow world-weary in quite this way—that it is, in fact, only the man of great sensitivity who can be brutal enough to long for a form of partial suicide:

'To let them alone, these things, the new things, let them utterly alone and see if that, by chance, wouldn't somehow prove the best way to deal with them: this fancy brushed his face for a moment as a possible solution, giving it, as so often before, a cool wave of air. Then he knew again as well as ever that leaving was difficult, leaving impossible—that the only remedy, the true soft effacing sponge, would be to *be* left, to be forgotten. There was no footing on which a man who had liked life—liked it at any rate as *he* had—could now escape it. He must reap as he had sown. It was a thing of meshes; he had simply gone to sleep under the net and had simply waked up there. The net was too fine; the cords crossed each other at spots near too together, making at each a little tight hard knot that tired fingers were this morning too limp and too tender to touch.'

Not until he had reached this extreme was Dane willing to accept the truth of the other side of his nature, to admit that it was 'the inner life, for people of his generation, victims of the modern madness, mere maniacal extension and motion, that was returning health'.

II

Some forty-five years ago, a critic of repute* found *Roderick Hudson* to be 'crammed with local colour like a schoolmistress's bedroom full of photographs of Rome'. The leisurely inventories of descriptive writing as practised in the Florence of 1874 by a young American of thirty-one do not always please modern tastes, though an acquaintance with the bread-and-butter narrative of some contemporary realists who cut their *tranches de vie* a little on the thick side should have taught us that this sort of thing is dreadfully easy to do badly and by no means easy to do well. The raptures of James's young American sculptor on being introduced to the culture of nineteenth-century Europe may

* Rebecca West: *Henry James* (1916).

tend to pall—though the creator of Roderick Hudson had for the feel and texture of that alien culture a romantic sensibility which at times produced writing of a flawless serene beauty. But the significance of this novel is not in the outward setting but in the inwardness of his apprehension of that selfish core, that adamantine foolhardiness at the heart of abnormal sensitivity, which can first fortify and then destroy both the possessor and the fascinated benefactor of a certain type of artistic genius.*

The role of hero is divided between Roderick Hudson, the headstrong sculptor of inspired rightness of touch, and his older friend Rowland Mallet who transplants him from a New England township, barren to his genius, to the richer artistic climate of Italy. Away in the far background there is Mary Garland who loves Roderick in silence and is silently loved by the self-abnegating Rowland. Miss Garland fails to interest us deeply. The reader feels a disinterested compulsion to respect her reticence, sharing the view that 'it was not a disadvantage to talk to a girl who made one keep guard on one's composure; it diminished one's usual liability to utter something less than revised wisdom'. But if Mary is 'boiled suet' (Miss West's phrase) it matters surprisingly little, for one feels that she figures merely as the remotest corner of a conventional triangle for the benefit of readers of the eighteen-seventies who must have a snack of that noble inarticulate sexual love which, as bogus now as it ever was among the 'unenlightened' Victorians, still lends the glow of false psychology and false ethics to the tears we shed as we watch Miss Bette Davis go through another 'it-hurts-me-more-than-it-hurts-you' performance. The tension in *Roderick Hudson* is not triangular, not even when Christina Light, a new and livelier young lady of shady European antecedents, captivates a Roderick open to the appeal of beauty from whatever source. The tension is bilateral; it is between Roderick and Rowland as they exemplify, like cousins german, contrasted expressions of a similar response to life and art.

It is at once clear that Rowland's avuncular affection renders him liable to unlimited hurt at the hands of his *protégé*. James

* For a note on the *structural* significance of the Roderick–Rowland relationship, as contrasted with the Milly Theale–Kate Croy relationship in *The Wings of the Dove*, see p. 220, below.

allows him the one protective fibre of his type—an ironic familiar awareness of his own nature:

'It often seemed to Mallet that he lacked the prime requisite of a graceful flâneur—the simple sensuous confident relish of pleasure. His was neither an irresponsibly contemplative nature nor a sturdily practical one, and he was for ever looking in vain for the use of the things that please and the charm of the things that sustain. . . . Oftener, perhaps, he wished he were a vigorous young man of genius without a penny. . . .'

No one could be less a flâneur than the man who could forget his own quite considerable grounds for grievance in the contemplation of the possible price Roderick would have to pay for the flowering of a genius which Rowland himself would die to possess:

'He often felt heavy-hearted; he was sombre without knowing why; there were no visible clouds in his heaven, but there were cloud-shadows on his mood. Shadows projected they often were, without his knowing it, by an undue apprehension that things after all might not go so ideally well with Roderick.

'He wondered gloomily at any rate whether for men of his companion's large easy power there was not a larger moral law than for narrow mediocrities like himself, who, yielding Nature a meagre interest on her investment (such as it was), had no reason to expect from her this affectionate laxity as to their accounts. Was it not part of the eternal fitness of things that Roderick, while rhapsodizing about Christina Light, should have it at his command to look at you with the eyes of the most guileless and unclouded blue, and to shake off your musty imputations by a toss of his picturesque brown locks?'

A superficial inference drawn from the great mass of his published fiction might lead us to suppose that the Roderick in James was stifled and petted out of existence by the Rowland. But to recall the unflagging creative power behind his writing life of half a century is to admit that there is a sense in which it takes a Roderick to *create* a Rowland. The impression of *Roderick Hudson* lingers strangely as one reads the other novels. As he develops more characters like Mallet, thoughtful, cultured, debonair, the author still keeps burning that flame of 'genius' he saw in Roderick. This may account for his occasional savage remarks about his later 'super-subtle fry'—Isabel Archer, in

The Portrait of a Lady, 'was often reminded that there were other gardens in the world than those of her remarkable soul'. To reduce the matter to a sentence: Gilbert Osmond, that 'sterile dilettante', could never have written *The Portrait of a Lady*, in which he figures with so chill an air of superior sensibility. The warmth of that extra quality separating Gilbert Osmond from the Osmond-like creator of Gilbert Osmond is the source of every minute accuracy of observation.

Already in *Roderick Hudson* is present that double quality enjoyed by all novelists of the first rank: the warm insight to penetrate deeply but without laceration into the secret heart (expressed by Chehov and one or two minor writers who have the faculty almost as a poetic gift), and yet the possession of that added and generally opposed talent for conscious expatiation on the human theme. It is that combination of primary genius (usually connected with love or loving-kindness as a poetic but particular reality) with secondary talent, which, after all, places Shakespeare and Proust in the serene first rank. In *The Princess Casamassima* (1885–86), that novel in which the promise of *Roderick Hudson* is so brilliantly fulfilled, James comes to excel in this combination of fresh insight plus mature appreciation, to a point unsurpassed by Proust himself. For with Proust the insight is so often into states and emotions which are not themselves fresh—are, indeed, curtained and musty. How different is the tender picture of Hyacinth Robinson, battered and perplexed by London and by life—a tender picture unsmeared by the clear varnish of articulated comment informing and preserving it. By this time the 'cousins' in the double nature of the author have come to figure as the illustration of a philosophy of art, if not of life itself, embracing as it does all the unashamed passion and poetry of direct feeling and also the willingness to *make* something of it.

Had the words been fashionable at the time, a reviewer might well have claimed to detect in Roderick and Rowland the expression of the author's 'unconscious' and 'conscious' attitude to life and art, might even have seen in Rowland the outcome of the home teachings of Henry James Senior, brimful of conscience and magnanimity, and in Roderick the spark of the born creator, owing nothing to conscious heredity. The full significance of the 'cousin' theme, if I have succeeded at all in defining so slippery a notion, comes out in Rowland's appreciation of that 'genius' in Roderick which he himself understood but did not possess, and which the lucky owner used with little conception of its source or even of its results. One of Roderick's fellow-artists gives a good working image for that enviable quality—' "Complete", that's what he is; while we little clevernesses are like half-ripened plums, only good eating on the side that has had a glimpse of the sun'—but it is left to poor talented Rowland to seize the implication:

'Suddenly he felt an irresistible pity for his companion; it seemed to him that his beautiful faculty of production was a double-edged instrument, susceptible of being dealt in back-handed blows at its possessor. Genius was priceless, inspired, divine; but it was also at its hours capricious, sinister, cruel; and men of genius accordingly were alternatively very enviable and very helpless.'

When, some thirty years later, Henry James wrote his Preface to this novel, he complained that 'the grounds of my young man's disaster [were] unquestionably meagre', and conceives of the reader as asking: 'On the basis of so great a weakness . . . where was your idea of the interest? On the basis of so great an interest, where is the provision for so much weakness?' To a sympathetic reader, this self-criticism is curiously beside the point. What Henry James had done had been simply to present an acutely moving picture of Rowland's 'constitutional tendency to magnanimous interpretations' expending itself in love and pity upon a subject—Roderick and the terrible loneliness of genius, whether genuine or illusory—wholly adequate to call forth love and pity. There is no question of taking sides between them; both are admirably 'sympathetic' in the sense that they are both understandable, and although straight 'sympathy' can hardly be claimed for Roderick, the relationship built up between the two is not one of simple give and take. For Rowland, indeed, it does seem all give and no take, and yet, when he looks on the dead body of Roderick* and realizes, like Othello, that his 'occupation's gone', he has grown in scope and stature as a direct outcome of his great outpouring of sensibility. Roderick would not, could not, respond in kind; his return

* 'After the collapse of his art and his love, Roderick falls over a precipice in a too minutely described Switzerland.' (Rebecca West, *op. cit.*).

was unconscious and consisted only, without intention, of providing a release for the love and pity. Rowland is the giver, but also, and much more than Roderick, he is the receiver too. Roderick could not 'receive'—he has the fundamental chill of the single-minded artist; even his impression of Christina Light is an aesthetic and selfish rapture.

All this atmosphere of sensibility is so subtly achieved, with nothing pointed out and nothing falsified by placards, that it is plain that the author, at the age of thirty-one at any rate, had not become so like his own Rowland that he had lost *direct* knowledge of his own Roderick. In later novels and stories, especially those dealing with the social difficulties of artists, we are compelled more and more to view the Roderick-like characters through the eyes of the Rowland-like characters; it is as though Henry James had decided to inhabit the body of one of his constituent 'cousins' and had kept in touch with the other only through a correspondence heavily weighted by the style of his conscious and critical half. But in *Roderick Hudson* direct emotion is deeply worked into the design. Certainly not before *Roderick Hudson*, and only rarely afterwards, does James flick psychological truth on the raw with such deceptive economy as in this single reaction of Roderick's to his friend's comment on his relationship with the young sculptor:

' "An egoist to whom you have made perpetual sacrifices?" He repeated the words in a singular tone; a tone that denoted neither exactly indignation nor incredulity, but (strange as it may seem) a sudden violent curiosity for news about himself.'

III

In the earlier novels and tales, the 'cousin' theme appears again and again, in several cases underlined by the antipathies and attractions of genuine consanguinity. *Watch and Ward*, a product of James's late twenties and the first of his full-length novels (printed serially in 1871 and in book form in 1878), is furnished with two pairs of genuine cousins whose interrelations make up the plot. It is a charming and underrated story, written with careful prentice skill and yet possessing a mature wit in human assessments. Nora, the heroine, has first of all a cousin, George Fenton, who represents—almost like a thumbnail sketch of the strapping Basil Ransome of *The Bostonians*—a masculine version of what she might wish herself to be if she were not a polite as well as a gifted young lady:

'It must be said that Fenton was not altogether unworthy of her favours. He meant no especial harm to his fellow-men save in so far as he meant uncompromising benefit to himself. The Knight of La Mancha, on the torrid flats of Spain, never urged his gaunt steed with a grimmer pressure of the knees than that with which Fenton held himself erect on the hungry hobby of success. Shrewd as he was, he had perhaps, as well, a ray of Don Quixote's divine obliquity of vision. It is at least true that success as yet had been painfully elusive, and a part of the peril to Nora's girlish heart lay in this melancholy grace of undeserved failure. The young man's imagination was eager; he had a generous need of keeping too many irons in the fire.'

The second pair of cousins, Roger and Hubert Lawrence, are both suitors for the lady's hand, and do in very truth make up between them the complete man to whom she would cheerfully surrender. Unhappily, the division of qualities between the two men vexes her judgement, and vexes them too—each wishing, at times, to be more like the other. Here is Roger:

'In trifling matters, such as the choice of a shoemaker or a dentist, his word carried weight; but no one dreamed of asking his opinions on politics or literature. . . .

'He of course had no imagination, which, as we know, should always stand at the right hand of charity; but he had good store of that wholesome discretion whose place is at the left. . . .

'He would now, he declared, cast his lot with pure reason. He had tried love and faith, but they would none of him. He had made a woman a goddess, and she had made him a fool. He would henceforth care neither for woman nor man, but simply for comfort, and, if need be, for pleasure. Beneath this gathered gust of cynicism the future lay as hard and narrow as the silent street before him. He was absurdly unconscious that good humour was lurking round the very next corner.'

Cousin Hubert, whose more vigorous attractions are agreeably disguised by his Christian name and his profession as clergyman, expresses sentiments well below the surface in Roger who, poor fellow, had to be informed by his inamorata 'with a kind of desperate abruptness, that her mother had been a public singer'. Hubert's self-assurance worries one of Nora's lady-friends—who has her own antithetical light to shed on the heroine: 'Between these two, though there was little natural sympathy, there was a wondrous exchange of caresses and civilities. They had quietly judged each other and each sat serenely encamped in her estimate as in a strategical position.' This good lady objects to Hubert on the following grounds:

'What is he, when you come to the point? . . . He is neither fish nor flesh, neither a priest nor a layman. I like a clergyman to bring with him a little odour of sanctity, something that rests you, after all your bother. Nothing is so pleasant, near the fire, at the sober end of one's drawing-room. If he doesn't fill a certain place, he is in the way. The Reverend Hubert is in any place and every place. His manners are neither of this world nor, I hope, of the next. Last night he let me bring him a cup of tea and sat lounging in his chair while I put it in his hand. O, he knows what he's about. He is pretentious, with all his nonchalance. He finds the prayer-book rather meagre fare for week-days; so he consoles himself with his pretty parishioners. To be a parishioner, you needn't go to his church.'

The reverend gentleman himself reveals, a few pages later, that he has enough of Roger in his make-up to feel divided in himself:

'I only half live; I am like a purse filled at one end with small coin and empty at the other. Perhaps the other will never know the golden rattle! . . . I had the wit to see, but I lacked the courage to do—and yet I have been called reckless, irreverent, audacious. . . . There are men born to imagine things, others born to do them. Evidently I am not one of the doers. But I imagine things, I assure you!'

Washington Square (printed serially in 1880 and in book form the following year), 'the perfect termination of Mr. James's first period of genius,'* has a similar triangular set-up, with cousins Arthur and Morris Townsend planted in similar relation to Catherine Sloper, a heroine plain and reserved almost to the point of neurosis. In its limpidity of style, recreating the atmosphere of old New York even to the smell of the Square's ailanthus trees, there is even in the unelaborated catalogues or

* Rebecca West, *op. cit.*

point-by-point descriptions, that uncompromising passion for accuracy which would later expand the sentences of Henry James as it expanded those of Proust. The chief characters, the timid young woman, an addle-pated fussy matron, a stern father, are all familiar enough. What is of greater interest is the moral problem posed here as a direct outcome of a more imaginative treatment of the established 'cousin' theme. Dr. Sloper's disapproval of Morris, the Townsend cousin favoured by his daughter, drives that young gentleman about his business when he discovers that the lady, whose dowry forms her sole attraction, would be disinherited by her father. The simple antithesis of character, adequately sketched in *Watch and Ward* nine years earlier against a similar American background, is here complicated by the intrusion of a more potent third party in the shape of Dr. Sloper. As a result, the reader is left not only with a handful of characters drawn with wit and irony, but also with a moral riddle larger than the book itself. Is it right to deny another person an experience which one knows very well to be harmful? Dr. Sloper is right in supposing that the amiable good-for-nothing would make a detestable husband:

'The sign of the type in question is the determination—sometimes terrible in its quiet intensity—to accept nothing of life but its pleasures, and to secure these pleasures chiefly by the aid of your complaisant sex. Young men of this class never do anything for themselves that they can get other people to do for them, and it is the infatuation, the devotion, the superstition of others that keeps them going. These others in ninety-nine cases out of a hundred are women.'

Yet is Catherine any happier for being protected? She could perhaps have 'helped' the prodigal; perhaps, too, his ill-treatment of her, much as it might have saddened the good Doctor, would have given her life a deeper purpose or even a tragic significance? Is it an infringement of individual rights to prevent a baby putting its hand in the fire? And which harms the baby more, a burn or the denial of experience?

In an indirect way the problem is resolved. We see Catherine's character, developed almost overnight in the course of her sudden achievement of womanhood as she faces the implications of her own choice between the types of character represented by the cousins, adjusting itself in the end quite naturally to spinsterhood—as it might, but for a hair's-breadth difference, have adapted itself to the lot of an ill-served wife. If ordinary lives are to be assessed not by what *happens* but by *how* they meet each accidental event and how they tread one or other of several possible paths, then it doesn't much matter what particular thing happens. This is no very fruitful doctrine for a teller of tales, and it is nowhere made explicit in *Washington Square*. Yet the full implication of James's antithetical approach to the creation of situation by the placing of his 'cousins' must be, in the end, that supremacy of personality over incident which, for all his endless manipulation of 'situations' and organization of 'ados', is typical of his best work.

From all the many versions of Henry James's international obsession we may pick for further illustration the quartet of cousins who confront one another with their American and European views of life in *The Europeans* (1878). This charming book has an American setting, as *The American* had a European. One could hardly invent a more romantic cousin for the sober New England Wentworths than Eugenia, Baroness Munster, morganatic wife of Prince Adolf of Silberstadt-Schrenckenstein. This elegant lady, *née* Young, suddenly appears with her brother Felix to ruffle in no uncertain fashion the quiet Wentworth dovecotes. Mr. Wentworth Senior is equipped to brace himself against the Continental airs of these native-born members of his own family; nephew Felix promptly marks him down as 'a tremendously high-toned old fellow; he looks as if he were undergoing martyrdom, not by fire, but by freezing.' Daughters Charlotte and Gertrude, on the other hand, are open in their several ways to the affront from Bohemia: cousin Felix at once puts his finger on their New England similarities:

'They are sober; they are even severe. They are of a pensive cast; they take things hard. I think there is something the matter with them; they have some melancholy memory or some depressing expectation. It's not the Epicurean temperament.'

Against their common background they have put forth some blossoms of individuality; but Charlotte and Gertrude are clearly blossoms on the same branch even if one should be a little less bud-like than the other. (It is because of this fraternal or sisterly closeness, even in contrarieties, that the 'cousin' relationship is a nearer approximation to that peculiar brand of close contradiction and distant affinity with which Henry James makes such reiterated and varied play.) When Mr. Wentworth warns his daughters that 'we are to be exposed to peculiar influences', the girls respond in contrasting tones, but they are both well within the charmed circle of home influences:

'Gertrude was silent for a moment, in deference to her father's speech; then she spoke in a manner that was not in the least an answer to it. "I want to see how they will live. I am sure they will have different hours. She will do all kinds of little things differently. When we go over it will be like going to Europe. She will have a boudoir. She will invite us to dinner—very late. She will breakfast in her room."

'Charlotte gazed at her sister again. Gertrude's imagination seemed to her to be fairly running riot. She had always known that Gertrude had a great deal of imagination—she had been very proud of it. But at the same time she felt that it was a dangerous and irresponsible faculty; and now, to her sense, for the moment, it seemed to threaten to make her sister a strange person, who should come in suddenly, as from a journey, talking of the peculiar and possibly unpleasant things she had observed. Charlotte's imagination took no journeys whatever; she kept it, as it were, in her pocket, with the other furniture of this receptacle—a thimble, a little box of peppermint, and a morsel of court-plaster.'

Gertrude, in short, is beginning to experience, across the strong pull of sisterly likeness, the counter-attractions of the distant, different, and yet fascinating magnetism of her strange cousins: like so many of James's characters, she is being deliciously and dangerously nipped by sudden twinges in her 'other self'. The canny Felix observes, after a short time, that one sister at least feels the attraction of the 'other life', and noting her struggles as she feels herself drawn, counts it as yet another illustration of the general principle that 'nothing exceeds the licence occasionally taken by the imagination of very rigid people'. Eugenia is less successful. All her charms break in vain upon the bleak highmindedness of the New England neighbour who had become her fascinated adorer; it is indeed in terms of unfriendly coastal imagery that she herself admits her failure:

'She found her chief happiness in the sense of exerting a

certain power and making a certain impression; and now she felt the annoyance of a rather wearied swimmer who, on nearing shore, to land, finds a smooth hard wall of rock when he counted upon a clean firm beach. Her power, in the American air, seemed to have lost its prehensile attributes; the smooth wall of rock was insurmountable.'

There has never been, however, the slightest suggestion that Robert Acton, who is no cousin by blood, is in any sense a cousin in spirit. In the different reactions of Gertrude and Acton, indeed, there is the clearest possible illustration of the thesis that although they share a common culture and are at first sight equally proof against the alien invasion, they are in a more important sense unlike in that one has the imagination to feel the claims of 'cousinship', and the other has not.

There are also the two young gentlemen of *Confidence* (1880), Gordon Wright the man of action and his friend Bernard Longueville of whom, when people asked the question 'why he didn't do something', it was generally accepted that 'he did more than many people in causing it to be asked'—and who, 'in spite of a great momentary appearance of frankness and a lively relish of any conjunction of agreeable circumstances,' enjoyed the disadvantages as well as the advantages of his double nature and 'had really little taste for giving himself up, and never did so without very soon wishing to take himself back'. It would be valuable, too, to set side by side Isabel Archer and Ralph Touchett, the cousins by blood in *The Portrait of a Lady* (1880–1881): Ralph being yet another incarnation of the type of sensitive invalid whose 'serenity was but the array of wild flowers niched in his ruin', and whose double nature is explicitly revealed to his cousin:

' "I keep a band of music in my ante-room," he once said to her. "It has orders to play without stopping; it renders me two excellent services. It keeps the sounds of the world from reaching the private apartments, and it makes the world think that dancing's going on within".'

(A much more mature version, one might think, of Benvolio's innocent self-deception.) Cousin Isabel, like Gertrude of *The Europeans*, 'was not accustomed to keep [her imagination] behind bolts,' but her fault—from which a larger dash of Ralph in her character would have saved her—was that 'she was always planning out her development, desiring her perfection, observing her progress. Her nature had, in her conceit, a certain gardenlike quality, a suggestion of perfume and murmuring boughs, of shady bowers and lengthening vistas, which made her feel that introspection was, after all, an exercise in the open air, and that a visit to the recesses of one's spirit was harmless when one returned from it with a lapful of roses' —and there follows that ironic comment about her 'remarkable soul' which has already been quoted.

So one could proceed, via the blood-cousins Julia Dallow and Nick Dormer of *The Tragic Muse* (1889–90), or the terrible struggles between the blood-cousins Olive Chancellor and Basil Ransome of *The Bostonians* (1885–86) as they outbid each other for the body and soul of Verena Tarrant, a sensitive girl who feels the attraction of both sides of that double life so savagely torn apart and shared between them—and text by text it would be possible to follow the developing theme right up to Milly Theale and Kate Croy of *The Wings of the Dove* (1902) and to the still later products of the full autumnal period. One early *nouvelle*, *Eugene Pickering* (1874), may be selected, finally, from among a host of tales embodying the author's obsession with the sensibilities of American tourists in Europe, and in which for the most part the contrast of cultures (in the strict anthropological sense of the word) overshadows our interest in people as people, rather than as Americans or Europeans. Eugene deserves mention as another version of the self-tormented 'split personality' sketched in Benvolio and perfected in Hyacinth Robinson, a version somewhere between the simple diagram and the later patient unravelling of complicated souls; a version invested with a rhetorical sympathy recalling again Henry James's own significant over-protestations concerning his choice of the spectator's role:

'I was like a poodle-dog that is led about by a blue ribbon, and scoured and combed and fed on slops. It was not life; life is learning to know one's self, and in that sense I have lived more in the past six weeks than in all the years that preceded them. I am filled with this feverish sense of liberation; it keeps rising to my head like the fumes of strong wine. I find I am an active, sentient, intelligent creature, with desires, with passions, with possible convictions—even with what I never dreamed of, a possible will of my own! I find there is a world to know, a life to lead, men and women to form a thousand relations with. It all lies there like a great surging sea, where we must plunge and dive and feel the breeze and breast the waves. I stand shivering here on the bank, staring, longing, wondering, charmed by the smell of the brine and yet afraid of the water. The world beckons and smiles and calls, but a nameless influence from the past, that I can neither wholly obey nor wholly resist, seems to hold me back. I am full of impulses, but, somehow, I am not full of strength. Life seems inspiring at certain moments, but it seems terrible and unsafe; and I ask myself why I should wantonly measure myself with merciless forces, when I have learned so well how to stand aside and let them pass. Why shouldn't I turn my back upon it all and go home to—what awaits me?—to that sightless, soundless, country life, and long days spent among old books? But if a man *is* weak, he doesn't want to assent beforehand to his weakness. . . .'

IV

From these few representative examples one or two notions emerge about Henry James's equipment as a novelist in the days before his famous style grew so luxuriant that it covered the ground of everything he wrote with a tropical carpet of undergrowth so thick that it is often difficult to know exactly what is underneath. The ground of the earlier work is covered by a rich but less obscuring verdure; the spring landscape reveals its contours, and Miss West's compliment* to *The Europeans* is thoroughly in keeping with the pastoral air: 'that is the pure note of the early James, like a pipe played carefully by a boy.' The 'boy' was 35 when he played that particular tune, but the image will stand without hurt if we recognize in *The Europeans* an example of a novel so close-packed, so sinewy, that its lean simplicity is the simplicity of a problem selected, posed, worked out, and resolved.

In the autobiographies Henry James recalled how from the very first he classed himself among 'those whose faculty for application is all and only in their imagination and their

* *Op. cit.*

sensibility'. Being, rather than doing, was his aim; speaking of himself as a child, he writes:*

'For there was the very pattern and measure of all that he was to demand: just to *be* somewhere—almost anywhere would do—and somehow receive an impression or an accession, feel a relation or a vibration. He was to go without many things, ever so many—as all persons do in whom contemplation takes so much the place of action; but everywhere, in the years that came soon after, and that in fact continued long, in the streets of great towns, in New York still for some time, and then for a while in London, in Paris, in Geneva, wherever it might be, he was to enjoy more than anything the so far from showy practice of wondering and dawdling and gaping. . . .'

How he dawdled and gaped at foreign cities is well enough known, but it is important to remember (as we certainly must when we share the adolescent bewilderment of his little Hyacinth Robinson, dawdling and gaping at life as he treads the pavements of London) the intense *human* curiosity of the dawdler and gaper. Curious first of all about himself—and at the age of 70 he can still be curious about that early curiosity:†

'I had rather a positive lack of the passion [jealousy], and thereby, I suppose, a lack of spirit; since if jealousy bears, as I think, on what one sees one's companions able to do—as against one's own falling short—envy, as I know it at least, was simply of what they *were*, or in other words of a certain sort of richer consciousness supposed, doubtless often too freely supposed, in them. They were so *other*—that is what I felt. . . .

'I never dreamed of competing—a business having in it at the best, for my temper, if not for my total failure of temper, a displeasing ferocity. If competing was bad snatching was therefore still worse, and jealousy was a sort of spiritual snatching. . . . A helpless little love of horizons I certainly cherished, and could sometimes care even for my own.'

'They were so *other*—that is what I felt'—but—'I never dreamed of competing.' Here, from long back, is the germ of George Dane's exhausted admission that 'everyone was a little someone else'. Here, rather than in his precocious zeal for Europe or his precocious mastery of language, was his first great gift as a novelist. And what is it, explicit in the quota-

* *A Small Boy and Others*, Ch. I. † *A Small Boy and Others*, Ch. XIII.

tions selected above and implicit in every novel or tale from which they are taken, what is it that enables his cherished created beings to step outside the inherited or conditioned bounds of their personalities and greet, across chasms however deep, the personalities of their spiritual 'cousins'? Simply the gift of Imagination in the full Coleridgean sense of the word—a point sufficiently proved by James's control of Fancy when Fancy is required. It was a gift universalized as he employed it, while thinking and writing about people rather than attempting to compete with them, to endow the creatures of that same imagination with little reflected imaginations of their own.

Of course, there is a 'catch in it', if you want to look for one. The rhetoric and self-dramatization of Benvolio may offer examples of wish-fulfilment, compensation, self-hallucination, or what you will. Hubert Lawrence, Gertrude Wentworth, Bernard Longueville, Eugene Pickering and all the rest—they may all, to an unfriendly eye, be extensions of the author's own desire to shout 'I'm the king of the castle because I can imagine myself to be you, and you're a dirty rascal because although you can *do* things you can't imagine them, so that I am two people and you are only one person.' The graver wisdom of *The Great Good Place* may foretell a spiteful nemesis for the doers—even if their doings are nothing more violent than indulgence in the more practical side of literary success.

I prefer to conclude, however, from the full evidence of his work, that Henry James's prime endowment was a compassionate imagination; that he brings renewed life to the old discarded image of hendiadys, whereby one and one make three when the simple word 'and', joining two contrasting nouns, turns the first into an adjective and transmutes the whole from antithesis to compound. I prefer to claim that he devoted much of his life and art to the belief that although, like the solitary islands of Matthew Arnold's poem, 'we mortal millions live alone,' there is nevertheless vivid to our imaginations, if we care to use them, the knowledge that we are still, however submerged may be our links, 'parts of a single continent.'

13

THE PRIVATE LIFE AND THE PUBLIC LIFE

The Princess Casamassima and *The Bostonians*

I

The two serene masterpieces of James's early maturity, *The Princess Casamassima* and *The Bostonians*, were published in book form in 1886 after serial publication the previous year. It is astonishing to contemplate the issue in one year of two major novels (they run to some 700 and 550 pages respectively in the Macmillan pocket edition), the prime quality of which—a quality strangely unsought and unrecognized by so many readers of Henry James—is 'the abundant, full-blooded life of well-nourished organisms'.* Yet a glance at the James bibliography reveals no trace of fallow period or exhausted soil in the years immediately preceding and following this bumper harvest.

There was no flagging, but there was a pained incredulous disappointment at their failure to make any impression on critics or general readers. 'I am still staggering a good deal,' he wrote† to W. D. Howells on January 2nd, 1888, 'under the mysterious and (to me) inexplicable injury wrought—apparently—upon my situation by my last two novels, the *Bostonians* and the *Princess*, from which I expected so much and derived so little. They have reduced the desire, and the demand, for my productions to zero. . . .' Twenty years later the disappointment was still fresh and still inexplicable; writing‡ to

* F. R. Leavis: *The Great Tradition*, 1948.
† *The Letters of Henry James*, edited by Percy Lubbock. Vol. I, p. 135.
‡ *Letters*, Vol. II, p. 100.

Howells on August 17th, 1908, he mentions his desire to revise and re-issue *The Bostonians* in the New York Edition, referring to the book as 'tolerably full and good', and admits that it had never, 'even to my much-disciplined patience, received any sort of justice.' A study of Henry James's progressively resigned dejection at never being rewarded by public enjoyment of his works would make an essay by itself—there would be plenty of texts in his letters and Prefaces, and a number of wry comments in the novels. But the cool reception afforded to his twin offerings in 1886 did not daunt him. In the first of the letters to Howells quoted above, he continues:

'However, I don't despair, for I think I am now really in better form that I have ever been in my life and I propose yet to do many things. Very likely too, some day, all my buried prose will kick off its various tombstones at once. Therefore don't betray me till I myself have given up. That won't be for a long time yet.'

He held manfully to his own view of these two novels. Of *The Bostonians* he wrote* to his brother William in February 1885: 'the story is, I think, the best fiction I have written.' As for *The Princess Casamassima*, it is included in the first of two 'short lists' of his novels, provided† as late as 1913 for the benefit of a young aspirant: its companions in the list 'not to be missed' being *Roderick Hudson*, *The Portrait of a Lady*, *The Wings of a Dove*, and *The Golden Bowl*.

II

The Princess Casamassima has, as a skeletal plot, a tale of metropolitan revolutionaries and the struggle to right the wrongs of the down-trodden, but, as Dr. Leavis observes, the novel brings 'little comfort to those who would like to justify James by his interest in the class-war'. Noting the 'earthy and sappy vitality' of the book, the same critic suggests that it derives, significantly, from a literary source—Dickens. There is ample evidence of James's habit of seeing the 'real' world through the derived world of art, and he has himself told us in *A Small Boy and Others* (the first of three autobiographical

* *Letters*, Vol. I, p. 117. † *Letters*, Vol. II, p. 333.

volumes), that as a child he would creep to a corner of the room, hidden behind a screen or table-cloth, to drink in enjoyment as a cousin read aloud to his mother the first instalments of *David Copperfield*. It is true, too, that on his first childhood view of London he found it 'extraordinarily the picture and the scene of Dickens, now so changed and superseded', and later recalls* his horrified fascination when, from the safe interior of an early Victorian four-wheeler, he watched 'swarming crowds . . . of figures reminding me of George Cruikshank's Artful Dodger and his Bill Sykes and his Nancy', figures looming suddenly in 'gas-lit patches . . . culminating, somewhere far to the west, in the vivid picture, framed by the cab-window, of a woman reeling backward as a man felled her to the ground with a blow in the face'. The childhood Dickensian view we may well accept, but James's mature view of London was entirely his own. This is made conveniently explicit in one of his generous letters to the young H. G. Wells. Praising that author's *Kipps* in 1905, he writes:†

'You have for the very first time treated the English "lower middle" class, etc., without the picturesque, the grotesque, the fantastic and romantic interference of which Dickens, e.g., is so misleadingly, of which even George Eliot is so deviatingly, full.'

'The very first time' is a phrase generous indeed: *The Princess Casamassima* pre-dated *Kipps* by some twenty years.

'The simplest account of the origin of *The Princess Casamassima* is, I think, that this fiction proceeded quite directly, during the first year of a long residence in London, from the habit and interest of walking the streets . . . the prime idea was unmistakably the ripe round fruit of perambulation.'

So it was, according to the later Preface, that little Hyacinth Robinson 'sprang up for me out of the London pavement'—not from Dickens, and still less from any narrow notion of society dominated by moral indignation.

It is, indeed, precisely on the ground that James's young hero was *not* Dickensian that some critics seem to be annoyed. Mr. Van Wyck Brooks quotes with vexation the young lad's habit of 'letting his imagination wander among the haunts of the aristocracy', a habit which he attributes solely to James's superstitious reverence for the 'noble blood' flowing in the poor young book-

* *A Small Boy and Others*, Ch. XXII. † *Letters*, Vol. II, p. 40.

binder's illegitimate veins. 'In real life,' cries the outraged Mr. Brooks* from the realistic side of the Atlantic (he cannot forgive James for leaving it), 'the last thing that would have occurred to a young man in Hyacinth's position would have been to "roam and wander and yearn" about the gates of that lost paradise: he would have gone to Australia, or vanished into the slums, or continued with the utmost indifference at his trade of binding books.' That may be indeed what he *should* have done, according to the set social tenets of Boston. Henry James knew better. He knew that the imagination of a child is not bounded by a nice sense of social status or republican zeal. He had only to recall his own childhood dreams, in far-off New York, over 'the full entrancing folios of Nash's lithographed *Mansions of England in the Olden Times*'†—another habit frowned upon by the incorruptible Mr. Brooks. Mr. Stephen Spender‡ goes one better in high-minded indignation and suggests that Hyacinth Robinson, 'might today have become a socialist Prime Minister: a Ramsay MacDonald, who, at the height of his power, would dismay his followers by going over to the other side and becoming the most frequent of visitors at large country houses and of dinners at Buckingham Palace.'

How wilfully irrelevant are these black-and-white political judgements in the face of Hyacinth's bewilderment between private dreams and public sympathies! It is the bewilderment, to quote the Preface again, that supplies the very germ and human quality of the novel; to read it as a political tract is to miss the whole meaning. As James admits, with that rueful cynicism which colours so many of the Prefaces:

'the wary reader for the most part warns the novelist against making his characters too *interpretative* of the muddle of fate, or in other words too divinely, too priggishly clever. "Give us plenty of bewilderment," this monitor seems to say, "so long as there is plenty of slashing out in the bewilderment too. But don't, we beseech you, give us too much intelligence; for intelligence—well, *endangers*; endangers not perhaps the slasher himself, but the very slashing, the subject-matter of any self-respecting story. It opens up too many considerations,

* *The Pilgrimage of Henry James* (1928), p. 82.

† *A Small Boy and Others*, Ch. II.

‡ In the Henry James number of *Hound and Horn*, April-June, 1934.

possibilities, issues; it *may* lead the slasher into dreary realms where slashing somehow fails and falls to the ground." '

When Hyacinth 'wanted to drive in every carriage, to mount on every horse, to feel on his arm the hand of every pretty woman in the place,' and felt bitter when 'these familiar phenomena became symbolic, insolent, defiant, took upon themselves to make him smart with the sense that *he* was out of it', it may be objected by unfriendly critics that the young man is suffering from delusions of grandeur. To which the answer is, of course, that some young men *do* suffer from delusions of grandeur (I have seen no pious outcry against *The Bulpington of Blup*, in which H. G. Wells gave us a full-scale study of the disease), and that it is the novelist's job to describe people as they are. Moreover, the reader's indignation against social injustice is more easily aroused by young Robinson's hurtful dreams than by his more overt ('Dickensian', if you like) references:

'. . . but a breath of popular passion had passed over him, and he seemed to see, immensely magnified, the monstrosity of the great ulcers and sores of London—the sick, eternal misery crying, in the darkness, in vain, confronted with granaries and treasure-houses and palaces of delight where shameless satiety kept guard.'

The Princess Casamassima is admittedly 'political' in plot and background, and when Miss Rebecca West complained* that James 'produced a picture-gallery when he had intended a grave study of social differences', she made a good point but with—I feel—the wrong emphasis. Let a man be never so deeply involved in political theory (and Hyacinth Robinson was not *deeply* involved), he will nevertheless see most clearly—if he has any eyes at all—the people among whom he lives and works; for political theory is something added to the normal human equipment and not something substituted in its place. It is indeed an additional merit in the novel that James has defined for his chief character, mainly by a superb series of portraits of various types of revolutionary zealot, a highly complex attitude towards politics. But this 'political' success, however indicative of a mature deftness of touch, is subordinate to the overall portrait of the whole humanity of his hero. No one can complain that Henry James, in the early novels at least, was not

**Henry James* (1916), p. 78.

helpful in supplying guides for the reader; even if we had missed the pervasive tone and the point of stress, there are signposts in plenty. Here is one:

'For this unfortunate but remarkably organized youth, every displeasure or gratification of the visual scene coloured his whole mind, and though he lived in Pentonville and worked in Soho, though he was poor and obscure and cramped and full of unattainable desires, it may be said of him that what was most important in life for him was simply his impressions.'

The opening chapters put us at once in possession, with rich and beautiful economy, of the 'private' and 'public' impressions of the boy. He is being brought up by Miss Pynsent, his dear 'Pinnie', a little dressmaker of modest means who lives with simple decorum in a decayed neighbourhood. She is as ' "lower middle" class, etc.' as you could wish, but James is hardly so insensitive as to set that particular placard over her devoted head. Instead, by a hundred kindly touches her portrait is built up, each touch adding something to the mixture of love and squeamish sense of the sordid which grew up side by side in the mind of her young *protégé*. Three illustrative snippets must suffice:

'Miss Pynsent could not embrace the state of mind of people who didn't apologize, though she vaguely envied and admired it, she herself spending much of her time in making excuses for obnoxious acts she had not committed.'

'Miss Pynsent esteemed people in proportion to their success in constituting a family circle—in cases, that is, where the materials were under their hand. This success, among the various members of the house of Henning, had been of the scantiest, and the domestic broils in the establishment adjacent to her own, whose vicissitudes she was able to follow, as she sat at her window at work, by simply inclining an ear to the thin partition behind her—these scenes, amid which the crash of crockery and the imprecations of the wounded were frequently audible, had long been the scandal of a humble but harmonious neighbourhood.'

'Though it was already November there was no fire in the neatly-kept grate beneath the chimney-piece, on which a design, partly architectural, partly botanical, executed in the hair of Miss Pynsent's parents, was flanked by a pair of vases, under glass, containing muslin flowers.'

This last passage reminds me forcibly of Mr. T. S. Eliot's *A Cooking Egg*, and I wonder how it is that the indulgent sarcastic inflation has been so rightly appreciated in the one American-born English author, and so signally missed in the other. Listen to the echo of Miss Pynsent in the more austere notes of Mr. Eliot on Pipit:

> *Pipit sate upright in her chair*
> *Some distance from where I was sitting;*
> Views of the Oxford Colleges
> *Lay on the table, with the knitting.*
>
> *Daguerreotypes and silhouettes,*
> *Her grandfather and great-great-aunts,*
> *Supported on the mantelpiece*
> *An* Invitation to the Dance.
>
> . . . . . .
>
> *But where is the penny world I bought*
> *To eat with Pipit behind the screen?*
> *The red-eyed scavengers are creeping*
> *From Kentish Town and Golders Green;*
> *Where are the eagles and the trumpets?*

'Where are the eagles and the trumpets?' is precisely what Hyacinth asked of his own Pipit, and asked in vain. He, too, turned to the 'weeping, weeping multitudes' drooping in the Victorian equivalents of 'a hundred A.B.C.s', found among them first his fellow outcasts, came to share their political attitudes, and finally died in the attempt to overthrow, in the interests of the weeping multitudes, the eagles and trumpets he so pathetically craved for himself.

The little boy's first view of social injustice (other than the undeserved straitness of poor Pinnie's circumstances) is described in a harrowing melodramatic scene; he is conducted to the prison where his mother lies dying. He is unaware that the gaunt foreign slattern is his mother, a French girl who had served a life-sentence for the murder of her lover (Hyacinth's unknown father), a mysterious 'Lord Frederick'. The scene is grim, ghoulish; dramatic ironies are piled as thick as one could wish, as when a fearful Mrs. Bowerbank, embodying Victorian morality, asks:

'Is there nothing the little gentleman would like to say, now, to the unfortunate? Hasn't he any pleasant remark to make to her about his coming so far to see her when she's so sunk? It isn't often that children are shown over the place (as the little man has been) and there's many that'd think themselves lucky if they could see what he has seen.

' "Mon pauvre joujou, mon pauvre chéri," the prisoner went on in her tender tragic whisper. . . .'

The scene may indeed be Dickensian in treatment, but I think we can trace its germ not to any bookish memory, but to that grim little scene in *A Small Boy and Others* (Chapter XIII) describing the impressions crowding in on the young Henry James when he himself was taken on a childhood visit to Sing-Sing.

The development of Hyacinth's political attitude (it is one of Henry James's better jokes, by the way, that the lad had no objection to his name, considering it to be quite masculine so long as it was not pronounced in the *French* fashion!) is illustrated almost entirely by means of the 'portrait gallery' to which Miss West took exception. To indicate something of the functional significance of these portraits it will be necessary to offer a fair number of quotations. It may be useful, first, to enumerate these characters as functional 'types' surrounding and vitalizing the figure of Hyacinth, before noting in how much more lively a form than 'types' they are in fact created. Millicent Henning, a warm-hearted vulgar girl, Miss Pynsent's nearest neighbour, who feels her excluded social status not at all, but glows with the life of her own rampageous London, and runs after the nobs, beaming with health and strength, for all she is worth—and for all *they* are worth; Anastasius Vetch, a gentle old fiddler equally content to espouse an old-fashioned Radical philosophy or to take tea with Miss Pynsent, and ever prompt to aid the young man whose genius he recognizes more clearly than do any of the more 'intellectual' characters; Eustache Poupin who reflects in an equally sedentary fashion the fire of the Paris Commune and who longs somewhat passively for the brotherhood of man; Paul Muniment, Hyacinth's contemporary, a young London Socialist of clear sight and hard head and a vivid incorruptibility which is in the event far more corruptible than Hyacinth's own second-hand resolves; his sister, Rose

Muniment, a bed-ridden cripple nauseatingly *au fait* with the affairs of the titled folk whom she affects to patronize; Lady Aurora Langrish, a self-conscious and wondrously sympathetic Lady Bountiful figuring as the distressed conscience of her gilded class; Captain Sholto, a hanger-on of that class who makes a much more effective alliance with the common folk via Millicent Henning; Diedrich Hoffendahl, the genuine article behind real revolution and unliterary assassination; and most seductive of all, the Princess Casamassima herself, who shares to a generous extent the hero's sensibility and who dramatizes both him and herself in her own bored efforts to 'climb down' as he, poor distracted fellow, is at once trying to climb up and, as it were, to blow up. A portrait gallery? Yes—and *what* a portrait gallery! Even if Miss West were right in supposing that they do not in sum help forward the 'grave study of social differences', she is certainly right in praising them as portraits.

If we look at them a little more closely we shall discover not only their liveliness but also their constructional effect, as each in turn illustrates one facet of the hero's 'bewilderment'. First, of more importance perhaps than any member of the above list, is the endearing figure of Pinnie, from whom, rather than from a shadowy melodramatic Lord Frederick, we may trace something of the quality of Hyacinth's Pentonville delicacy (a point, incidentally, which would have been perceived by Mr. Van Wyck Brooks if he had known his English social types half as well as Henry James knew *his*):

'His attention, however, was mainly given to Pinnie: he watched her jealously, to see whether, on this important occasion, she would not put forth a certain stiff, quaint, polished politeness, of which she possessed the secret and which made her resemble a pair of old-fashioned sugar-tongs.'

As the plot unfolds itself, Hyacinth is called upon to invest emotional capital in very many contrasting human beings, but there is in his life no more genuine understanding than that existing between the prim dressmaker and her little waif. One slight passing comment pierces to the heart of this relationship in that felicitous manner which seems indeed for so many readers to function not as a revelation but as an over-successful camouflage:

'One of the things she loved him for, however, was that he

gave you touching surprises in this line, had sudden inconsistencies of temper that were all for your advantage. He was by no means always mild when he ought to have been, but he was sometimes so when there was no obligation. At such moments Pinnie wanted to kiss him. . . .'

Hyacinth's upbringing unfits him for a genuine companionship with Millicent Henning, who played with him as a child and would gladly prolong their games beyond adolescence:

'There were things in his heart and a hidden passion in his life which he should be glad enough to lay open to some woman. . . . The answer was not in this loud, fresh laughing creature, whose sympathy couldn't have the fineness he was looking for, since her curiosity was vulgar. Haycinth objected to the vulgar as much as Miss Pynsent herself; in this respect she had long since discovered that he was after her own heart.'

But he was grateful for Millicent's warmth of heart, and esteemed that quality even while acknowledging its physical basis. This is done with a wry twist significant of the early James: a single sentence which would have been expanded to a chapter in the later novels, in which the wryness might remain as a confusion in the reader's mind and the direction of the twist be concealed except from the most assiduous scrutineer:

'She was bold, and free, and generous, and if she was coarse she was neither false nor cruel. She laughed with the laugh of the people, and if you hit her hard enough she would cry with its tears.'

'If she had been ugly he couldn't have listened to her; but her beauty glorified even her accent, intensified her cockney genius with prismatic hues, gave her a large and constant impunity.'

'No one but a capital girl could give herself such airs,' Hyacinth remarks in a later generous mood; it is refreshing to see how deeply his creator could appreciate common vitality, and the following paragraph should be of interest to those who still maintain that Henry James did not like or understand ordinary common folk:

'An inner sense told him that her mingled beauty and grossness, her vulgar vitality, the spirit of contradiction yet at the same time of attachment that was in her, had ended by making her indispensable to him. She bored him as much as she irritated him; but if she was full of execrable taste she was also full of life, and her rustlings and chatterings, her wonderful stories, her bad grammar and good health, her insatiable thirst, her shrewd perceptions and grotesque opinions, her mistakes and her felicities, were now all part of the familiar human sound of his little world.'

Millicent, clearly, was hardly likely to encourage a young man to desperate deeds against society: she would always, in Spenderian analysis, vote solid Tory. The thoughtful reserve of Mr. Vetch made him, too, a most congenial member of the forces of discontent. He is prepared to play his fiddle in the capitalist theatre so long as he can think his private thoughts and indulge, in Pinnie's 'dismal, forsaken bower', in 'so many sociable droppings-in and hot tumblers'. He voices very clearly one aspect of Hyacinth's inherent resistance to the revolutionary creed: 'The way certain classes arrogate to themselves the title of the people has never pleased me.' As for the gallant Monsieur Poupin, he is a retired and exiled member of the Old Guard who has already shot his bolt; his portrait is indeed a luxury, and a splendid example of the young novelist's high spirits:

'M. Poupin was a socialist, which Anastasius Vetch was not, and a constructive democrat (instead of being a mere scoffer at effete things), and a theorist and an optimist and a visionary; he believed that the day was to come when all the nations of the earth would abolish their frontiers and armies and customs-houses, and embrace on both cheeks, and cover the globe with boulevards, radiating from Paris, where the human family would sit, in groups, at little tables, according to affinities, drinking coffee (not tea, *par exemple!*), and listening to the music of the spheres. Mr. Vetch neither prefigured nor desired this organized felicity; he was fond of his cup of tea, and only wanted to see the British constitution a good deal simplified. . . .'

In Paul Muniment the straightforward political theorist is shown to best advantage; Hyacinth falls quickly under the spell of the young man who reminds the reader of the simplified intellectual life enjoyed by those of his modern brothers who echo his opinion that 'one must be narrow to penetrate'. After a time, however, the negative austerities of his creed give Hyacinth pause:

'. . . he moved in a dry statistical and scientific air in which it cost Hyacinth an effort of respiration to accompany him . . . he sometimes emitted a short satiric gleam which showed that his esteem for the poor was small and that if he had no illusions about the people who had got everything into their hands he had as few about those who had egregiously failed to do so.'

This sort of perception has far more effect on the reader's understanding of Hyacinth's character than any later chink in the young revolutionary's armour required by the exigencies of the plot. Sister Rose, presented on her sick-bed as an object of pity, succeeds in filling the reader with a reluctant shamefaced distaste, so that it is a positive relief to discover, in a chance tone of irony, that the author is of the same way of thinking:

' "Well, I have told you often enough that I don't go with you at all," said Rose Muniment, whose recumbency appeared not in the least to interfere with her sense of responsibility.'

Long before the appearance of the Princess Casamassima herself (she is that same Christina Light who was the downfall of Roderick Hudson, but that fact is of no more significance than as an author's weakness for a created character), Hyacinth is perplexed by the conflict between the views of his friends, who all for different reasons desire the collapse of capitalist society, and his own excluded response to the finer fruits of that society. There, of course, lies his tragedy in the 'plot'—that it should be Hyacinth who has to become an assassin and who kills himself rather than go through with it. The deeper tragedy of 'character' (so exhausting the reader's emotional response that the melodramatic ending somewhat misses fire) lies in the boy's aspirations. To these, even the sympathetic interest of the Princess is no more than a fortunate following wind—and this in spite of her own desire to play at liberty, equality and fraternity. It is of the other conspirators, without any guidance from this condescending love-hunting lady, that he first grows tired:

'He wondered at their zeal, their continuity, their vivacity, their incorruptibility; at the abundant supply of conviction and prophecy which they always had on hand. He believed that at bottom he was sorer than they, yet he had deviations and lapses, moments when the social question bored him and he forgot not only his own wrongs, which would have been pardonable, but those of the people at large, of his brothers and sisters in misery.'

When he is enabled to take a short holiday on the Continent, his own Pentonville imagination has prepared him for a response quicker and more piercing than that of a dozen Princesses:

'. . . as he lingered, before crossing the Seine, a sudden sense overtook him, making his heart sink with a kind of desolation—a sense of everything that might hold one to the world, of the sweetness of not dying, the fascination of great cities, the charm of travel and discovery, the generosity of admiration.'

and he slashes out, in his bewilderment, at Paul Muniment, who 'would cut up the ceilings of Veronese into strips, so that every one might have a little piece'.

It is significant that, in attempting the briefest *précis* of this novel, it is to the 'portraits' that one turns and not to the melodramatic 'plot', full as it may be of surprises and coincidences and unnecessary devices to keep alive an interest already and otherwise fully quickened. What Hyacinth had precisely to *do* soon slips from our memory; we recall him as a prim unhappy little bookbinder and forget his embroilment in underground machinations while remembering his endowment with an eye for character and a soul stirred by any manifestation of the beautiful or the moving. If he has a 'split personality' it is only the ambiguity of full sanity, of

'the rather helpless sense that, whatever he saw, he saw (and this was always the case) so many other things beside. He saw the immeasurable misery of the people, and yet he saw all that had been as it were rescued and redeemed from it; the treasures, the felicities, the splendours, the successes, of the world.'

He can grasp on the instant that sense of injustice towards which his fellow-conspirators had laboured long, but at a crisis in their plotting he can cry out with exasperated impatience: 'Isn't it enough, now, to give my life to the beastly cause . . . without giving my sympathy?' His ambivalence is his tragedy, it is also his inner strength of private glory amid public woe as his creator progressively reveals 'the torment of his present life, the perpetual laceration of the rebound'.

The vivid evocative quality of Hyacinth Robinson's impressions, then, are illustrated by his sense of the characters of his associates, to which he gives his whole mind and heart, rather than by the overt political attitudes to which he gives half his mind and as much of his heart as he can spare. The liveliness of Hyacinth himself and the authenticity of his claim to be (as a created character) alive in the real world and therefore *available* to all these impressions, are established primarily through his creator's ability to recreate the sights and sounds and smells of Hyacinth's London, and (still more important) the manner in which an adolescent of unusual sensibility might react to those sights and sounds and smells. We have Henry James's word for it* (almost, indeed, his last word) that 'the mid-Victorian London was sincere—that was a vast virtue and a vast appeal'. In those same mellow autobiographical pages† he has told us how in a certain eating-house of the very old English tradition 'I said to myself under every shock and at the hint of every savour that this was what it was for an exhibition to reek with local colour, and one could dispense with a napkin, with a crusty roll, with room for one's elbows or one's feet, with an immunity from intermittence of the "plain boiled", much better than one could dispense with that;' he has gone still further and admitted again (as plainly as in the Preface to *The Princess*) his determination to *do* something with this acute receptivity to atmosphere:

'If the commonest street-vista was a fairly heart-shaking contributive image, if the incidents of the thick renascent light anywhere, and the perpetual excitement of never knowing, between it and the historic and determined gloom, which was which and which one could most "back" for the general outcome and picture, so the great sought out compositions, the Hampton Courts and the Windsors, the Richmonds, the Dulwiches, even the very Hampstead Heaths and Putney Commons, to say nothing of the Towers, the Temples, the Cathedrals and the strange penetrabilities of the City, ranged themselves like the rows of great figures in a sum, an amount immeasurably huge, that one would draw on if not quite as long as one lived, yet as soon as ever one should seriously get to work.'

It is to this kind of sensibility, rather than to sour notions of what a young revolutionary should or should not think or dream, that a wise reader will relate Hyacinth's longings for the world represented in his untutored mind by the figure and setting of the Princess Casamassima; it is in this divided sympathy, and not in any technical deviation from the views of Paul

* *The Middle Years* (1917), p. 24.
† *Op. cit.*, pp. 44, 54–55.

Muniment or Diedrich Hoffendahl, that lies the tragic weakness —and thus the human kinship—of the little Pentonville bookbinder. At the same time, it has been pointed out* that although the politics of his friends had nothing in common with modern revolutionary Communism, Hyacinth was in fact placed in a 'classic Anarchist situation' in keeping with the political assassinations and other acts of terrorism prevalent in the 1880's, and that *The Princess Casamassima* shows James to have been capable of producing 'a first-class rendering of literal social reality'.

III

If, in *The Princess Casamassima*, there are pain, pathos, evocative twinges of childhood and adolescence, flashes of intuition in the private and public impressions of a sensitive youth, in *The Bostonians* there are all these things plus passion pure and simple, passion of the kind we mean when we talk about (usually without having re-read) *Wuthering Heights*. It is one of the most powerful novels in our language; that it is not generally recognized as such can only be due to a general conspiracy (headed by the author himself) to hide or disguise the central theme.

The Bostonians bears a striking resemblance to *The Princess Casamassima* in certain matters of tone and in the evocation of that strained human anguish between the conception of a 'political' ideal and its execution in the face of contrary 'private' impulses. The impression of both books that remains most vividly in the reader's mind is just this strained grey quality of the prose—relieved by some amazing 'set-pieces' of character-drawing. Nowhere in the later novels did Henry James so demonstrate his power to introduce into the very texture of his writing all the tension of his characters as they 'slash out in the bewilderment' of the contrast between life as a conscious political effort towards an attitude, and life as a more complex and aching system of personal desires and denials which may run, if not in direct opposition to the conscious will, at least in a direction oblique enough to cause a harsh grating of responses.

In both novels, the subtler tension in the central character is made more easy to appreciate by the placing, as an immediate

* By Lionel Trilling (*Horizon*, Vol. XVII, No. 100).

background, of some more overt but not quite crude instance of a similar unsteadiness of purpose. To set off the social perplexities of Hyacinth Robinson, striving to rise from poverty to the *beau monde* against his conviction that the *beau monde* should be destroyed, there is the less complicated social urge of the Princess Casamassima, striving to climb down in the other direction to satisfy a passing whim; there is also the more active revolutionary zeal of Paul Muniment and his friends, itself somewhat tangled with personal implications and thrown into relief by the more mature (if less precise) commentary of Anastasius Vetch and Pinnie. So here, in *The Bostonians,* the conflict in the mind of Olive Chancellor is thrown against the background of a much less complicated instance in the person of Miss Birdseye, the true Bostonian reformer.

It is worth noting the extraordinary tenderness of the portrait of Miss Birdseye, from the very beginning. We are guided to see courage and honest value in the dim drapery of a foolish old woman fumbling in a muddle-headed way with causes beyond her scope. Her detailed portrait, that great set piece framed in a description of her apartments all prepared for yet another meeting in aid of some good cause, is one of the finest passages of Henry James's early maturity. It overflows with adjectives, but there is no straining after effect: the adjectives tumble out as though the author is quite saturated with his 'appreciation' of her.

'She was a little old lady, with an enormous head; that was the first thing Ransom noticed—the vast, fair, protuberant, candid, ungarnished brow, surmounting a pair of weak, kind, tired-looking eyes, and ineffectually balanced in the rear by a cap which had the air of falling backwards, and which Miss Birdseye suddenly felt for while she talked, with unsuccessful irrelevant movements. She had a sad, soft, pale face, which (and it was the effect of her whole head) looked as if it had been soaked, blurred, and made vague by exposure to some slow dissolvent. The long practice of philanthropy had not given accent to her features; it had rubbed out their transitions, their meanings. The waves of sympathy, of enthusiasm, had wrought upon them in the same way in which the waves of time finally modify the surface of old marble busts, gradually washing away their sharpness, their details. In her large countenance her dim little smile scarcely showed. It was a mere sketch of a smile, a kind of instalment, or payment on account; it seemed to say that she would smile more if she had time, but that you could see without this, that she was gentle and easy to beguile.'

Henry James, struck 'deadly sick' when his brother William wrote a letter accusing him of painting in Miss Birdseye a recognizable portrait of the respected Bostonian philanthropist Miss Peabody, categorically stated* that 'Miss Birdseye was evolved entirely from my moral consciousness, like every other person I have ever drawn.' He goes on to claim that 'though subordinate, she is, I think, the best figure in the book,' and—which is more to our present purpose—'she is represented as the embodiment of pure, the purest philanthropy.'

But tender though the portrait is, it is important to recognize in Miss Birdseye a kindly example of those professional reformers who, deep in magnanimous schemes for 'foreigners' and others with whom they have no valid individual contact, fail entirely to establish for themselves any true personal relationship with the world and with their fellows: a judgement summed up in the observation that the legend of an *affaire* between Miss Birdseye and a Hungarian refugee must have been apocryphal because 'it was open to grave doubt that she could have entertained a sentiment so personal.' This manner of life, however kindly displayed in the person of Miss Birdseye, clearly represents to the author a fatal error in the investment of emotional capital—and this manner of life is what Olive Chancellor wished to persuade herself was admirable. Her tragedy is greater than that of Miss Birdseye, not because her sense of values was any less mistaken, but simply because she was unable to pursue her mistaken course with anything like success. Temperament and history alike had aided Miss Birdseye, so that her eccentricity took on, at the last, an aura of honesty and integrity, and made her possibly as happy as she could ever have been in any other mode of life. But with Olive, the personal heresy which she strove to damp down by denying herself any relations with men (an unsympathetic tribe represented by her cousin Basil Ransom) and devoting herself single-mindedly to Women's Rights, flared up again with a terrible intensity in her love for Verena Tarrant, flared up inside

* *Letters*, Vol. I, p. 115.

and destroyed the very holy sanctuary of their mutual and vowed devotion to an impersonal 'cause'.

With Miss Birdseye fresh in the mind, it is convenient to draw attention to another instance of James's detached sympathy in the delineation of minor figures, introduced in *The Bostonians* (as so often elsewhere) in a series of sketches to the splendid *economy* of which his long sentences and inflated periphrasis so oddly and actively contribute. It is a quality of tone to be seen to great advantage in the gentle ironical humour of the portraits of Selah Tarrant, the mesmeric healer, and his wife, daughter of Abraham Greenstreet the Abolitionist. It comes out in a kind of amused outrage at their pathetic poverty of taste, their shoddy system of pretences and makeshifts. One doesn't in the least resent the narrator's tone of superiority: one *has* to feel superior to such fry, if one is to make anything of them at all, and there is a caressing humour about it all which never declines into a snigger. Underneath, one is always conscious of a deep human sympathy, a beautiful apprehension of the tortured twists and quirks producing all this corrugation of personality. The portrait of Verena Tarrant's mother, admirable in itself, has much functional significance. It helps to explain the girl's willingness to leave home in order to live as Olive Chancellor's guest, it certainly provides her with an incentive for her final desertion of 'public life' for a private career as Mrs. Basil Ransom, and it offers, in its very tone, another clear indication of the author's disapproval of those who allow amateur and ineffective gestures towards the political life to diminish whatever chance they may have of developing a rich private integrity.

'She was a queer, indeed . . . a flaccid, unhealthy, whimsical woman, who still had a capacity to cling. What she clung to was "society" and a position in the world which a secret whisper told her she had never had and a voice more audible reminded her she was in danger of losing. . . . Verena was born not only to lead their common sex out of bondage, but to remodel a visiting-list which bulged and contracted in the wrong places, like a country-made garment. As the daughter of Abraham Greenstreet, Mrs. Tarrant had passed her youth in the first Abolitionist circles, and she was aware how much such a prospect was clouded by her union with a young man who had begun life as an itinerant vendor of lead-pencils (he had called at Mr. Greenstreet's door in the exercise of this function), had afterwards been for a while a member of the celebrated Cayuga community, where there were no wives, or no husbands, or something of that sort (Mrs. Tarrant could never remember), and had still later (though before the development of the healing faculty) achieved distinction in the spiritualistic world.'

We can read this sort of sketch (and it is only one of many aspects of Mrs. Tarrant, cumulative in their effect) with an indulgent smile, confident that Henry James will never be so crude as to betray our mood and suddenly turn on us with sermons about 'motives' or 'compensations' or 'wish-fulfilments'. This confidence is implicit, and the humour and the sympathy co-exist without embarrassment. It is largely the inflation that brings the smile, and there is no cruelty about *that*. As an 'itinerant vendor of lead pencils', Selah is both funnier and more dignified than as a 'pedlar,' for instance. If the Greenstreets objected to mesmeric healing as 'manual activity', there is rich comedy in the inflation and yet the term suits both their own and Selah's view of his exercises. The tattered garments of pretence are held up to ridicule, but they are not still further rent; James restores them to their wearers for whatever warmth they may still afford, and does not (like a Swift) leave his models entirely naked and comfortless.

Selah Tarrant himself is a medium for a double assault on the less rooted forms of 'public' life; he is not only, like his wife, a camp-follower of the irregular skirmishers among the intellectual forces, but also a fascinated devotee of the power of the American Press, that lusty organ of collective vulgarity which Henry James viewed with peculiar aversion:

'The newspapers were his world, the richest expression, in his eyes, of human life; and for him, if a diviner day was to come upon earth, it would be brought about by copious advertisement in the daily press. . . .

' . . . . the places that knew him best were the offices of the newspapers and the vestibules of the hotels—the big marble-paved chambers of informal reunion which offer to the streets, through high-glass plates, the sight of the American citizen suspended by his heels. Here, amid the piled-up luggage, the convenient spittoons, the elbowing loungers, the disconsolate "guests", the truculent Irish porters, the rows of shaggy-backed men in strange hats, writing letters at a table inlaid with advertisements, Selah Tarrant made innumerable contemplative stations.'

In these and other portraits from *The Bostonians* there emerges an expression of Henry James's own strong desire—more familiarly documented in his letters, essays in autobiography, and in the long series of novels and tales devoted to what may be termed his international obsession—to escape from all this sort of thing to a more civilized sphere. A wincing appreciation of every last scrap of vulgarity in nineteenth-century American domestic conversation, whether exemplified in Matthias Pardon the slick reporter or Mrs. Tarrant the addle-pated explainer-away of social awkwardnesses, is set down with tormented accuracy. No wonder, the reader cannot help but feel, no wonder Henry James was so much in love with the European style of conversation recorded by the European novelists; no wonder he was determined to find it and in the end make his own characters speak always with point, always in the spirit of 'revised wisdom', and not merely, like Mrs. Tarrant, making an ado about offering a piece of apple-fritter, or 'taking a gossip's view of great tendencies' like Matthias Pardon.

Olive Chancellor herself is one of the great tragic heroines of fiction. Her plight is so intrinsic, so affects every page of the novel with a sense of tension and strain, that one does not miss, here, an elaborate late Preface which would have pointed out and underlined all one's own unaided responses to the powerful theme—except to note in its absence a further indication that the 'failure' of the book was due very largely to its unusual theme. (Mr. Edmund Wilson recalls* that 'when Henry James was selecting the material for his collected edition, he was forced by the insistence of his publishers . . . and against his own inclination, to exclude *The Bostonians* from it.' Miss Theodora Bosanquet told me that it would probably have been the next novel to be honoured with a Preface, if he had allowed himself time for the task. In a letter† of August, 1915, he still admits how much he would have enjoyed 'making it a much truer and more curious thing—it was meant to be curious from the first'.)

Olive's tragedy is fairly simply that of self-delusion, but the self-delusion itself is anything but simple. It is soon clear that

* *Hound and Horn*, April-June, 1934. † *Letters*, Vol. II, p. 498.

love and jealousy prompt all her actions with regard to Verena: the stresses and strains are pitiable to recognize. But it is altogether too easy a matter to point a finger at the raw spot and to say: 'She was in love with Verena and was ashamed of it, or perhaps did not really admit it to herself, but covered it up with all sorts of rationalizations which in turn were directed against man, the natural and favoured enemy of her unnatural passion.' Henry James himself certainly stoops to no such crude analysis. Her consequent morbidity of temperament is not, even for Basil Ramsom, a matter for superior comment—'any sufficient account of her must lie very much to the rear of that.' Henry James returns here, with more profound and ambitious mastery, to the theme he had so brilliantly sketched in *Roderick Hudson*: the relationship between a conscientious thoughtful moralist and a creature of grace and personal fascination whose lack of those same qualities of moral high-seriousness alternately infatuate and disgust the pursuer. The essential lack of balance in the human situation was clear enough in *Roderick Hudson*, but it was not there developed on the plane of tragedy. Here, it indubitably *is*.

It adds to the complexity of the situation that Olive Chancellor does honestly believe in her 'cause'. We see her deeply devoted to it before ever Verena Tarrant steps on to the stage. We see her instinctive fear of Basil Ransom, that bright-eyed exponent of personal arrangements and the anti-progressive enemy of 'causes', long before that fear becomes a dread that he will steal Verena away from her. Indeed, if his intrusion were the only fear, Olive would, even in the face of the successful conclusion of his outrage to her happiness, lose tragic stature. It is so much more than that. We are shown that Verena was bound in the end to disappoint her protectress, with or without assistance from that lady's cousin. If Olive had her own tragic flaw, so—from Olive's point of view—had Verena. It was the flaw most likely to strike against Olive's own, and wound her at her weakest point.

In her previous shy attempts to nourish her sad courage on something more tangible than 'causes', Olive had found the young women whom she approached all 'odiously mixed up with Charlie', and had retired conscious of defeat. With Verena there was no 'Charlie'. She was not just another 'pale shop-maiden' who 'couldn't make out what she wanted them to do'. Verena, who had 'sat on the knees of somnambulists, and had been passed from hand to hand by trance-speakers', had been hitherto defended from that particular danger by the accident of her eccentric upbringing. It soon becomes evident that it *was* only an accident, and Olive's first major self-delusion was in setting any store by it. Olive's sister Mrs. Luna, that bedizened arch-priestess of *la vie intime*, was not wholly prejudiced when she announced that Verena was 'an artful little minx and cared as much for the rights of women as she did for the Panama Canal', and added: 'She will give Olive the greatest cut she has ever had in her life. She will run off with some lion-tamer; she will marry a circus-man!' Coming quite early in the novel there is a significance—sinister for Olive—in one brief sentence about Verena, a sentence gaining point from its position at the end of a chapter: 'Her ideas of enjoyment were very simple; she enjoyed putting on her new hat, with its redundancy of feather, and twenty cents appeared to her a very large sum.' The redundancy of feather, that gay straw in the wind of Verena's freshness, implies a potential 'Charlie', that figure appearing to Miss Chancellor's distressed imagination as 'a young man in a white overcoat and a paper collar'.

The recurring theme, in Henry James's novels, of the relationship between two contrasted and mutually attractive types (the integrated moralist and the wavering child of genius or intuition) had already been worked out between man and man in *Roderick Hudson*, between man and woman in *The Portrait of a Lady* and elsewhere, and is now worked out in *The Bostonians* between woman and woman. The early short story *Benvolio* had posed the problem in its simplicity, where the two 'types' are united in one person. There it was a legend, developed on the plane of a fairy-story. The symbolism of the bright young man's two rooms—one large gay room for entertaining his friends and one small solitary room for study and composition, the former overlooking a fashionable street and the latter giving on a walled garden—is symbolism simple but quintessential. The 'ambiguity' of Henry James is progressively revealed as a tormented uncertainty of purpose, of wish, in himself; no novelist has ever described the state so often or so well, with all those vague gradations of mood somehow absorbed into the very texture of his prose and never forced—to their inevitable destruction—into a harsh code of pros and cons. Here, it is Verena who is ambiguous. *Her* aims are, at first, truly mixed, for her *capacities* are, at first, truly mixed. With Olive herself the intuitive free 'personal' life could never have succeeded, and it was her tragic delusion to make that attempt. The 'person' Olive fell in love with was the brilliant accidental personification of her own left-handed craving for a 'personal' life. That she could never honestly allow for the flowering of the free personal life in Verena herself was not only fatal to the false relationship of compromise between them (a relationship based, for a time steadily enough, on mutual admiration); it also proclaimed her own *inability* to love freely, free from her morals, free from her programme, free from her other self. Courage she had in plenty, but not that saving disgrace of moral slovenliness that would bid her follow the moment's whim. When she has achieved her aim and has quite literally bought Verena from her parents (a curious relapse into bondage for a grand-daughter of Abraham Greenstreet the Abolitionist), she still shows every sign of resisting her personal motives—for it is not until the very end that Olive's passion breaks through her own defensive positions. Meanwhile, with this impressionable girl her prisoner, with this Bohemian wayward unorthodox object of her affection living as her friend and *protégée,* Olive manages to convince herself (and, for a long time, Verena too) of the high morality of her programme:

' "We will work at it together—we still study everything." Olive almost panted; and while she spoke the peaceful picture hung before her of still winter evenings under the lamp, with falling snow outside, and tea on a little table, and successful renderings, with a chosen companion, of Goethe; almost the only foreign writer she cared about; for she hated the writing of the French, in spite of the importance they had given to women.'

Olive's loss of Verena to Basil Ransom reaches the plane of stark tragedy only in those harrowing closing chapters of the novel where the strain breaks at last in shrill hysteria like the shriek of an unlubricated engine. Henry James, with that customary embarrassment which overwhelmed him always on such occasions, calls in the aid of rhetoric, even of melodrama.

It is all competently done, but on what a disappointing level, after the sustained critical poise of the rest of the novel:

'The expression on her face was a thing to remain with him for ever; it was impossible to imagine a more vivid presentment of blighted hope and wounded pride. Dry, desperate, rigid, she yet wavered and seemed uncertain; her pale, glittering eyes strained forward, as if they were looking for death. Ransom had a vision, even at that crowded moment, that if she could have met it there and then, bristling with steel or lurid with fire, she could have rushed on it without a tremor, like the heroine that she was.'

With Verena, for a time, there had been a balance, a poise of warring elements. Like a needle between two magnets she could swing freely, now to Olive, now to Basil Ransom. It is not too much to say that in the end she swung home to that magnet whose forces were constant, undivided: she could with her 'personal' life love Basil on his own terms and find in the end her 'Charlie': she could possibly with her 'public' self have loved Olive on Olive's 'public' terms. It was the essence of Olive's tragedy that when she in turn attempted to put out a personal attraction, the needle flickered awhile and then finally came to rest where that particular pull was strongest and simplest—not in Olive against whom no needle sensitive to manifold impulsions and repulsions could ever quietly nestle, but in Basil whose powers were concentrated in a single attraction.

IV

Miss Rebecca West was of the opinion* that *The Bostonians*, in spite of descriptive passages of great beauty, failed to 'come off', and renewed the kind of charge we have seen brought against *The Princess Casamassima*: 'this musical disclosure of fine material is interrupted past any reader's patience by a nagging hostility to political effort.' Mr. Edmund Wilson, however, although he contrives to find Olive Chancellor 'horrid' and 'clammy', delivers the judgement that in these two novels and in *The Tragic Muse* Henry James gave 'his clearest and most elaborate criticism of life'—a judgement recalling the author's own admission† that in these three novels 'I "go behind" right

**Henry James* (1916), p. 71. † *Letters*, Vol. I, p. 324.

and left'. And Mr. Van Wyck Brooks, by no means an over-sympathetic critic, asks:* 'Who that recalls *The Bostonians*, that picture of a world which seems to consist of nothing but hands, reproving, pushing, pulling, exploiting hands, can doubt that, in all this, James was inspired by the sacred terror of his own individuality?'

Here, I think, we have the germ of the matter. But the germ is largely hidden by conditions which are, for the reader, all gain. I agree with Miss West that there are passages in *The Bostonians* 'that one would like to learn by heart'. By 1886, at the age of 43, James had found himself as a novelist and was writing with fluent mastery. There is observable in both *The Princess Casamassima* and *The Bostonians* an exuberance only superficially at variance with the strained strenuous themes. This conscious pleasure in creative achievement not only endows minor characters with a quality of life far in excess of anything required by purely structural considerations (and of this vivid quality we have seen but a few examples only), but also peppers the two novels with wholly gratuitous felicities. Miss Birdseye can be claimed as essential to the pattern, but what are we to say of that superb caricature Mrs. Farrinder, who 'laboured . . . to give the ballot to every woman and to take the flowing bowl from every man'—except that although unnecessary she is wonderfully welcome, and would have served, along with other free marginal sketches, to make the reputation of a lesser novelist? Henry James could be a 'popular' novelist today if his readers first discovered Mrs. Farrinder and Doctor Prance and Matthias Pardon, or Anastasius Vetch and Pinnie, *before* setting out with *The Ambassadors* or in quest of *The Golden Bowl*.

Is there not in all this wealth of personal observation any object-lesson by James himself in the precept, so largely smothered by his own enthusiastic practice, that until man is at home in his immediate social life he cannot hope to derive sufficient inner nourishment to be strong enough to face, let alone think of contributing towards the solution of the problems of his larger political setting? If there is a 'message' in these masterpieces of the novelist's art, it is surely: 'Put your own house in order.' We need not (*pace* Miss West) be unfriendly to political progress in order to understand Basil Ransom's

* *The Pilgrimage of Henry James* (1928), p. 46.

view: 'He, too, had a private vision of reform, but the first principle of it was to reform the reformers.' And just as Hyacinth Robinson's plight is in effect a far more damning indictment of the Victorian social system than any speech from the lips of Paul Muniment, so even Basil Ransom himself, constitutionally averse to schemes of amelioration, gives us a personal wince at the unfairness of things as he looks about him in the rich home of his reforming cousin:

'He ground his teeth a little as he thought of the contrasts of the human lot; this cushioned feminine nest made him feel unhoused and underfed. Such a mood, however, could only be momentary, for he was conscious at bottom of a bigger stomach than all the culture of Charles Street could fill.'

The author's sympathy goes out, of course, to his chief figures, bewildered in their 'public' world—to Hyacinth and to Olive. But he cannot conceal his sidelong admiration for those happier mortals who have come to terms with their environment —for Pinnie in *The Princess Casamassima*, and in *The Bostonians* for such a person as Doctor Prance, that trim little female physician who wins the esteem even of Basil Ransom, a Southerner through and through and the bitter masculine enemy of Women's Rights:

'She stood there an instant, turning over the whole assembly a glance like the flash of a watchman's bull's-eye, and then quickly passed out. Ransom could see that she was impatient of the general question and bored with being reminded, even for the sake of her rights, that she was a woman—a detail that she was in the habit of forgetting, having as many rights as she had time for. It was certain that whatever might become of the movement at large, Doctor Prance's own little revolution was a success.'

This sneaking sympathy for people who are competent in small matters is matched in innumerable instances by a cynical irritation aroused by people who are incompetent in larger affairs. Mrs. Luna laughs at sister Olive's 'thoughtfulness': 'That's what they call in Boston being very "thoughtful",' Mrs. Luna said, 'giving you the Back Bay (don't you hate the name?) to look at, and then taking the credit for it.' Olive herself winces at vulgarity and is virtuously ashamed of her every wince ('in a career in which she was constantly exposing herself to offence and laceration, her most poignant suffering came from the injury of her taste'), whereas her adored Miss Birdseye, for whom 'there was a genius in every bush', 'was always trying to obtain employment, lessons in drawing, orders for portraits, for poor foreign artists, as to the greatness of whose talent she pledged herself without reserve; but in point of fact she had not the faintest sense of the scenic or plastic side of life.' Selah Tarrant, for all his pretensions, 'couldn't hold the attention of an audience; he was not acceptable as a lecturer,' and as for his wife, 'she knew that he was an awful humbug,' and she herself was not worthy of Verena's gifts: 'the commonness of her own surface was a non-conductor of the girl's quality.' Matthias Pardon, representative of the Great American Press, 'regarded the mission of mankind upon earth as a perpetual evolution of telegrams,' and it was only the 'newest thing' that 'came nearest exciting in his mind the sentiment of respect'. The whole caricature of Mrs. Farrinder is etched with enjoyable malice, and even Mrs. Burrage, the female Anti-Feminist rampant, represents the domestic hearth at its most complacent but does not escape the barb of James's satire, directed in *The Bostonians* against all those who adopt a rigid attitude to life based on insufficient personal grounds: 'she could fancy how Mrs. Burrage would be affected by the knowledge that her son had been refused by the daughter of a mesmeric healer. She would be almost as angry as if she had learnt that he had been accepted.' Finally, the gaunt tragic figure of Olive Chancellor is sometimes shown in a light not so much unsympathetic as 'critical' in the somewhat academic sense of the word. In the first introductory sketch we are told that 'it was the usual things of life that filled her with silent rage; which was natural enough, inasmuch as, to her vision, everything that was usual was iniquitous'. She and Verena, congratulating themselves on 'the wonderful insight they had obtained into the history of feminine anguish', nevertheless plan their future activities with unbruised will, and there is some savagery in the comment: 'A person who might have overheard some of the talk of this possibly infatuated pair would have been touched by their extreme familiarity with the idea of earthly glory.' To hunt no further afield, there is even at times a direct charge against Olive's intellectual integrity: 'I have said that it was Miss Chancellor's plan of life not to lie, but such a plan was compatible with a kind of consideration for the truth which led her to shrink from producing it on poor occasions.'

These instances of narrative comment lend plausibility to the view that Henry James was speaking his own mind (or part of it) when he puts tart observations into the mouth of Basil Ransom. This thoughtful Southerner disliked 'mediums, communists, vegetarians', was sensitive to the wrongs suffered by the defeated Confederate States, but refrained from 'prating in the market-place'. Yet we are explicitly informed that 'he had always had a desire for public life; to cause one's ideas to be embodied in national conduct appeared to him the highest form of human enjoyment.' At the same time (and here the personal views of his creator are surely apparent?) 'he thought [his age] talkative, querulous, hysterical, maudlin, full of false ideas, of unhealthy germs, of extravagant, dissipated habits, for which a great reckoning was in store,' and we are made to feel that it was from this caricature of the public life, the 'windy, wordy reiteration of inanities', as well as from the personal clutches of Olive Chancellor, that he wished to rescue Verena.

Such an account might lend colour to Miss West's view that *The Bostonians* has an infuriating 'nagging hostility to political effort', were it not for the ample evidence of James's complementary sympathy for his band of suffragettes. Basil Ransom immediately sensed his cousin's intense gravity: 'the simplest division it is possible to make of the human race is into the people who take things hard and the people who take things easy. He perceived very quickly that Miss Chancellor belonged to the former class.' And a little later: 'she gave him an uneasy feeling—the sense that you could never be safe with a person who took things so hard.' We are left in no doubt as to her private psychology: she complains to Verena that 'you don't dislike men as a class', and yet it is carefully pointed out that 'it was a curious incident of her zeal for the regeneration of her sex that manly things were, perhaps on the whole, what she understood best'. But far more evocative of the reader's sympathy than any clumsy indication of her half-recognized 'motives' is the slow cumulative weight of Olive's conscious braveries and a certain undeniable 'quality'. She is credited with 'a gentle dignity, a serenity of wisdom', and 'the detachment from error, of a woman whose self-scrutiny had been as sharp as her deflexion'. Verena speaks for the reader when she tells her friend 'you have a fearful power of suffering'—and suffering of such intensity would, we feel, be neither humanly possible nor artistically effective in a character of less than Olive's stature. She is, no less than the 'battered, unpensioned' Miss Birdseye herself, a representative of the 'heroic age of New England'.

The scattered quotations in these notes on *The Bostonians* and *The Princess Casamassima* will have given small notion of the fluent rich elegance of the early Jacobean style; there are whole chapters in which subtlety and dignity combine to form a medium of quite astonishing self-sufficiency. I would invite attention to a single aspect of this prose of James's early maturity, mainly for the explanatory light it may throw on his later, more 'difficult' mode of communication. I have already suggested that the 'inflation' in the portraits of the Tarrant family has a function as well as (for readers who enjoy stylistic jokes) a gratuitous delight. We may smile at Verena's 'perpendicular journeys' strap-hanging in a tramcar, and even more when, on boarding a similar vehicle, Miss Birdseye was 'insert[ed] . . . into the oblong receptacle'; Mrs. Tarrant doesn't merely enjoy the paper—'from this publication she derived inscrutable solace'; Ransom's Southern relations exist on a 'farinaceous diet' and Olive's conscience is indicated as 'that attentive organ'; in a poor quarter of a town little children become 'the infant population' and the grass 'thin herbage'; the erratic violence of Verena's education is deemed to show 'a want of continuity', and Matthias Pardon's gossip columns are devoted 'to the great end of preventing the American citizen from attempting clandestine journeys'. Sarcasm is altogether too simple a label for these apparent verbal absurdities; there is a very real sense in which each one of them is *true*, more true than the simpler paraphrase, because in smiling at them we remember that from the inside of the mind of the character concerned there is nothing funny in the tone. Mrs. Tarrant may never have used the words, but she did somehow see herself, pompously, as 'deriving inscrutable solace' rather than just reading the paper—as anyone will agree who has ever been irritated by the complacent smirk of some clubman behind his copy of *The Times*.

In the second volume of *The Princess Casamassima* there is a subtler instance rather more indicative of the controlled conscious 'inflation' of the later style. The Prince and Madame Grandoni are sitting in Hyde Park, watching the riders jogging up and down. The state of mind of these self-conscious observers, meeting to debate in solemn ceremony some matter which in our less stately age would be disposed of in a few words of psycho-analytical slang, is indicated with beautiful *economy* (there is the signal point) in the half-amused half-serious tone of the narrator: they sat 'amid a wilderness of empty chairs and with nothing to distract their attention from an equestrian or two left over from the cavalcades of a fortnight before, and whose vain agitation in the saddle the desolate scene seemed to throw into high relief.' If there are *not* states of mind in which jogging riders appear accurately and vividly as agitated equestrians, then I am a poor reader and Henry James a pompous ass.

14

THE WINGS OF THE DOVE

A Study in Construction

I

From the flimsiest *nouvelle* to the longest novel, everything Henry James wrote was checked and weighed and spaced out in homage to an immense meticulous critical consciousness. Of all his novels, *The Wings of the Dove* is his most successful 'creation'—but because of its very qualities it is primarily valued as a novel of character rather than of situation.

This aspect of James's masterpiece may be illustrated by a preliminary glance at another novel of much the same period in which a not dissimilar 'situation' quite overshadows the 'characters', pointing the useful moral that a good *dramatic* construction is not necessarily a good basis for a novel. Indeed, to select *The Other House* (1896) for complementary reference is almost to invite the charge of cheating, for it was 'first written as a play-scenario under the title of *The Promise*, turned into a novel and then, after the lapse of more than a decade, reconverted into a play.'* James found the work of dramatization 'ferociously difficult', but he makes it plain (in a letter† of 1909 which contains some admirable good sense on plays in general) that the problem is not a matter of dramatic form but of human credibility: 'If I can go on *believing in* my subject I can go on treating it; but sometimes I have a mortal chill and wonder if I ain't damnably deluded.' In the event, *The Other House* is a disappointing novel of the middle period, a stage play sketchily cast in novel form by plentiful admixture of the James 'style'—and

* Leon Edel, Introduction to *The Other House* (reprint of 1948).
† *Letters*, Vol. II, pp. 129–131.

by no means his best. His old propensity to melodrama had returned in full force, and a bare outline of the plot will indicate the full domination of situation over character in a manner miraculously overcome, a few years later, by the author of *The Wings of the Dove.*

Tony Bream gave his wife Julia a deathbed promise that he would not marry again during the lifetime of their little daughter, Effie. The sudden death of Julia was entirely unexpected, but it is assumed throughout that Tony's promise, given in a spirit of an almost light-hearted humouring of the whim of an invalid, is morally binding. (This, more than any subsequent extravagance, is the real weakness in the motivation of the plot; in *The Wings of the Dove* a somewhat similar treatment of an invalid's desires is made credible by the credibility of the characters themselves.) Rose Armiger, Julia's friend, is staying with the Breams at the time of the exacted promise, and just before Julia's death Rose rejects the proposal of Dennis Vidal, who has been seeking her hand for a long while. The widower is now the object of the veiled attentions of Rose, and also of Jean Martle, the young friend of his neighbour, Mrs. Beever. Jean Martle rejects the hand of Paul, Mrs. Beever's son, who has proposed to her at the instance of his domineering mother, but who is in fact in love with Rose.

An interval elapses (it is significant that in writing a *précis* of the narrative, the conventions of the stage come so easily to mind), and we find the main characters assembled in Mrs. Beever's garden at Eastmead, divided from Tony's house by a bridge over a stream. Rose hints to Tony that Jean might do an injury to little Effie in order to remove the obstacle to her marrying him. Unseen by the others, Rose takes Effie across the bridge. The child is found drowned. Rose meanwhile has told the others that Jean was last seen with the child. Tony, distraught, thinks Jean has been guilty, and publicly confesses that he himself was responsible for the child's death. Dennis Vidal, home from China whither he repaired after his dismissal by Rose, has secretly seen Rose and Effie on the bridge together. In a scene of some obliquity, Rose shares with him her guilty secret. Still loving her, although appalled by her callousness, he promises to protect her. He will take her away, and announce that they are to be married.

A family council, played out in twos and threes on the stage with the assistance of the family doctor, tacitly agrees that the whole affair be hushed up. The murderess, in failing to implicate Jean, has in fact made it possible for Jean to marry Tony. A parting interview reveals that Paul, too, would have shielded the guilty woman, if asked. She leaves with Dennis. The curtain descends on a rueful admission by Tony that the tragedy has been due to the unfortunate fact that people 'like him too much':

' "I mean you'll have such a pull. You'll meet nothing but sympathy."

'Tony looked indifferent and uncertain; but his optimism finally assented. "I daresay I shall get on. People perhaps won't challenge me."

' "They like you too much."

'Tony, with his hand on the door, appeared struck with this; but it embittered again the taste of his tragedy. He remembered with all his vividness to what tune he had been "liked", and he wearily bowed his head. "Oh, too much, Paul!" he sighed as he went out.'

All this would have made a passable *drame*, but it fails as a novel. The extent of its failure will become apparent in a study of *The Wings of the Dove*, where a contrived and potentially melodramatic theme is made credible because Henry James concentrates on personality—near-perfect though the careful elaboration of plot may be. In *The Other House*, where the accent is on situation, the whole thing is a sham—or if considered seriously, distinctly unpleasant.

There are, of course, as in everything James wrote, flashes of the novelist in the sketches of minor characters. Mrs. Beever, 'like an odd volume, "sensibly" bound, of some old magazine,' is one of a long series of self-possessed matrons with a store of worldly wisdom and astringent valuations: 'Mrs. Beever had once said with regard to sending for [Dr. Ramage]: "It isn't to take his medicine, it's to take *him*. I take him twice a week in a cup of tea".' But the hero himself comes to life only at rare moments when he loses his galvanic 'stagey' property and becomes the subject of commentary, as when it is noted that he had 'a certain quality of passive excess which was the note of the whole man and which, for an attentive eye, began with his neckties and ended with his intonations'. The other chief character, Rose Armiger, 'a person constitutionally averse to making unmeasured displays,' has in her cold self-sufficiency many sisters in the earlier novels; only dimly does she adumbrate Kate Croy in *The Wings of the Dove*. Her effect on poor Dennis Vidal is not unlike that of Kate Croy on Merton Densher—a repellent fascination; but Vidal's 'sense that in a single hour she had so altered as to be ugly' is a bleak statement beside that slow change of attitude towards Kate which Densher will share only step by step with the reader, in an unfolding of character unsurpassed elsewhere by this master of the gradual revelation.

II

To attempt a synopsis of a major James novel, where by his own confession there is ever 'an inch of canvas to an acre of embroidery', is always difficult. From two fat volumes of *The Wings of the Dove* one could extract something like this as the theme.

Merton Densher and Kate Croy are secretly engaged to be married, secretly because she is living with her rich and domineering Aunt Maud who has in view more distinguished game in general and a certain Lord Mark in particular. The lovers, with harmonious common-sense, are content to wait until something shall turn up to render their union less inapt. One could hardly put it less indefinitely than that: they are prepared to jog along with an occasional meeting in the Park until they can 'square' Aunt Maud. For Densher, a poor journalist, cannot hope by his own efforts to attain to the required financial standards of Lancaster Gate.

Upon this grey but fallow scene enter two new characters: Mrs. Susie Stringham, an American, being an old school-friend of Aunt Maud's, and her younger friend Milly Theale. During a journalistic tour in the United States, Densher had met Milly in New York, where, as a notoriously rich young hostess, she had given him passing hospitality.

Sponsored by an enthusiastic Aunt Maud, Milly (a 'princess' to her devoted Mrs. Stringham, a 'dove' to her new friend Kate) becomes the success of the London season. Densher, more by his ability to 'talk America' than his relationship with Kate (for that is still their guarded secret), sees something of these ladies during their modest conquest of London. But Milly's triumph is more arranged for her by other people than enjoyed by herself. Her health is very low and she nourishes a private melancholy. A visit to Sir Luke Strett, a distinguished and sympathetic physician, brings her bitter hope: she must be off at once to Venice for a change of climate. Before *leaving* it, she must bestir herself to *face* life. Sir Luke perceives that she is in love. We, by this time, know her to be in love with Merton Densher.

So the ailing 'princess' sets up her household in the Venetian Palazzo Leporelli, the stricken 'dove' retires to balance her will to live against her wish to die. Aunt Maud and Kate go with the party: the two elder and the two younger ladies have become 'inseparable'. Merton Densher also appears in Venice, and his visits to the palace provide Milly with her only real pleasure in the gathering gloom of her unspoken malaise. Insidiously at first, and then explicitly, we have become aware that Kate is directing Densher to woo and marry the slowly dying Milly, from whom, as from everyone else, their private engagement is still concealed. Kate is prepared to wait, in fine, until the poor journalist has become a rich widower—it is thus that Aunt Maud shall be 'squared'.

We are left slightly puzzled as to the precise degree of Densher's compliance in this morbid scheme until the point when Kate has demanded from him complete trust and obedience, and in surrendering his will to hers he claims her bodily surrender. Kate and her aunt return to England, leaving Densher to provide in his loved presence Milly's last relaxing grip on life. He feels abject in his ambiguous role, but the beautiful reticence of Milly's behaviour supports him, and he stays.

Lord Mark, who has danced attendance on all the ladies during the London season, now appears in Venice and brings the uneasy calm to an end. He proposes to Milly, and, when not accepted (for 'rejected' would be too harsh a term for their little scene), reveals to her the true relationship between Kate and Densher. (This is done behind the scenes: the reader is made aware of the consequences, but is not made privy to the fatal part of their interview.) Apprised that his presence is now no longer welcome—but feeling himself technically innocent of any mortal hurt—Densher returns to London. Left alone with her faithful Susie, Milly dies in Venice.

On Christmas Eve, Densher receives from Venice a letter in Milly's handwriting. On the same day, Kate and her aunt receive news of her death. Guessing only too clearly the contents of his own letter, realizing with shame that the dying 'dove' has made him rich so that he can marry Kate, he confronts his betrothed. There are unspoken—and spoken—recriminations. How, asks Densher, was Lord Mark, just after he had been refused by Kate, in a position to rush to Venice and, with a revealing word, end Milly's happiness and her life? He will not touch the money; the letter is burned unread. Later, legal documents from New York put the matter beyond all doubt. But for Merton Densher, now, with the memory of Milly ever before him, the fruit is too bitter. He would still marry Kate, but he will have none of the money. She will not have him without it. They part.

Doubly disconcerting, such a résumé. In the first place, the bare plot is undubitably 'nasty'. It is shocking, thus baldly told, as it is never shocking in the novel itself. In the second place, the whole tone and art of the book are quite omitted. For by now the renowned 'later style' is richly in evidence, and what one really remembers of *The Wings of the Dove* is not the plot, nor even specifically the 'parts' played by the characters, but the delicacy with which so fragile a web of human entanglement has been constructed. As a work of art, *The Wings of the Dove* is elaborately wrought, but the author's aim is the same as ever: to show the individual consciousness in its most secret development, to repeat yet again, behind a new veil of obscurity and indirectness, his impression of the hunted yet defiant spirit 'slashing out in bewilderment'. Mr. Edmund Wilson* has put this intention—and this success:

'Milly Theale, for example, is one of the best pictures of a rich New Yorker in fiction: when we have forgotten the cloudy integument through which we have been obliged to divine her, we find that she remains in our mind as a personality independent of the novel, the kind of personality, deeply felt, invested with poetic beauty and unmistakably individualized, which only the creators of the first rank can give life to.'

**Hound and Horn*, April–June, 1934. (Henry James number).

That is partly true. But there is an error of judgement, a misplaced emphasis, rare indeed in Mr. Wilson's criticism. For it is through the medium of, and not in spite of, that cloudy integument that the character of Milly and the whole effect of the novel are achieved, and remembered. Once 'forgotten', the spell has vanished and the shape behind the opacity is meagre indeed. One may go further: the shape would be not only meagre but false. Henry James was not so artless as not to make proper allowances for his own apparatus of perspective and divination. The cloudy integument may indeed be between the reader and the subject, but he knew about it, and the integument is in truth a very important part of the subject. One might as well complain of the bloom on a peach.

With this most important reservation made and with a full consciousness of the danger and delicacy involved, it is helpful to go in some detail into the construction of this novel. Two points support the venture in the case of this particular novel as representing James's art at its finest.

First, the very sense of discouragement that attends an effort at paraphrase, that feeling of loss and vandalism when the matter and the form have, as it were, been prised apart—these ineptitudes have their positive contribution to one's appreciation. These first feelings of loss offer to the formal critic or to the fascinated but not quite comprehending reader perhaps the most easily localized illustration in Henry James's fiction of the creative value of his 'cloudy integument' (call it what one will—indirectness, opacity, timorousness, craftsmanship, squeamishness, insight, poetry, or guff, according to one's taste and mood). It is a demonstration arithmetically simple. Subtract from the prodigious total of one's impressions of the novel all that sum which may be classed under the heading of plot and narrative skill—no trivial constituent. Then the *remainder*—still ampler—falls into some other category flowering from a mature but still passionate scholarship in the field of human experience and behaviour. It is this remainder that provides a wealth of matter for appreciation. For in *The Wings of the Dove*, as Mr. Wilson has pointed out in a somewhat back-handed way, the separation indicated above is a relatively simple affair. Perhaps because of the very 'ripeness' of the novel, the two constituent elements fall apart at the least tap. Putting it quite bluntly, Mr. Wilson's admirably concise sketch of the main character—'the pathetic Milly Theale . . . who wastes away in Venice and whose doctor recommends a lover'—is so central and yet so loose a part of the mechanism of the whole that one may slide it in and out without any fear of abrasion.

Secondly, and more immediately to the purpose, Henry James has himself provided in the Preface to *The Wings of the Dove* his own considered version of the novel's theme and his own inimitable account of its development. This Preface is 'closer' to its novel than most of the others: it is possibly the only example of a James Preface which could be read with advantage before embarking on the novel itself. The others deal largely with critical theories for which references to the work in hand are used as instances and starting-points: here the relation of the Preface to its own book is more tightly enforced. These detailed notes on the author's intention and execution beautifully preserve something of the quality of *The Wings of the Dove*—a quality to be savoured in advance or retasted, according to the order of reading.

III

Some writers are so silent about their own work that a critic may with some impunity speak in terms of formal construction and development. Try this with James, and you will be embarrassed or comforted, according to the degree of confirmation involved, to have your commentary drowned by the deep authoritative tone of his own auto-criticism. At times he can be hard on himself, and with a firmer hand than most other critics would care to bring to the task of chastisement. (It is a remarkable thing to watch him, in the ample Preface to an almost over-ample novel, rapping himself over the knuckles for skimpiness of treatment.) And because he so clearly knew what he was doing and so judicially viewed the whole and the parts of the whole, his praise too is more informed and certainly more illuminating than anything an outsider could supply. That quality of ever-wakeful ever-watchful *consciousness* that gives him stature as a man and artist is demonstrated in its least adulterated form in the Prefaces, where his permanent love of insisting, of pointing it out and rubbing it in, appears as an all but perverse self-indulgence of commentary and soliloquy. His familiar yet respectful handling of what in a letter he called 'my poor blest old genius' should preserve any other reader from the fear of spoiling the freshness of an impression by over-attention to detail, even if detailed attention had not been so serenely and explicitly called for as in this passage:

'Attention of perusal, I thus confess by the way, is what I at every point, as well as here, absolutely invoke and take for granted . . . The enjoyment of a work of art, the acceptance of an irresistible illusion, constituting, to my sense, our highest experience of "luxury", the luxury is not greatest, by my consequent measure, when the work asks for as little attention as possible. It is greatest, it is delightfully, divinely great, when we feel the surface, like the thick ice of a skater's pond, bear without cracking the strongest pressure we can throw on it. The sound of the crack one may recognize, but never surely to call it a luxury.'

A man is pretty sure of his point of view when, having stated it dogmatically, he can thus immediately accept it as an assumption and turn to that use of irony which indicates the rooted security of a private prejudice.

Here, then, is 'The Dove', in the inspired *procédé* of her creator:

'The idea, reduced to its essence, is that of a young person conscious of a great capacity for life, but early stricken and doomed, condemned to die under short respite, while also enamoured of the world; aware moreover of the condemnation and passionately desiring to "put in" before extinction as many of the finer vibrations as possible, and so achieve, however briefly and broken, the sense of having lived.'

The theme, thus presented, verges on the melodramatic. One can imagine how an inferior artist would have approached the clean-cut drama of the situation—or how, for that matter, the Henry James of the early tales and of *The American* would have attacked it. But here, immediately, with one self-confident stroke, we are presented with a clue to that 'tone' which will bulk so much larger in the total impact of the novel than the plot itself; we are introduced, in other words, to the feel and function of the cloudy integument:

'It involved, to begin with, the placing in the strongest light a person infirm and ill—a case sure to prove difficult and to require much handling; though giving perhaps, with other matters, one of those chances for good taste, possibly even for the play of the very best in the world, that are not only always to be invoked and cultivated, but that are absolutely to be jumped at from the moment they make a sign. . . .

'Why should a figure be disqualified for a central position by the particular circumstance that might most quicken, that might crown with a fine intensity, its liability to many accidents, its consciousness of all relations? This circumstance, true enough, might disqualify it for many other activities—even though we should have imputed to it the unsurpassable activity of passionate, of inspired resistance.'

But such a figure, the very essence of which is fragility and an indistinctness of outline, is to be apprehended and given 'position' by reference to other more definite characters, whose inter-relations with Milly, and even with one another, will provide the movements we shall expect to find mirrored in the pool of Milly's consciousness. (The advantages and dangers of such a method of showing forth one's central figure provide elements for a discussion of the high art and aim of fiction which would bear crucially on the final assessment of Henry James in the hierarchy of novelists. Here, it is necessary only to be assured that he himself, for better or worse, chose his own method with deliberate care and judged its advantages to outweigh its dangers.) Kate and Merton Densher, then, are to be the figures of harder outline in relation to whom the configuration of Milly will begin to take shape:

'If her impulse to wrest from her shrinking hour still as much of the fruit of life as possible, if this longing can take effect only by the aid of others, their participation (appealed to, entangled and coerced as they find themselves) becomes their drama too—that of their prompting her illusions, under her importunity, for reasons, for interests and advantages, from motives and points of view, of their own. Some of these promptings, evidently, would be of the highest order—others doubtless mightn't; but they would make up, together, for her, contributively, her sum of experience, represent to her somehow, in good faith or in bad, what she would have *known*.'

And because these agents in turn are 'bribed away, it may even be, from more prescribed and natural orbits, inheriting from their connexion with her strange difficulties and still stranger opportunities, confronted with rare questions and called upon for new discriminations', then in order to take up our own position and point of view in relation to *them*, we must be allowed to see them at some length and grow familiar with them *before* they meet Milly. We are, in short, to have an opportunity to examine the springs and mechanism of that double trap in which our 'dove' is predestined to be caught.

'I had secured my ticket over the tolerably long line laid down for *The Wings of the Dove* from the moment I had noted that there could be no full presentation of Milly Theale as *engaged* with elements amid which she was to draw her breath in such pain, should not the elements have been, with all solicitude, duly prefigured.'

'If, as I had fondly noted, the little world determined for her was to "bristle"—I delighted in the term!—with meanings, so, by the same token, could I but make my medal hang free, its obverse and its reverse, its face and its back, would beautifully become optional for the spectator. I somehow wanted them correspondingly embossed, wanted them inscribed and figured with an equal salience; yet it was none the less visibly my "key", as I have said, that though my regenerate young New Yorker, and what might depend on her, should form my centre, my circumference was every whit as treatable. . . . one began, in the event, with the outer ring, approaching the centre thus by narrowing circumvallations.'

But how these very supporters and supernumeraries, when they in turn come up for handling and treatment, are dealt with! Kate and Merton Densher themselves, in the process of being independently 'fixed' before they are confronted with Milly and the possibilities for their life inherent in her state as a 'princess' and her nature as a 'dove', have become prime figures. One can almost feel Henry James straining after new sub-supporters through whose perceptions they too may more fully be apprehended.

' . . . the whole preliminary presentation of Kate Croy . . . from the first, I recall, absolutely declined to enact itself save in terms of amplitude. Terms of amplitude, terms of atmosphere, those terms, and those terms only, in which images assert their fullness and roundness, their power to revolve, so that they have sides and backs, parts in the shade as true as parts in the sun—these were plainly to be my conditions, right and left. . . .'

For Kate, the amplitude and atmosphere lie ready to hand in her family. Lionel Croy, her discredited father, forms indeed the very covers or endpapers of the novel. We meet him in the first chapter, we are conscious—to the point of embarrassment—of his presence in the last chapter, and throughout all the intervening space we fumble back to him in memory, from time to time, as to a yardstick for Kate. That indeed is how Henry James intended him to be of service. The amount of aid we are able to summon from that shadowy figure as we seek now to excuse the developing hardness and cruelty of Kate and now to discover some alleviating source for her controlling avarice, does vindicate her creator's contention that once one is committed to the roundabout method of presentation, all these references and cross-references are no luxury, but serve an indispensable function. (*Given* the method, there is no other way; the validity of the method must for the moment beg the question, since Henry James only poses it in this Preface in order to bring forward fresh arguments for its rightness. For their immediate purpose they are satisfying and convincing arguments: whether the necessity so staunchly to defend his creative principles indicates a deep-seated uncertainty, is another and a larger problem.) How much wider a function, then, the author would have wished Lionel Croy to serve, had he but secured ample room and verge enough, is made explicit in this illuminating passage:

'The building up of Kate Croy's consciousness to the capacity for the load little by little to be laid on it was . . . to have been a matter of as many hundred close-packed bricks as there are actually poor dozens. The image of her so compromised and so compromising father was all effectively to have pervaded her life, was in a certain particular way to have tampered with her spring; by which I mean that the shame and the irritation and the depression, the general poisonous influence of him, were to have been *shown*, with a truth beyond the compass even of one's most emphasized "word of honour" for it, to do these things. But where do we find him, at this time of day, save in a beggarly scene or two which scarce arrives at the dignity of functional reference? He but looks in, poor beautiful dazzling, damning apparition that he was to have been. . . .'

Should even this 'functional reference' fail of full explanation there are sister Marian and Aunt Maud ever available to figure, on either side of Kate's strenuous manipulations, like heraldic emblems of poverty at its most crippling and repulsive, and wealth with all its gracious appointments.

For Merton Densher no such apparatus of localization and reference is set up. Indeed, the lack of it is itself effective and noteworthy. We feel to the full the independent and unattached state of the young journalist from the first moment of his appearance, and in that state we can appreciate how it is that Aunt Maud, though she fears him in theory and honestly likes him in practice, can never really come to take him seriously, since for her a person without relations, in both the family and the general meaning of the word, is automatically—and this in no actively pejorative sense—insignificant. Equally we are made to feel that this same state is, in other directions, his strength. It is for this, we feel, that Milly loves him; it is this conscious aimlessness of his that allows him to become so closely attached to Kate that he will give the appearance—and it *is* only an appearance—of having made over his will to her entirely. With these advantages (as a character in a novel) springing from his 'free' state, one does not rate too seriously his creator's later and nostalgic wish, in the Preface, that he too had been embellished with a more elaborate setting:

'The who and the what, the how and the why, the whence and the whither of Merton Densher, these, no less, were qualities and attributes that should have danced about him with the antique grace of nymphs and fauns circling round a bland Hermes and crowning him with flowers. One's main anxiety, for one's agents, is that the air of each shall be *given*; but what does the whole thing become, after all, as one goes, but a series of sad places at which the hand of generosity has been cautioned and stayed.

'. . . the pattern of Densher's final position and fullest consciousness was to have been marked in fine stitches, all silk and gold, all pink and silver, that have had to remain, alas, but entwined upon the reel.'

The 'attentive' reader of *The Wings of the Dove* will not, I suggest, echo that rueful 'alas!' Indeed, one may sometimes complain of Henry James that 'the hand of generosity' is too infrequently stayed, or even that it becomes in the later novels the hand of mistrust, over-anxious to point out nuances and transitions which we might safely have been left to descry for ourselves. One moves on safer and freer ground in *Roderick Hudson*, for instance, than when one is being so solicitously guided through the later novels by a veritable cat's-cradle of leading-strings. Here at any rate is an instance (and there are others) where James the creator is wiser than James the critic. It is surely well for the structure of this great novel that Densher's pink and silver embroidery remained on the reel, and that James should have turned instead, especially in Book First, to establish 'the associated consciousness of my two prime young persons, for whom I early recognized that I should have to consent, under stress, to a practical *fusion* of consciousness', and should have spent his pains on producing, in the undoubted success of his attempt to render the nature of the close but unofficial tie between them, what in a later passage of the Preface he terms 'the full impression of its peculiar worried and baffled, yet clinging and confident, ardour.'

'They are far from a common couple, Merton Densher and Kate Croy . . . but what they have most to tell us is that, all unconsciously and with the best faith in the world, all by mere force of the terms of their superior passion combined with their superior diplomacy, they are laying a trap for the great innocence to come.'

But not every piece of adverse self-criticism in the Preface (or in other Prefaces) can thus be dismissed as showing less tactful wisdom than is displayed in the creative writing. In *The Wings of the Dove*, as in so many of the other novels, the reader feels vaguely that the wonderful apparatus of introduction is not fully used in the later sections, that the richness of the atmosphere is somehow thinned away, that the unsurpassed delineation and shading of the major characters fits them for a fuller and more active life than they are afterwards called upon to live out in the comparatively short space allotted to narrative after we have grown intimate with the men and women who are to be involved in that narrative. (One must be careful, in fairness to other novelists who have been satisfied with fewer pages and who yet have succeeded in shaping proportions better pleasing to themselves, to add that qualification '*comparatively* short'. For although the reader may sometimes indulge a momentary restless complaint that the game is hardly worth the candle—or rather the magnificent candelabra that would in truth make any game seem embarrassingly wasteful—and the author himself with more vigorous reproaches explicitly bewail his own lack of proportion, it is only fair to remember that the narrative through parts of which we stir uneasily and the scope of which Henry James considers to be inadequate, is in fact housed in a couple of ample volumes.) We must face the fact, as he himself fairly faced it (with amusing unconvincing excuses), that the first part of a James novel is almost always better than the second part. Almost without exception, his opening paragraphs set the scene with a combined richness and economy quite unrivalled in English or American fiction; almost without exception, the closing chapters seem either to trail away or to be cut short as in disappointment or despair of rounding off the whole.

'*The Wings of the Dove* happens to offer perhaps the most striking example I may cite . . . of my regular failure to keep the appointed halves of my whole equal . . . . Nowhere, I seem to recall, had the need of dissimulation been felt so as anguish; nowhere had I condemned a luckless theme to complete its revolution, burdened with the accumulation of its difficulties . . . in quarters so cramped.'

'The latter half, that is the false and deformed half . . . bristles with "dodges" . . . for disguising the reduced scale of the exhibition, for foreshortening at any cost, for imparting to patches the value of presences, for dressing objects in an *air* as of the dimensions they can't possibly have.'

The most ardent admirer of Henry James's art, then, may willingly concede the faults of construction which he himself not only recognized but for which he was eager on many occasions to perform 'public penance', with most sincerity perhaps in the present Preface, and with wry humour in the Preface to *The Tragic Muse*:

'Time after time, then, has the precious waistband or girdle, studded and buckled and placed for brave outward show, practically worked itself, and in spite of desperate remonstrance, or in other words essential counterplotting, to a point perilously near the knees—perilously I mean for the freedom of those parts.'

For in *The Wings of the Dove*, any failure in the 'brave outward show' is, after all, only a minor foreshortening in a novel so wonderfully constructed as to make most others appear in very truth like 'large loose baggy monsters'—to use an ungracious phrase he once applied to the works of Tolstoy. Indeed, in making the concession, one is able in a sense to turn the tables on those detractors of Henry James who hold (as most of his detractors do hold) that he has undoubted craftmanship to offer and nothing much else. 'On the contrary,' one might argue, 'in *The Wings of the Dove* the slight awkwardness of construction is more than compensated by the extraordinary warmth and subtlety of the content—that raw material which your concentration on the obvious *form* of the novel passes over without comment.'

A study of Henry James's own Preface, then, brings to light something of those qualities of literary construction and human insight which elaborated so slight a theme into so rich a work. That second quality is impossible to assess with any finality, but the first is at least demonstrable. If *The Wings of the Dove* is one of the most difficult of his novels, it is also one of the most revealing. No analysis of any other James novel could provide a better example of his power of making much out of little, or illustrate how much 'portentous' importance is attributed by the novelist to every minor encounter and every slight change of position of the characters whose interrelations make up his tale.

IV

Once again, as in so many of James's novels, the prime interest lies in the relationship between people of two contrasted types, types at the same time mutually attractive and mutually inimical and even destructive. Here, in *The Wings of the Dove*, is yet another study in opposed ways of living, the hard and the soft, the arranged and the unarranged life. Here again, for long periods, we are, with the author, asked to espouse now one way and now the other. Our sympathies, though clear in the end, are for long divided.

It is interesting, and unexpected, to notice that by comparison with the much earlier novel *Roderick Hudson* the counters are less intricately shuffled. It is fair to suggest that in *Roderick Hudson* the problem was subtler. For there, James confronted us with what may be termed a soft and arranged life in Rowland Mallet, and a hard and unarranged life in Roderick Hudson. The potential mutual attraction and mutual destruction was stronger for that reason. The 'arranged' life of Rowland could yearn nostalgically after what he considered to be the spontaneous genius of Roderick, and at the same time the essential selfish 'hard' core of his hero, while hurting him bitterly, was yet enough akin to his own feeling for order and conscious planning to forbid that simple disgusted reaction which might have severed their relationship and so put an end to his suffering. There were times, indeed, when Rowland sincerely wished that he too *could* become hard, could lose his 'constitutional tendency to magnanimous interpretations' and gain that clarity of selfishness which might have transmuted his talents to something like his friend's genius. Allow that these feelings were in the opposite direction engaging the consciousness of Roderick himself—that he was at once repelled by the complacency and attracted by the security of Rowland's way of life, and we are immediately presented with that quadruple stress which will always remain as the cause of that novel's extraordinary power, and which elevates it to a very high place in the long James canon.

The Wings of the Dove treats with greater elaboration of detail an essentially simpler 'diagram'. The hard and arranged life of Kate comes into contrast and conflict with the soft and unarranged life of Milly: the likelihood of hurt is one-sided. It is not until the very end of the book that we see Kate lose her objective as inevitably as Milly lost hers; and a sudden reversal of fortune, as Aristotle and common-sense decree, does not work on the imagination as powerfully as prolonged strain. If Milly is a dove, then Kate is immediately accepted as a more metallic creature—like the Emperor's clockwork nightingale in the fairy-story, with springs and bright metal parts suggesting a trap in which a dove could be, and was, caught.

To Henry James the interest lay in the progressive development of these characters side by side in a certain pattern of construction: that 'double or alternating centre' described at some length in the Preface. But the astonishing thing about

The Wings of the Dove is not the construction (which does at times falter), but the author's renewed demonstration of a familiarity with the mental processes of two opposed human types, his ability to pop from inside one to inside the other with, in spite of an enormous elaboration of presentation, a minimum of outside commentary. (Indeed, as will be noted later, a lack of external precision detracts from the final impact of this and other later novels.) It is the *inwardness* of it all that makes the novel, that reconciles the reader to so much pother. Milly's yielding softness and Kate's hard clarity are so inwardly done that we view the events of the book through their eyes—or, to change the metaphor and quote a Prefatory remark about Kate, 'we surrender again to our major convenience . . . that of drawing breath through the young woman's lungs.' What we thus gain in intensity of feeling is only partially offset by the loss of any consistent *picture* of these characters (just as in real life we can have no very true objective picture of ourselves). We see *through* Kate and Milly, we do not see *them* very clearly. This is made plain when we consider the bright particularity of the minor figures—Aunt Maud or Susan Stringham—who are wholly consistent and yet have no more of the caricature about them than is needed to give stability to minor characters drawn from the outside.

The 'inward' apprehension of Kate Croy is not however attempted until we have had an initial introduction from the outside, in the first two Books: this is no doubt why always throughout the novel her figure is one degree clearer than Milly's. We see her in relation to her father, her sister, her aunt. There are, very early in the book, one or two hints that she has only recently, and by force of pressing circumstances, decided to take up a firm line in creating an individual life for herself. Other people had clearly until now (until the novel opens, that is) dominated her. 'It wouldn't be the first time,' we are told in an early soliloquy (Book First, Chapter 2), 'she had seen herself obliged to accept with smothered irony other people's interpretation of her conduct. She often ended by giving up to them—it really seemed the way to live—the version that met their convenience.' Aunt Maud had been from the beginning a repressive influence: 'The main office of this relative for the young Croys—apart from giving them their fixed measure of social greatness—had struck them as being to form them to a conception of what they were not to expect.' As for sister Marian, she had drained her sympathy without giving anything in return:

'[Kate] noticed with profundity that disappointment made people selfish; she marvelled at the serenity—it was the poor woman's only one—of what Marian took for granted: her own state of abasement as the second-born, her life reduced to mere inexhaustible sisterhood. She existed in that view wholly for the small house in Chelsea; the moral of which moreover, of course, was that the more you gave yourself the less of you was left. There were always people to snatch at you, and it would never occur to *them* that they were eating you up. They did that without tasting.'

Marian also provides a terrible warning against the penalties incurred by marriage to a poor man:

'Mr. Condrip's widow . . . was little more than a ragged relic, a plain prosaic result of him—as if she had somehow been pulled through him as through an obstinate funnel, only to be left crumpled and useless.' (Book First, Ch. 2).

These are fair indications, and fair excuses. But at first Kate needs no lenience of judgement. Her relationship with Merton Densher, which later seems to deteriorate and harden into that between schemer and agent, is at first presented in a far more attractive light. She sees in his vague but spontaneous qualities something to which she can cling, something to save her from that harsh material outlook which circumstances are forcing upon her.

'She had observed a ladder against a garden-wall and had trusted herself so to climb it as to be able to see over into the probable garden on the other side. On reaching the top she had found herself face to face with a gentleman engaged in a like calculation at the same moment, and the two inquirers had remained confronted on their ladders.'

'They had accepted their acquaintance as far too short for an engagement, but they had treated it as long enough for almost anything else, and marriage was somehow before them like a temple without an avenue. They belonged to the temple and met in the grounds; they were in the stage at which grounds in general offered much scattered refreshment.' (Book Second, Ch. 1).

When we remember that Merton Densher is introduced as

looking 'vague without looking weak—idle without looking empty', it is a tribute to Kate that, in her narrow plight, we feel her to be in full sympathy with the tone of the rest of his portrait:

'He suggested above all, however, that wondrous state of youth in which the elements, the metals more or less precious, are so in fusion and fermentation that the question of the final stamp, the pressure that fixes the value, must wait for comparative coolness.' (Book Second, Ch. 1).

It is Kate's tragedy, and a tragedy demonstrably to be accounted for by the circumstances which, like her father's corrupting influence, had 'tampered with her spring', that she attempted to stamp on Merton Densher's character an unworthy denomination of value which in the end it was not willing to receive. With Aunt Maud as model and guardian, and with a father and a sister alike persuading her to accept that model, it was the only value she had left to play with. In the end it is Milly who stamps *her* value on Densher, and his acceptance of *her* standards rather than Kate's manages to keep him, still dominated by Kate, in the reader's sympathy.

Ten Books run their course, however, before Kate's scheme is shown up and finally defeated. Meanwhile, the better side of her character is as a guide and a beacon to the true heroine, the 'dove', who sighs in vain to secure for herself something of its poise. Softness of outline and hesitancy of plan make up Milly's own 'tone', and we are made to feel its attraction from the first. It is warm and unspoiled and unformulated; it calls for careful guarding, for protection.

'She had arts and idiosyncrasies of which no great account could have been given, but which were a daily grace if you lived with them; such as the art of being almost tragically impatient and yet making it as light as air; of being inexplicably sad and yet making it as clear as noon; of being unmistakably gay and yet making it as soft as dusk.' (Book Third, Ch. 1).

Yet although Milly at no point forfeits our sympathy, we never lose sight of her millions and of her protected state—so protected, indeed, that she hated it herself and felt in her faithful Susie Stringham a positive need to treat her like a princess:

'Susan had read history, had read Gibbon and Froude and

Saint-Simon; she had high lights as to the special allowances made for the class, and, since she saw them, when young, as effete and over-tutored, inevitably ironic and inevitably refined, one must take it for amusing if she inclined to an indulgence verily Byzantine. If one *could* only be Byzantine!—wasn't that what she insidiously led one on to sigh?' (Book Fifth, Ch. 4).

So that when the two women meet, in that 'compact constructional block' (to quote the Preface again) provided by the dinner-party at Lancaster Gate, 'where all the offered life centres, to intensity, in the disclosure of Milly's single throbbing consciousness,' it is Milly who is bowled over by Kate:

'She thrilled, she consciously flushed, and all to turn pale again, with the certitude—it had never been so present—that she should find herself completely involved: the very air of the place, the pitch of the occasion, had for her both so sharp a ring and so deep an undertone.'

'Mrs. Lowder and her niece, however dissimilar, had a least in common that each was a great reality . . . yet she none the less felt Mrs. Lowder as a person of whom the mind might in two or three days roughly make the circuit. She would sit there massive at least while one attempted it; whereas Miss Croy, the handsome girl, would indulge in incalculable movements that might interfere with one's tour.' (Book Fourth, Ch. 1).

And again later:

'Kate had for her new friend's eyes the extraordinary and attaching property of appearing at a given moment to show as a beautiful stranger, to cut her connexions and lose her identity, letting the imagination for the time make what it would of them —make her merely a person striking from afar, more and more pleasing as one watched, but who was above all a subject for curiosity.' (Book Fifth, Ch. 1).

From that Lancaster Gate dinner-party onwards, as Milly falls more and more under the spell of Kate's apparent firmness of purpose and makes the attempt to stiffen her own failing existence with purposeful splints, the reader finds much 'constructional' support from the first chapter in Book Third where Miss Theale and her confidante are first presented. In particular we recall that curiously evocative scene (it does not yield to quotation, for it is thickly shrouded with the cloudy integument and needs its context) where Milly is discovered gazing from an Alpine crest and seems to be facing for a moment alone Life with a capital 'L'. For it is one of Henry James's recurring felicities of touch that he will always in part present his prime figures before they come into contact, in order to correct too easy or exaggerated impression of their later mutual influence or interdependence. Just as in *The Bostonians* we are introduced to an Olive Chancellor whose psychology is already fairly clear *before* her discovery of Verena Tarrant, so here Milly's Alpine meditation gives us a clue to her problem before she meets Kate—and (although we are aware of a previous passage in New York) before, in the pages of the novel at least, she meets Merton Densher. Milly's later head-on encounter with Life and Death as she sits in Regent's Park *after* having met the persons who are most to influence the remaining months of her existence, gains immensely in power thereby.

It is not until after she has come into the orbit of Kate and renewed her acquaintance with Merton Densher that Milly is made conscious in Sir Luke Strett's consulting room—a room 'somewhat sallow with years of celebrity'—of the ironic fact that her new pathetic attempt to order her life has not got under way before that life is condemned.

'It would be strange for the firmness to come, after all, from her learning in these agreeable conditions that she was in some way doomed; but above all it would prove how little she had hitherto had to hold her up. If she was now to be held up by the mere process—since that was perhaps on the cards—of being let down, this would only testify in turn to her queer little history. *That* sense of loosely rattling had been no process at all; and it was ridiculously true that her thus sitting there to see her life put into the scales represented her first approach to the taste of orderly living. Such was Milly's romantic version . . .' (Book Fourth, Ch. 3).

The full force of that word 'romantic' is difficult to assess. Her visits to the great specialist, seen through her own eyes, are blurred with a kind of fascinated mystification. She does not seem to listen with much attention to what he has to say (perhaps the very vagueness of his utterances is to be attributed to her own version of them?), but she is swept away by his presence and the comfortable feeling that he will somehow 'help' her. She has not won any clearer notion of her state of health, but—

what she seems to need even more urgently—she has in her own soft romantic fashion achieved a new 'relation' with someone:

'. . . . the relation was the special trophy that, for the hour, she bore off. It was like an absolute possession, a new resource altogether, something done up in the softest silk and tucked away under the arm of memory. She hadn't had it when she went in, and she had it when she came out . . .' (Book Fourth, Ch. 3).

The reader who protests that this is not how a perfectly normal young woman comes away from her doctor will have made a comment of no small value, perhaps, to an understanding of the pathetic nature and character of 'The Dove'. At all events, whether we take these pages at their face value or read something else into them, the next chapter brings us to the heart of Milly's malaise and to that section of the novel where Henry James throws aside the veil and moves from a treatment of peripheral states of consciousness to the very centre of human vulnerability. We are back on familiar ground; this is the creator of Roderick Hudson and of Hyacinth Robinson speaking. The beauty of the revelation demands, at some length, his own words:

'No one in the world could have sufficiently entered into her state; no tie could have been close enough to enable a companion to walk beside her without some disparity. She literally felt, in this first flush, that her own company must be the human race at large, present all round her, but inspiringly impersonal, and that her only field must be, then and there, the grey immensity of London.'

'The beauty of the bloom had gone from the small old sense of safety—that was distinct: she had left it there behind her for ever. But the beauty of the idea of a big adventure, a big dim experiment or struggle in which she might more responsibly than ever before take a hand, had been offered her instead. It was as if she had had to pluck off her breast, to throw away, some friendly ornament, a familiar flower, a little old jewel, that was part of her daily dress; and to take up and shoulder as a substitute some queer defensive weapon, a musket, a spear, a battle-axe—conducive possibly in a higher degree to a startling appearance, but demanding all the effort of a military posture.'

'Here (in Regent's Park) were benches and smutty sheep;

here were idle lads at games of ball, with their cries mild in the thick air; here were wanderers anxious and tired like herself; here doubtless were hundreds of others just in the same box. Their box, their great common anxiety, what was it, in this grim breathing-space, but the great practical question of life? They could live if they would; that is, like herself, they had been told so: she saw them all about her, on seats, digesting the information, recognizing it again as something in a slightly different shape familiar enough, the blessed old truth that they would live if they could. All she thus shared with them made her wish to sit in their company; which she so far did that she looked for a bench that was empty, eschewing a still emptier chair that she saw hard by, and for which she would have paid, with superiority, a fee.' (Book Fourth, Ch. 4).

In his own stilted fashion Henry James has, in this passage and that describing Milly's Alpine vigil, come as near as any novelist to a statement of the general human predicament—seen not in terms of high drama of decision, but as a sudden void in the heart which can afflict a gentle grey-habited young lady with an irresistible desire to claim for herself, for an instant, some part in human kinship.

Milly's unaided striving for a new sense of order is clearly doomed to failure: she can only look longingly at what she considers to be order in other lives. Her own flinching interest in Merton Densher, the only emotion that had any real chance of shaping a new 'order' for her, can never compete with Kate's. (This is so apparent that we feel Kate's wicked 'plan' to be particularly wicked because it was so unnecessary: 'The Dove' could surely have been easily separated from her cash without having her spirit murdered in the process.) Entering the National Gallery to seek composure and stability, Milly turns away even from the pictures as from too rich a diet:

'She really knew before long that what held her was the mere refuge, that something within her was after all too weak for the Turners and the Titians. They joined hands about her in a circle too vast, though a circle that a year before she would only have desired to trace. . . . She marked absurdly her little stations, blinking, in her shrinkage of curiosity, at the glorious walls. . . .' (Book Fifth, Ch. 7).

Instead, she finds a passing envy for the poor circumscribed lives of the lady-copyists there, who simply because they lacked her own embarrassing material and spiritual resources, seemed to be the better able to cope with what little they did have:

'It was immense, outside, the personal question; but she had blissfully left it outside, and the nearest it came, for a quarter of an hour, to glimmering again into view was when she watched for a little one of the more earnest of the lady-copyists. Two or three in particular, spectacled, aproned, absorbed, engaged her sympathy to an absurd extent, seemed to show her for a time the right way to live. She should have been a lady-copyist—it met so the case. The case was the case of escape, of living under water, of being at once impersonal and firm. There it was before one—one had only to stick and stick.' (Book Fifth, Ch. 7).

We remember that contrasting but mutually attractive types are a very keynote of Henry James's art: it is more than usually dangerous to look for traces of the author's own personality on any one side of the diptych. But is it fanciful to recall the similar impression created in the mind of Christopher Newman of *The American* as he watched Noémie Nioche at work in the Louvre, and to suggest that the creator of both Newman and Milly was himself, in certain moods, peculiarly susceptible to the attractions of the small neat organized life?)

It is here, in the National Gallery, when she surprises Kate and Merton Densher together, that Milly enjoys by contrast with her own helplessness a fresh sense of Kate's superb 'management' in the smoothing away of what might have been an awkward situation:

'It was perhaps only afterwards that the girl fully felt the connexion between this touch and her own already established conviction that Kate was a prodigious person; yet on the spot she none the less, in a degree, knew herself handled and again, as she had been the night before, dealt with—absolutely even dealt with for her greater pleasure. A minute in fine hadn't elapsed before Kate had somehow made her provisionally take everything as natural.' (Book Fifth, Ch. 7).

We feel that it is Milly's neurotic desire to be 'managed' rather than any specific duplicity on Kate's part which allows her so readily to accept Kate's artificial version of their situation *vis-à-vis* the passive Merton Densher:

'Little by little indeed, under the vividness of Kate's behaviour, the probabilities fell back into their order. Merton Densher was in love and Kate couldn't help it—could only be sorry and kind: wouldn't that, without wild flurries, cover everything? Milly at all events tried it as a cover, tried it hard, for the time; pulled it over her . . . drew it up to her chin with energy.' (Book Fifth, Ch. 7).

Kate is, in short, beginning to manage Milly, as she has all along manipulated Merton Densher; there is a malleability in both characters which allows—indeed, asks for—such treatment. We remember that gold is malleable and cast-iron is not, and although there must be from time to time in the reader a genuine annoyance at the softness or weakness of the only two sympathetic figures in a novel full of coarsening lives, it is already beginning to dawn on us that what is fine in Milly and in Densher will draw them together, even while Kate's more powerful will is driving them apart. Book Sixth, which has its strain and its *longueurs*, shows Kate coming more and more into the open with her hard plans, with Milly and Densher alike grudgingly succumbing to *force majeure* and in the process sensing in one another a kinship which neither has the will to acclaim, but which will effectively, in the end, lose them both to Kate. In the very next chapter after the National Gallery episode, where Milly's strength and weakness were revealed in her beautiful yet almost craven behaviour in asking the couple back to luncheon and engaging Merton in tourist gossip about America, we are shown by a well-placed stroke how this new interest in Milly fills him with an increasing resentment against Kate, makes him bitterly conscious at last of every 'irritating mark of her expertness'.

'This expertness, under providence, had been great from the first, so far as joining him was concerned; and he was critical only because it had been still greater, even from the first too, in respect of leaving him.' (Book Sixth, Ch. 1).

Let Kate expertly reveal a few more details of her programme, and he is bitter to the point of mutiny:

'He walked up the Bayswater Road, but he stopped short, under the murky stars. . . . He had had his brief stupidity, but now he understood. She had guaranteed to Milly Theale through Mrs. Stringham that Kate didn't care for him . . . she had described Kate as merely compassionate, so that Milly might be compassionate too. "Proper" indeed it was, her lie—the very properest possible and the most deeply, richly diplomatic. So Milly was successfully deceived.' (Book Sixth, Ch. 4).

And when, his will still subject to Kate's, he calls on Milly to play the first strokes of the game laid down for him, his sympathies are already on the side of the intended victim:

'Since it was false that he wasn't loved, so his right was quite quenched to figure on that ground as important; and if he didn't look out he should find himself appreciating in a way quite at odds with his straightness the good faith of Milly's benevolence. . . . If it wasn't proper for him to enjoy consideration on a perfectly false footing, where was the guarantee that, if he kept on, he mightn't soon himself pretend to the grievance in order not to miss the sweet?' (Book Sixth, Ch. 5).

In six Books, then, the characters are made ready. The remaining four need little more commentary than has been provided in the foregoing synopsis. The texture of the writing grows ever richer, the serenity of intuition ever clearer, the fastidious avoidance of over-emphasis yet more delicate, as throughout the mounting tension and up to the *dénouement* itself we are invited to concentrate our attention not on scenes of overt recrimination and retribution but rather on the small inward adjustments of sensibility, so faintly perceptible that even in our own lives we can hardly discern them—those adjustments and readjustments that cause the final human cleavages or fusions, and are in themselves of so much more value to a novelist of James's gifts than the actions to which they lead. Brief illustrations of his treatment of two major themes for the novel—the veiled jealousy of Kate for Milly and Milly for Kate, and the final change of heart in Merton Densher—must suffice here to demonstrate that remarkable artistic mastery.

Kate's jealousy is the simpler: it is financial jealousy providing the mainspring of a novel which *in toto* might be considered, from the strictly 'outside' or social point of view, as a morality play on the evils of money. It is this simpler jealousy that shapes the plot. But its subtler effects shape the human tragedy, and in a very different direction. These effects are best shown at the evening party given by Milly at her Venetian Palazzo Leporelli, a party the significance of which—if we had missed it—the Preface makes unmistakably explicit:

'It is in Kate's consciousness that at the stage in question the drama is brought to a head, and the occasion on which, in the splendid saloon of poor Milly's hired palace, she takes the measure of her friend's festal evening, squares itself to the same synthetic firmness as the compact constructional block inserted by the scene at Lancaster Gate.'
But even more, it is in Merton Densher's consciousness of Kate's consciousness:

'Yet he knew in a moment that Kate was just now, for reasons hidden from him, exceptionally under the impression of that element of wealth in [Milly] which was a great power, and which was dovelike only so far as one remembered that doves have wings and wondrous flights, have them as well as tender tints and soft sounds.'

'It might have been in her face too that, well as she certainly looked in pearls, pearls were exactly what Merton Densher would never be able to give her. Wasn't *that* the great difference that Milly tonight symbolized?' (Book Eighth, Ch. 3).
And the *effect* on Merton Densher—for that is the true value of the scene:

'So at all events he read the case while he noted that Kate was somehow—for Kate—lacking in lustre. As a striking young presence she was practically superseded . . . she might fairly have been dressed tonight in the little black frock, superficially indistinguishable, that Milly had laid aside.' (Book Eighth, Ch. 3).

Milly's frailer jealousy of Kate, a self-effacing view bereft of the animus normally associated with the word, comes out characteristically in the scenes when she is aware of Kate as Kate must appear to the eyes of Densher, scenes which convey some of the most quietly brutal touches of pathetic jealousy I have met in any fiction. In the first scene, Milly is looking through her window at Kate, who waves to her from the pavement:

'What was also, however, determined for her was, again, that the image presented to her, the splendid young woman who looked so particularly handsome in impatience, with the fine freedom of her signal, was the peculiar property of someone else's vision, that this fine freedom in short was the fine freedom she showed Mr. Densher. Just so was how she looked to him, and just so was how Milly was held by her—held as by a

strange sense of seeing through that distant person's eyes.' (Book Fifth, Ch. 4).
In the second, Kate is standing by the window and Milly, watching her, knows by some unspoken sense that Densher is in London:

'... [Kate] hovered there with conscious eyes and some added advantage. Then indeed, with small delay, her friend sufficiently saw. The conscious eyes, the added advantage were but those she had now always at command—those proper to the person Milly knew as known to Merton Densher. It was for several seconds again as if the *total* of her identity had been that of the person known to him—a determination having for result another sharpness of its own. Kate had positively but to be there just as she was to tell her he had come back.' (Book Fifth, Ch. 5).

Between the claims of Innocence and Experience, where is the author's sympathy? It wavers, as in other novels. *The Portrait of a Lady* is especially close to *The Wings of the Dove* in this respect. There, it was Madame Merle who represented to Isabel Archer the advantages of the ordered life but who was never so hide-bound as to be insensitive to the delicate preoccupations of the heroine. Here, it is Aunt Maud who gains admiration for a prodigious calm and who figures to the elated imagination of Mrs. Stringham from New England as 'a projectile, of great size, loaded and ready for use' or as 'some great sleeping fortress', and yet is no monster of callousness. Even Mrs. Lowder's restrictions are deliberate, political, and not merely poverties of spirit:

'It had never been her pride, Maud Manningham* had hinted, that kept *her* from crying when other things made for it; it had only been that these same things, at such times, made still more for business, arrangements, correspondence, the ringing of bells, the marshalling of servants, the taking of decisions. "I might be crying now," she said, "if I weren't writing letters".' (Book Seventh, Ch. 1).

Merton Densher is the symbol of that wavering sympathy between the two views of life. He is the quiet centre of the storm—a storm, an unfriendly reader might exclaim, in a tea-cup. He is the *punctum indifferens*, the mere male among all the petticoats ('They were all *such* petticoats!' the poor man wails,

* The maiden-name of Mrs. Lowder.

at the crisis of his Venetian ordeal.) It is curious that the wretched dominated fellow doesn't lose more of our sympathy than he does. In the morality play, at least, he represents a condemnation, not so much of riches as of the crippling limitations of poverty, and his feeling of helplessness in the rich vulgarity of the Lancaster Gate drawing-room is less like Kate's envy of Milly's fortune than the frustrations of Hyacinth Robinson of *The Princess Casamassima*—a character who never lost our sympathy even in his weakest moments. During the tension of the last scenes with Kate, Densher plays Macbeth to her Lady Macbeth, still feeling the old admiration for her spirit but feeling now too the power of Milly's goodness. Yet it is never so much the horror of their guilt that drives Densher to repudiate his lover, as the less spectacular but infinitely more human growth of his exasperation at her 'Call me a good cab!' moods. Milly does all unconsciously exert 'the shaping spirit of Imagination', while Kate, like Coleridge's Fancy, has 'no other counters to play with but fixities and definities.' The Milly who could—on the Alps or in Regent's Park—experience a poetic mysticism akin to the promptings of his own timorous sensibility, becomes the mistress of his ideals, while Kate holds him to the end a slave to her will.

V

The quotations embodied in the foregoing notes are too few to indicate with any persuasion Henry James's essentially poetic approach to fiction. They may however suffice to illustrate the strength and weakness of his now steady concentration on peripheral states of consciousness. The whole 'ado' has been organized with a lack of direct exposition or even direct presentation of motive and emotion: to discover what one person is thinking or feeling we are compelled to look through another pair of eyes, to arrive at an appreciation by means of 'reflectors' working 'in arranged alternation'. It is a wilful and at times a fatal limitation. Not to know at first hand, for example, what Milly thought and felt during her last weeks of life at Venice, is a perverse denial for which no amount of peeping and cross-inferences can atone. It is for this reason above all that the later novels lack 'freshness', lack certainly the evocative powers of

Roderick Hudson or *The Princess Casamassima* where Henry James was willing to grapple overtly and spontaneously with life instead of moving always by hints and side-steps.

All this raises the question of his 'morbidity'—a quality hardly to be detected in the bright glowing light of, say, *Roderick Hudson*. Is it true that the early James was a keen observer and the later James something of a *voyeur*? Such an accusation would find more ample substance in the later short stories, but already in *The Wings of the Dove* the deliberate idiosyncrasy is marked enough to give rise to such a comment as this by Mr. Edmund Wilson:

'He was squeamish about matters of sex, it is true—and the people he wrote about were squeamish. And it is true that much of his contact with life was effected, not at close quarters, but through long infinitely sensitive antennae. Yet why, in a given story, should he leave us in doubt as to the facts, as to what kind of people we should think the actors?'

—a complaint provoked, it is true, by the ambiguity of *The Turn of the Screw*, but entirely relevant.

But if, as another critic* remarks, Henry James 'had lived cloistered too long and had actually forgotten the things people do', he never forgot how people *feel*. The essence, the fugitive perfume of life he never missed: it almost becomes a choice between flowers without scent or scent without flowers. Other novelists without number can present us with scentless accurate drawings or photographs of flowers; if Henry James with enormous industry preferred to offer instead a small phial of scent, we can be confident that the essence is never synthetic, but that to the very last, even in his most introspective moments, the uncomfortable odours will have been distilled from real life as we know it. Another metaphor, developed in the Preface, indicates that the author himself was aware how the real quality of his work could not be explained fully as the sum of its carefully joined parts, and that the final unity had a functional strength as well as a beauty not readily to be reduced to its elements. He is speaking of the artist at work:

'He places, after an earnest survey, the piers of his bridge—he has at least sounded deep enough, heaven knows, for their brave position; yet the bridge spans the stream, after the fact, in

* H. R. Hays, in *Hound and Horn*, April–June, 1934.

apparently complete independence of these properties, the principal grace of the original design. *They* were the illusion, for their necessary hour; but the span itself, whether of a single arch or of many, seems by the oddest chance in the world to be a reality; since, actually, the rueful builder, passing under it, sees figures and hears sounds above: he makes out, with his heart in his throat, that it bears and is positively being "used".'

It could never be claimed, then, that *The Wings of the Dove* is in any simple sense a moving or stirring novel. It excels rather in the emotional presentation of very quiet and secret states of consciousness, unfamiliar in fiction not because they are unworthy of presentation, but rather because so few novelists have been brave enough to face the exacting and so largely unrewarding task. It has, certainly, its Proustian *longueurs.* ('Proustian' I use advisedly and in the spirit of propaganda, for we should not refuse to one great artist the tolerant patience we are prepared to extend to another.) But it does report with unflinching honesty the frightening amount of emotional capital expended on residual or peripheral contacts, and demonstrates (as for instance through the experiences of Kate and Milly at the same dinner-party) how the deep better-known emotions are poured out, only very thinly disguised, in these border areas—'border' indeed, for here people touch, here above all they are, as Henry James so often puts it, 'in relation'. It is against that background of honesty that stand out most vividly—as in the case of the Regent's Park episode—those fearful flashes of reality which afflict us perhaps at moments of grief or exaltation, but even more poignantly as we turn restlessly between sleep and waking.

So that although, in discussing *The Wings of the Dove*, one can only deplore the distant wandering away from prime sources, further away than in any of his novels up to that date; and although one must admit that its position is well over the watershed dividing his first artistic period from those so maliciously (and in some moods of the reader, so aptly) called 'James the Second' and 'The Old Pretender'; yet it seems not so much to throw a shadow over the earlier lucidities as to light up with a wiser autumnal glow from that same stupendous sun of consciousness the still murkier tracts of his creative genius which lie ahead.

INDEX